To those believers, who like Daniel, live their lives with a "two-world view": having an eye on the world to come which enables them to live with excellence in this present world.

God's Man with God's Message

AN EXEGETICAL AND DISPENSATIONAL
COMMENTARY ON DANIEL

PAUL BENWARE

DISPENSATIONAL
PUBLISHING HOUSE, INC.

Copyright © 2018 Paul Benware
Cover and Illustration: Leonardo Costa
Cover and Illustrations © 2018 Dispensational Publishing House, Inc.

All rights reserved. This book or any portion thereof may not be reproduced or used in any manner whatsoever without the express written permission of the publisher except for the use of brief quotations in a book review.

"Scripture quotations taken from the New American Standard Bible® (NASB),
Copyright © 1960, 1962, 1963, 1968, 1971, 1972, 1973,
1975, 1977, 1995 by The Lockman Foundation
Used by permission. www.Lockman.org"

ISBN: 978-1-945774-22-5

Dispensational Publishing House, Inc.
PO Box 3181
Taos, NM 87571

www.dispensationalpublishing.com

Ordering Information:
Quantity sales. Special discounts are available on quantity purchases by churches, associations, and others. For details, contact the publisher at the address above.

Orders by U.S. trade bookstores and wholesalers. Please contact the publisher:
Tel: (844) 321-4202

2 3 4 5 6 7 8 9 1

Table of Contents

Introduction 1

Daniel 1: Coming To Babylon 27

Daniel 2: Dreaming Of Empires 45

Daniel 3: Educating A King 77

Daniel 4: Saving a King 93

Daniel 5: Ending An Empire 105

Daniel 6: Defying a Decree 123

Daniel 7: Dreaming of Beasts 139

Daniel 8: Observing Some Horns 171

Daniel 9: Couting The Years................................197

Daniel 10: Ministering to Daniel 237

Daniel 11: Preparing For The End 253

Daniel 12: Finishing The Prophecies 293

INTRODUCTION

INTRODUCING DANIEL: THE MAN AND HIS MESSAGE

Rarely in the Bible are we given a close and revealing look at the life of an individual whose personal history is free from major sins much less minor blunders. Rarely are we given the word from heaven that we are looking at a person who is considered very special by the Lord God Himself. Rarely does a man prosper materially and have great political power and yet remain authentically righteous in his life as well as consistently loyal to his God. And rarely does a man who does possess power, prestige and wealth become a primary channel for critical revelation from God. But such a man is Daniel. He uniquely is a man of God with a message from God. And, though rare it is, we have been given an opportunity to look at a man who honored the Lord wonderfully and to whom was given revelatory truth to benefit others throughout the ages. We will observe that this Book of Daniel contains both powerful prophetic revelations as well as crucial information about a life that pleases the Lord. The man Daniel gives us a wonderful example of those elements that are essential for living a life that honors the Lord and one that is so available to the Lord for His use.

The Purposes of Bible Prophecy

The Book of Daniel is a key book in the overall study of Bible prophecy. But frankly, this reality does not seem to motivate many believers to study this book. For them, it seems, time is not well spent trying to figure out the meaning of a goat with one big horn or a terrible looking beast who has ten horns. It is all so incomprehensible to them that many have marginalized Bible prophecy suggesting that it is not all that important and relevant, even saying that we need to live right now in this world and not focus on some distant future events. Others have taken the stance of "eschatological agnosticism" indicating that we really cannot know for sure so many of these things that have not yet happened, and so, investigating prophecy will have little value.

So why should we give attention to a study of Daniel and of Bible prophecy? There are a number of answers to this question. But one absolutely critical answer of scripture is that prophecy is designed to change the way we think and the way we live *at the present time*. It is not to satisfy our curiosities but to alter our priorities and our decision making right now. It is to develop and mature a "two world view" in our lives. A "two world view" can be described as living well in **this world** because there is a clear focus on the **world to come**. This is THE biblical approach to living life right now here on earth, and it is the way in which the Apostles lived, and how they exhorted other believers to live. For example, the Apostle Paul rebuked those who "set their minds on earthly things" and reminded believers that "our citizenship is in heaven, from which also we eagerly wait for a Savior, the Lord Jesus Christ". He had just told them that he focused on the "goal for the prize of the upward call of God." (cf. Phil. 3:14, 20, 14). The Apostle Peter notes that since the Father "impartially judges according to each man's work", you believers are to conduct yourselves "in fear during the time of your stay on earth" (1 Pet. 1:7). The Apostle also exhorts us to live with excellence right now in view of our future evaluation by the Lord (cf. 1 Pet. 4:7, 17; 2 Pet. 3:10-14). And James concurs when he reminded believers that we patiently deal with life when we remember that the Judges' coming is imminent (Jas. 5:7-9). If believers do have a clear focus and understanding of the world to come (and believe it!), their lives will be lived with greater authenticity and with greater consistency.

Having this "two world view" assists us in establishing **proper priorities** in this life. It helps to remind us daily of what is truly important and what we should give our lives to. The choices we make are better and the focus of our lives dramatically improve when a vibrant "two world view" is present in our thinking (cf. Jas. 1:12; Heb. 11:13-16, 35).

Having a "two world view" aids us in our lifelong struggle with **personal purity**. Serious believers are aware of the "sin which so easily entangles us" (Heb. 12:1), but understand that focusing on the Lord's return and our appearance before Him, which could occur at any moment, is a great help in dealing with personal sinning (cf. 1 John. 2:28-3:3). We can say "no" to a lot of things in this world when we live with an eye on the world to come. When we consciously live with the appearance of the Lord Jesus in mind, it does aid us in our personal battle with sin.

Having the "two world view" helps us obey the Word that tells us to live life with **diligence, alertness and seriousness** (cf. 1 Thes. 5:4-8). It gives that needed guidance in prioritizing life. We are to bring help, strength and encouragement to other brothers and sisters in Christ, and we are to share the good news about the Savior with lost people whose futures are bleak without Him. Each of us has divinely assigned tasks that we are to do with focus and energy. And living and obeying day after day receives needed motivation and energy from the two-world perspective. We all can get weary in well doing and having this two-world view is of great help in this marathon of life. Of course, all of this serious work does not mean that the child of God cannot enjoy the good gifts that come down from our Heavenly Father (e.g. Jas. 1:17; 1 Tim. 4:4-5). Clearly it is our Creator God that has provided all of these blessings for His creation. But it does mean that the believer remembers that Satan remains for now as the "god of this world". It is unwise to view this world as a playground forgetting that it really is a battleground. Good soldiers of the Lord Jesus do not forget this and they labor for Him, maintaining this critically important "two world view." It is clear that Daniel had a two-world view as he lived in Babylon, and yet, anticipated the day when Israel's Messiah would come and establish His marvelous kingdom on this earth.

The Importance of the Book of Daniel

Certainly every book in the Bible has an important contribution to make in our understanding of God's plan and purposes. In Genesis 1 and 2, we observe that God created mankind in His own image; and He did this so that man would be able to fellowship with Him, to rule the planet and to enjoy a physical paradise (Eden). When man made that terrible decision to disobey God, mankind lost everything: fellowship with God, rulership of the planet and life in paradise. At that point, God could have destroyed everything and started all over again. Instead, He chose to restore and reconcile all that was lost in Eden. That restoration is the story of the Bible. And when we look at the last three chapters of the Bible, we discover that those three main things lost in Eden are going to be restored, and even enhanced (Rev. 20-22). Jesus, son of man, will rule taking that authority back from Satan; giving the privilege of ruling back to faithful believers. Man will enjoy an enhanced fellowship with God as His righteous children. In the Garden of Eden, Adam and Eve met with God in the cool of the day, but in Revelation God will come and dwell among His redeemed ones. And thirdly, a new heaven and new earth will be created (after the great messianic kingdom of Jesus) which will be as the Garden of Eden. At the time of the Fall in Eden, God declared that the "seed of the woman" would solve this problem. That was further defined later when the "seed" was narrowed to Abraham and his descendants through Isaac and Jacob. When the "seed of Abraham" (Jesus) entered the world, the way of salvation and return to God was completely provided for. On the basis of the cross of Christ, God could now restore and reconcile. As the storyline unfolded, Daniel would make a significant contribution to our understanding of how this would come to fruition in the end of times. Specifically, there are several important contributions that Daniel makes.

First, the Book of Daniel provides a comprehensive view of the movement of the history of gentile nations. This is done through the lens of the nation of Israel. As noted above, after the fall of man (Gen. 3), instead of destroying man and the universe and starting over again, God chose to embark on the course of reconciliation and restoration. Israel would be the key to this work of God. But when God entered into His covenant with Abraham, He made it very clear that He was not just interested in Israel, but in the gentile nations. Twice God declared that in Abraham all the gentile nations would experience blessing. Gentile nations, including Babylon and its first great king, Nebuchadnezzar, was the object of God's grace. God indeed loves gentiles too!

Second, the Book of Daniel gives many key elements essential to an understanding of prophecy in both the Old and New Testaments. Daniel's revelations of the coming kingdom, of the future tribulation, of the "abomination of desolation" and of the coming Antichrist are built upon by the Apostles and Jesus Himself. And Daniel's "seventy weeks" prophecy is the foundation for Revelation 6-19 and other prophetic portions of scripture. And Daniel 2 (and other chapters) make it clear that when God's kingdom comes, it is an eternal kingdom which will never be superseded by any other kingdom.

Third, the Book of Daniel gives some insight into the Israelites' experience during their captivity in Babylon. While this is not a book of history per se, it does give some snapshots of the nation in that land in the years between the Old Testament books of 2 Kings and Ezra. The book does make it clear that God is not done with His disobedient nation and that there is hope and that they do have a future.

Fourth, in a practical way, the book shows that God does honor those who honor Him (1 Sam. 2:30). Daniel is an example of such a person. The book reveals many of the ways that Daniel honored God and how God, in turn, honored Daniel. God declares that Daniel was a "highly esteemed" man (cf. Dan. 9:23; 10:11, 19). The book provides us with an outstanding model of living godly and righteously in a world that is not conducive to such a lifestyle.

INTRODUCING THE BOOK: BACKGROUND TO THE BOOK OF DANIEL

Authorship and Date of Writing

Taken at face value, the statements within the book itself make it abundantly clear that the author was Daniel, a man who lived throughout the Babylonian captivity of Judah. Daniel was about 15 years old when the captivity began in 605 BC and he lived throughout the entire period with the last time notation in the book being 536 BC (Dan. 10:1). The time notations given throughout the book leave no doubt that the visions and events come out of the sixth century BC, specifically that time between 605 BC and 536 BC (Dan. 1:1; 2:1; 5:31; 6:28; 7:1; 8:1; 9:1; 10:1; 11:1). The book declares that the author did experience life during the reigns of several kings of Babylon and Medo-Persia who reigned in the sixth century BC.

Although the use of the first person in this book does not begin until chapter 7, the statement that Daniel was to "conceal these words and seal up the book" (Dan. 12:4) tells us that he is being presented as the author of the entire book. He certainly knew well the people mentioned in the book as well as being knowledgeable of the customs and events surrounding the times of the Babylonians and the Persians. All this points to the author living and writing in the sixth century BC and not to someone living many centuries later.

We conclude that Daniel lived and wrote this book during the sixth century BC. This has been the consistent viewpoint of the Church and the scholars of Israel. The Lord Jesus Himself pronounced the book as a genuine work of Daniel when He specifically referred to "Daniel the prophet" (Matt. 24:15) and Daniel's word about the "abomination of desolation." Jesus, who only quoted from canonical writings, put His stamp of canonicity on this book. Also Ezekiel, a contemporary of Daniel in the captivity period, speaks of the godliness and wisdom of Daniel (Ezek. 14:14, 20; 28:3). He places Daniel squarely in the time frame claimed by the book and its author. So in declaring that Daniel wrote this book in the sixth century BC, we are on solid ground, joining with those who for millennia have proclaimed the same thing.

The above position was held for many centuries (with only few exceptions, and those exceptions were in the ranks of known heretics) until questions were raised by theological liberals. It has become the position of modern liberal criticism that the book of Daniel was actually written by an anonymous author about 167 BC during the Maccabean period. It was during the Maccabean period that the Jews were revolting against the wicked king Antiochus IV (Epiphanes) and fighting against the terrible atrocities of his rule. The view of these liberal theologians is that Israel needed a hero. And this document (the book of 'Daniel') was intended to encourage these righteous Jewish rebels in their struggle against this extremely wicked king. It is said that Daniel's name was invoked to give credibility to the document. One author holding to this position puts it this way:

> Daniel is a non-historical personage modeled by the author(s) of the book after the ancient worthy who is linked in Ezekiel 14:14, 20 with righteous Noah and righteous Job, and who is described (Ezek. 28:3) as a wise man. As is the case with other Jewish apocalyptic writings, an ancient saint and sage has been selected to be the bearer of a message to an audience living in a totally different era.[1]

---

1 W. Sibley Towner, *Daniel*, (Louisville: John Knox, 1984), 5.

He then goes on to say that the author, or authors, spoke of loyalty to the Lord in the midst of difficult times, emphasizing "the people who are wise" and "those who are wise." He explains that this kind of emphasis points to some sectarian group in second century BC Judaism. (A conclusion that is neither compelling nor logical). He concludes that the writers were likely "*hasidim*, spiritual ancestors of the Qumran community."[2]

The case presented for this late date by an anonymous author, however, is not at all strong and lacks credibility. So, why then would these liberal scholars go against thousands of years of scholarship? First, it must be understood that those holding to this late date for Daniel do not do so because of overwhelming evidence that compels them to take that position. They have established this view and tenaciously hold to this position because of their strong bias against the possibility of predictive prophecy, and their resistance to anything miraculous. They are committed to an anti-supernatural position because of their commitment to a rationalistic philosophy. As one has observed, "Naturalism and rationalism are ultimately based on faith rather than on evidence; therefore, this faith will not allow them to accept supernatural predictions."[3] And no amount of evidence seems to affect this "faith" position of theirs.

This "faith" colors their approach to the events and prophecies of the book of Daniel. For example, in Daniel 11, there are dozens and dozens of specific persons and events referred to. These statements are so clear in what they refer to that all, whether liberal or conservative, agree on what king or what event is being spoken about in any given verse. Many of these events took place during the fourth and third centuries BC and all took place after the sixth century BC. Since Daniel wrote in the sixth century BC, all of these would be prophetic statements. But if there is no such thing as predictive prophecy, as the critical scholars claim, then they must be written after the

---

2 Ibid., 8.
3 Bruce Waltke, "The Date of the Book of Daniel," *Bibliotheca Sacra*, Vol.133 (1976): 329.

events themselves. Thus, the liberals assign a date of around 167 BC for the writing of this book in order to make these events in Daniel 11 historical and not prophetic. To move even a few years back towards the orthodox view cannot be done without a number of statements immediately becoming prophetic in nature. And their bias against predictive prophecy will not allow this. It is interesting to observe that what they seemingly have failed to appreciate is that even assigning a date of 167 BC to this book does not totally deal with the issue. There remains many more of Daniel's prophecies that are predictive, especially those related to the Messiah's coming kingdom. As another example, Daniel 9:24-27 with great accuracy predicts the exact time of the Messiah's death.

One claim of support that is consistently made by the liberal critics for their late date is the presence of three Greek and a few Persian words in the book of Daniel. According to their position, this forces the interpreter to a late date. This view was enshrined as absolute truth in S. R. Driver's oft quoted phrase. The Persian words "presuppose" a period after the Persian empire had been established; the Greek words "demand" a date "after the conquest of Palestine by Alexander the Great" (332 B.C.).[4]

This idea, that the presence of these loan words requires the conclusion that Daniel was written after the Persian period and after the conquests of Alexander the Great, is an assumed fact by critical scholars. However, such a conclusion is not at all accurate much less required.

---

4 S. R. Driver, *Introduction to the Literature of the Old Testament*, 5th ed. (New York: Meridian, 1960), 508

These words simply reflect an interchange between cultures that had been going on for centuries. It is known that Greek mercenaries served in the armies of Assyria long before the sixth century; that Greek artisans were employed by King Nebuchadnezzar of Babylon; and that Greek pottery and musical instruments had wide distribution long before Daniel lived.[5] So to say that the presence of a few Persian and Greek words demands a late date is overlooking the usual interchange of cultures that has always existed. It would be like someone saying that because "Toyota" and "Honda" are part of the vocabulary of Americans, this presents positive proof that Japan conquered the United States sometime in the past. No one would say such a thing because they recognize the interchange between cultures brought the words (and the cars) to America. In a concluding thought to his scholarly analysis of the problem of Greek loan words, Dr. K. A. Kitchen states that "the idea that Greek words and influence *could not* affect the Near East or appear in Aramaic before Alexander the Great *must* be given up."[6]

Furthermore, a number of conservative scholars have made the observation that we would actually expect to find many more Greek and Persian words in Daniel if, in fact, the book was written after the Persian period and after the conquest by Alexander and the armies of Greece.

> Perhaps the most important point to consider in this great controversy is that the book of Daniel would have been saturated with Greek terms if it were written as late as 167 B.C. in Palestine, where Greek-speaking (Hellenistic) governments had controlled the entire region for more than 160 years. Instead of this, we find just two or three technical terms referring to obviously foreign cultural objects.[7]

---

5 K. A. Kitchen, *"The Aramaic of Daniel: Notes on Some Problems in the Book of Daniel*, (London: Tyndale Press, 1965, 44-48.
6 Kitchen, 47.
7 John C. Whticomb, *Daniel*, (Chicago: Moody, 1985), 56.

Another line of evidence that is made by those who insist on a 167 BC date is the point that the book of Daniel was placed by the Jews in the third section of their canon, the Writings. The point being made is that the book of Daniel was not placed in the second, prophetic section (which was allegedly closed between 300-200 BC). They argue that if Daniel had been written in the sixth century then the Jews would have put Daniel in with the prophets. But since that section of the canon was already closed, the book was placed in the third section with later writings. In response it is helpful to make certain basic observations. First, the divisions within the Hebrew Scriptures are not necessarily chronologically based. On this matter, Dr. John Walvoord says:

> Further, the Writings were not so classified because they were late in date, inasmuch as they included such works as Job and 1 and 2 Chronicles, but the division was on the classification of the material in the volumes. More important, the Writings were considered just as inspired and just as much the Word of God as the Law and the Prophets. This is brought out by the fact that Daniel is included in the Septuagint along with other inspired works, which would indicate that it was regarded as a genuine work of inspiration.[8]

It is worth observing that Daniel was different from the writing prophets in a number of ways. Since the content of Daniel included much historical information and since the prophetic portions were as much directed to the gentiles as to Israel, Daniel was somewhat different than Ezekiel or Jeremiah. And this may have been a factor in the placement of this book. Second, it is believed by many that Daniel was actually listed with the prophets but was "only shifted to another category of canonical books by Hebrew scribes in the fourth century AD."[9] Third, and of particular significance is the point that it

---
[8] John F. Walvoord, *Daniel: The Key to Prophetic Revelation*, (Chicago: Moody, 1971), 19.
[9] Whitcomb, 15.

was the status of the writer that caused the Jews to place books into certain divisions of the Scriptures and not the order of writing. Daniel is presented as a government official (a godly one, of course). We know of no place where he was commissioned by God to enter the specific office of prophet. There is no evidence that Daniel received a definite call or was appointed by God to the office of prophet. Daniel was not like Isaiah or Jeremiah who were raised up to be prophets of God. The Jews recognized that Daniel's status was that of a government official and not that of a prophet and so put his work alongside of Ezra and Nehemiah. So the placing of Daniel in The Writings does not at all mean it was written late in the time of the Maccabees.

Those who insist on a late date for Daniel have raised numerous other issues as well. It is said that the Aramaic found in the book of Daniel is more like the Aramaic from the first or second centuries. If this is true, of course, then a sixth century date for the writing of Daniel is highly unlikely. But this position has been refuted by Kenneth A. Kitchen who, in great detail, notes that the Aramaic of Daniel is consistent with Aramaic texts from the 5th to the 9th centuries BC, clearly opening the way for a 6th century date for the book of Daniel.[10]

Furthermore, it is claimed by critical scholars that the book contains a number of historical errors such as calling Nebuchadnezzar the father of Belshazzar; the mention of 'Darius the Mede'; the apparent inaccuracies in dating; and the identity of Belshazzar. But these have been dealt with quite adequately by conservative scholars and will be discussed in the appropriate sections of this commentary.

There is much more that could be said here, but there is no real need to do so since there are excellent books on introduction and background that deal with these matters in great detail. However, one final point should at least be noted here concerning the Dead Sea scrolls. The scrolls have provided an interesting refutation to the critical late date of Daniel. Portions of the book of

---

10 Kitchen, 31-79.

Daniel were discovered at Qumran along with those of other Old Testament books. These scrolls were probably copied in the second century BC by those living in the Qumran community. Since the Qumran scrolls are copies and not the original writings, this has forced many critical scholars to reconsider their views on the late dating of such books as Psalm and Chronicles. They correctly reason that if *the copies* are dated from the Maccabean period then *the originals* were not written in that period. This would mean that the originals were written before the Maccabean period. The result has been to give earlier dates to a number of books. This, of course, makes a great deal of sense. "But critical scholars have refused to draw the same conclusion in the case of Daniel even though the evidence is identical."[11] It is obvious that such reasoning is not applied to the book of Daniel because to do so would place Daniel long before 167 BC and predictive prophecy would become a key element in the book of Daniel. The bias against predictive prophecy is so clearly evident on this point.

So, we conclude that the evidence is strong, and it is compelling for this book being written by the godly man Daniel in the sixth century BC. This has been the consensus for thousands of years and there is nothing in the weak, biased critical approach which causes us to change.

The Purpose of the Book

When looking at the contents of the book of Daniel as well as observing the historical setting in which this book was written, there are a number of likely reasons why Daniel was guided by the Holy Spirit to write this book. First, the book certainly must have been written *to encourage the nation of Israel.* In their Babylonian captivity the great question that weighed heavily on the hearts of these Israelite captives was "is God through with us?" Israel's disobedience and unbelief had brought the severe discipline of the Lord God on them and it was natural to wonder if God was finished with them. But Daniel, along with his

---
11 Waltke, 322.

contemporary Ezekiel, was quite clear that God had not set them aside. Daniel's amazing prayer, found in chapter 9, asks God to faithfully fulfill His promises to Israel. His prayer is based squarely on the fact that God is a righteous God who keeps His word; and His word was that He would restore Israel. Because of the grace and faithfulness of God to His covenant commitments, they did have an amazing future as the events of the future recorded in this book made clear. What an encouragement this would be to the Jews of that time.

A second purpose was *to provide a prophetic framework* that would be important to the understanding of other prophecies given before Daniel's time as well as prophecies given centuries later. Daniel's prophecies would particularly give a framework for that era known as "the times of the gentiles" (cf. Luke 21:24). During this period gentile nations would exercise dominance over Israel culminating in the final seven years of human history commonly known as The Tribulation. Without Daniel, many prophecies, in the Book of Revelation and other books, would be quite obscure and we would be forced to speculate about them.

A third purpose for Daniel's book is *to reveal with absolute clarity the sovereignty of God over men and nations.* The Lord God of Israel is not simply the God of Israel. He is not some tribal deity but the sovereign God of all the earth. Several of the Old Testament prophets have sections in their writings where gentile nations are addressed (e.g. Isa. 13; Amos 1). Although the messages to those gentile nations may not have actually been delivered to them, these messages let Israel know that in spite of the power of these gentile nations, it is the sovereign Lord who has absolute power and authority. So, in spite of the authority and power of Satan and the armament of nations, the Lord God of Israel is the One who sets kings up and takes them down, as Daniel 2 so eloquently declares. Eventually every nation of men as well as the forces of the devil will be forever destroyed. All authority resides in the Lord God of Israel, as Nebuchadnezzar learned firsthand. Every knee will indeed bow before the God of Israel.

A fourth purpose of the book of Daniel is *to provide another illustration of God's faithfulness to His covenant promises made with Abraham.* In the Abrahamic covenant, God had committed Himself to bring blessing to both Israel and the nations. And the Scriptures proclaim that reconciliation and restoration would occur through "the seed of Abraham"; that is, the Messiah. The fulfilling of these covenant promises ultimately depended on God's faithfulness and not on the faithfulness and obedience of Israel. Daniel joins with many other voices in the Old and New Testament in declaring that God will do what He said He would do in and through Israel. God will be absolutely faithful to His covenant commitments.

The Languages Used in the Book

The Book of Daniel is somewhat unique in that it was written in two languages, Hebrew (the language of the Jews) and Aramaic (the standard official language of that day). Similarly, the book of Ezra was written mainly in Hebrew, but it also contained an Aramaic portion (cf. Ezra 4:8-6:18; 7:12-26). Why the Holy Spirit led Daniel to do so is somewhat of a mystery to us. However, our best guess is that it has to do with the subjects of the various sections of the book of Daniel. The use of the Aramaic is in the section (Dan. 2:4-7:28) that focuses on the domination of the gentiles over Israel and the rise and fall of several gentile nations. It would be logical that the section concerning the gentiles would be written in a language they could understand. The remainder of the book is written in Hebrew with a Jewish audience in view as the emphasis is on Israel, Jerusalem and the relationship between Israel and gentile nations.

The Historical Setting of the Book

Daniel lived in Jerusalem during the last days of the Southern Kingdom of Judah. His life intersected a number of kings and prophets during those critical last days in the national life of God's people. It is important to have some understanding of the conditions and events that took place in Daniel's nation as well as among the gentile nations.

During the eighty years before the Babylonian captivity, Judah's spiritual situation was primarily characterized by religious defection. After the reign of the godly king Hezekiah (728-686 BC), Judah endured the long evil rule of Hezekiah's son Manasseh. Unfortunately for the nation, Manasseh followed in the footsteps of his wicked grandfather, Ahaz, rather that in the steps of his righteous father, Hezekiah. The testimony of scripture is that Manasseh did everything in his power to destroy the true worship of the Lord and to establish idolatry throughout the land. He excelled in evil.

> He restored the offensive cultic objects which Hezekiah had destroyed, placed altars of Baal throughout the land and even in the Temple, and recognized the Ammonite deity, Molech, by sacrificing children in the Valley of Hinnom. He approved various forms of pagan divination, and even erected an image of the Canaanite goddess, Asherah, in the Temple. Those who protested, he killed, thus shedding much innocent blood.[12]

He killed untold numbers of godly people as well as prophets and priests of the Lord thus effectively removing any righteous influence from Judah's national life. Manasseh's actions were so evil that it was declared that he was just like the wicked Canaanites, yet worse, because he sinned in the light of the knowledge of God. In all of the 450-year monarchy period in Israel there was no one who rivaled him in evil. And for this, God pronounced irreversible judgment on Judah. The nation of Judah was doomed and headed for captivity (e.g. 2 Kgs. 21:1-16).

After a very brief reign by Manasseh's wicked son, Amon, the Lord blessed Judah by establishing Josiah as king (640-609 BC). As it turned out, Josiah was the last godly king in the monarchy period. He brought a revival to Judah, but unfortunately it was basically external. There were activities such

---

12 Leon Wood, *A Survey of Israel's History*, (Grand Rapids: Zondervan, 1971), 364.

as the tearing down of images and burning objects of idolatry and observing biblical feasts. But the hearts of the people were generally untouched. Josiah himself was a truly godly man but the hearts of the people were far from the Lord and their turning back to the Lord was simply outward. The reality, of this superficial revival, was noted by Jeremiah the prophet (Jer. 3:10). And so, even though revival had come, the clouds of judgment began to gather on the horizon. The Lord did declare that because of Josiah's righteousness, he would not personally see the captivity of Judah. But the captivity would eventually come because of the sins of Manasseh (cf. 2 Kgs. 23:26; 24:3).

YEAR B.C.	EVENT	DANIEL'S AGE	KING OF JUDAH	KING OF BABYLON
620	Birth of Daniel	-------	Josiah	Nabopolassar
609	Josiah killed by Pharoah Necho. Battle at Haran.	11	Jehoahaz, second son of Josiah	Nabopolassar
609	Pharoah Necho in control in Judah replaces Jehoahaz	11	Jehoiakim (i.e. Eliakim) oldest son of Josiah.	Nabopolassar
605	Jerusalem falls to Babylon. **Daniel taken captive.**	15	Jehoiakim (who swears loyalty to	Nabopolassar/ Nebuchadnezzar
603	In Babylon, **Daniel finishes training**	17	Jehoiakim	Nebuchadnezzar

It was during the rule of Josiah that Daniel was born (c. 620 BC). So Daniel was born during that one brief period of time in Judah's latter history where the Word of God and the God of the Word were exalted in Judah. This, no doubt, greatly influenced the spiritual life and character of the boy

Daniel growing up in Jerusalem. During those years in Judah, young Daniel benefited from the godly leadership of both king and priests and from the prophetic ministries of men like Jeremiah, Zephaniah and Habakkuk.

On the world scene, the Assyrian empire had dominated the ancient near east for centuries. But their power was declining, and other forces were at work. The Median peoples gained their independence from Assyria (c.650 BC) and the Chaldeans (Babylonians) revolted throwing off the yoke of Assyria (c.625 BC). Kyaxares of Media and Nabopolassar of Babylon joined forces to attack Ninevah, the capital city of Assyria in 612 BC.

> Nabopolassar, instead of holding Babylonia for Assyria, had turned against it, and made common cause with the enemy, cementing the new alliance by the marriage of his son, Nebuchadnezzar, with Amytis, the daughter of Kyaxares. The two armies now marched against Ninevah, which made brave resistance.[13]

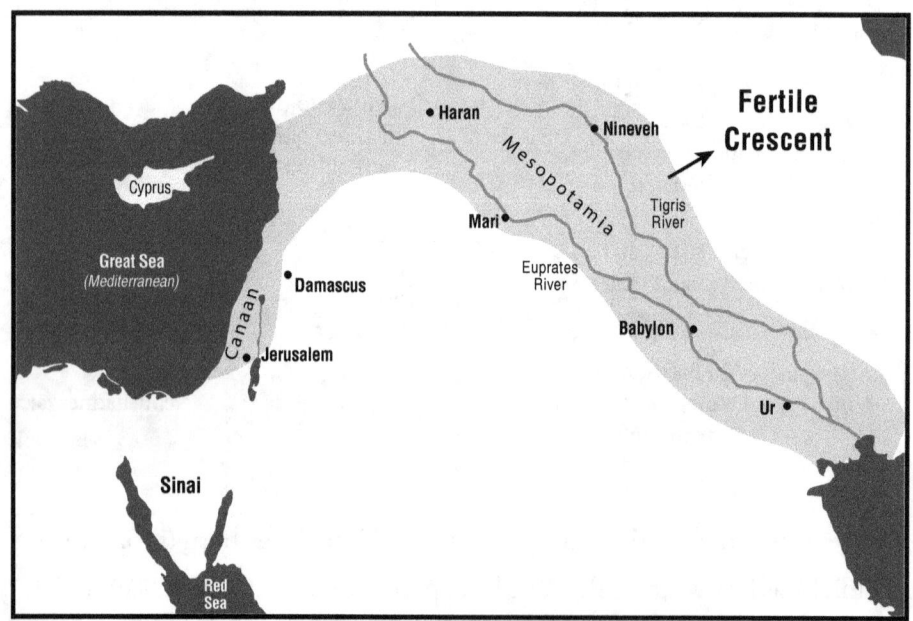

---

13 Alfred Edersheim, *Bible History: Old Testament*, (Peabody, Mass.: Hendrickson, 1995), VII: 965.

In spite of this brave resistance, Nineveh fell under the combined assault. This victory took place in 612 BC and fulfilled the prophecy of Nahum. A remnant of the Assyrian army, under Ashur-uballit II, fled westward to temporary safety in the ancient city of Haran. Pharoah Necho of Egypt, fearing the rising power of Babylon, went to the aid of the Assyrians. But in spite of his support, in 609 BC, Haran fell to Nabopolassar, king of Babylon. It should be observed here that in his march northward to Haran to help the Assyrians, Pharoah Necho was challenged by King Josiah of Judah, who for reasons that are not entirely clear, tried to keep the Egyptians from helping the Assyrians. In that confrontation, King Josiah was killed and Judah lost their last good and godly king. This was a tragedy of monumental proportions since King Josiah was the one barrier to Judah's captivity. This is reflected in the annual national mourning (2 Chron. 35:25; Zech. 12:11). And now that that barrier was removed by the death of the godly Josiah, captivity was only four years away.

In the year 605 BC, Nebuchadnezzar replaced his aged father Nabopolassar at the head of the armies of Babylon and led them against the weakened Assyrians who were again joined by the Egyptians. This battle took place at Carchemish on the Euphrates River. From the Babylonian Chronicles it can be ascertained that this battle took place in May-June of 605 BC.[14] The Babylonians completely destroyed their enemies and established themselves as the power in the world. After the battle of Carchemish, Nebuchadnezzar moved quickly to control all the land of Syria and Israel. He marched south and arrived at Jerusalem and brought about its submission. While the Babylonian Chronicles do not specifically say that Jerusalem was besieged in the year 605 BC (as stated in Dan. 1:1), it certainly allows for it when it declares that all of Hatti-land (i.e. Syria-Palestine) was defeated by the Babylonian armies. At this point the Babylonian Chronicles are focused

---

14 D.J. Wiseman, *"Some Historical Problems in the Book of Daniel"* (London: Tyndale Press, 1965), 16-18.

on the primary matter of the major defeat of the Egyptians and does not go into how Jerusalem and other places met their fate. Furthermore, instead of Jerusalem being "besieged", the text of Daniel 1:1 could be translated "cut it off" or even "showed hostility towards it."[15] The main point is that in August of 605 BC Jerusalem fell to the Babylonians and it is at this time that the lives of Daniel and Nebuchadnezzar intersect for the first time.

> As Nebuchadnezzar moved through the newly-won country, he desired not only the submission of leading cities but also the procurement of able young men, whom he might relocate in Babylon as prospective government personnel. It is likely that each city was forced to give him their finest. Among those from Jerusalem were Daniel and his three friends, Hananiah, Mishael, and Azariah.[16]

It is at this moment in time that the book of Daniel opens with the statement that Nebuchadnezzar came to Jerusalem in the third year of King Jehoiakim's reign over Judah; that is, the year 605 BC.

Interpreting the Book of Daniel

It is true that Bible prophecy presents some challenges to the interpreter. But when we approach the prophetic portions of Scripture, like those found in Daniel, we need to remember several basic truths. First, prophecy was given by God to be understood. It may take some diligence and skill on our part to come to an understanding, but God wants us to know about these matters. Second, the Holy Spirit as been given to us to help us understand God's truth. We have been given divine assistance in order that the truth might be grasped. And third, the very words of the prophetic scriptures are inspired by God and are, therefore, important. We must never dismiss some detail, symbol or imagery as silly, incomprehensible or without real value,

---

15 Ibid., 17-18.
16 Wood, 373.

unless we believe that the Holy Spirit unnecessarily gave these details. No, these are the very words of God and contain the truths that God wants us to understand. They are, therefore, worthy of our time, attention and best efforts. Some very basic rules of interpretation need to be remembered.

First, prophetic passages are to be interpreted literally. Of all the rules for interpreting prophecy, this is the greatest one. We simply mean by this that we approach the prophetic passages in the same basic way that we would any other literature or any ordinary conversation.

> The literal method of interpretation is that method that gives to each word the same exact basic meaning it would have in normal, ordinary, customary usage....It is called the grammatical-historical method to emphasize...that the meaning is to be determined by both grammatical and historical considerations.[17]
>
> In order to determine the normal and customary usages of Bible language, it is necessary to consider the accepted rules of grammar and rhetoric, as well as the factual historical and cultural date of Bible times.[18]

As we come to the text of Daniel, we must come with a literal mindset and the commitment to approach these chapters in this way. Of course, much of Daniel's book is the story of historic events and poses no real problem for most interpreters. When Daniel records his appearance before Nebuchadnezzar to interpret his dream, or when his friends are placed into the furnace of fire, there is no difficulty in understanding the meaning of the text. We interpret it all according to the normal rules of language. But this must be true of the prophetic portions as well. Without this basic approach there is no reliable check on an interpretation, and the result is that the interpreter actually becomes the final authority, and not the Scriptures themselves. We come to Daniel, therefore, committed to understand the text according

---
17 Paul Tan, *The Interpretation of Prophecy*, (Winona Lake: BMH Books, 1974), 9.
18 Bernard Ramm, *Protestant Biblical Interpretation*, 3rd rev. ed. (Grand Rapids: Baker, 1973), 121.

to the accepted laws of language and not to seek some mystical or figurative interpretation. Once inside this literal system we deal with specific words or phrases, deciding whether or not they are symbols or figures of speech.

A second important principle to remember while interpreting the prophetic sections of Daniel relates to symbols. Symbols are found throughout this book as communication devices. "A symbol is a graphic representation of an actual event, truth, or object....Symbols can be *words* or *acts*...Proper names are sometimes used as symbols in prophetic Scripture. The context and the analogy of prophecy will generally bring these out."[19] Symbols communicate truth concisely, and they communicate it graphically. They help listeners retain far more information because they "see" it along with hearing it or reading about it. Since the prophets did not use graphs and charts and did not have "power point" or other technological tools, they had to rely on the language that they used. When Daniel speaks about a four-headed, four-winged leopard (Dan. 7:6), we know he is using symbolic language since leopards simply do not come equipped like that. This leopard and the other strange looking animals in this book are representing different nations. We know this because the interpreting angels give assistance in helping Daniel understand (Dan. 7:17-23). And quite often the meaning of the symbols is to be found within the book of Daniel itself. Other symbols, such as the "great sea" (Dan. 7:2) can be understood as a picture of the gentile nations from previous prophecies (cf. Isa. 17:12) and even confirmed for us by later prophecies (cf. Rev. 17:15). But the point is that these symbols represent something literal and very often something already established. A symbol does not give the interpreter license to make it mean whatever he wishes. It is the task of the interpreter to investigate this figurative language to discover what literal truth is there.

A third interpretive principle that we must employ when coming to the book of Daniel is the well-known principle of interpreting by comparing

---

19 Mal Couch, *An Introduction to Classical Evangelical Hermeneutics*, (Grand Rapids: Kregel, 2000), 71.

scriptural prophecy with scriptural prophecy. God did not give all prophetic information to any individual. Rather, through many authors over a period of time the prophetic picture developed and became more complete. So we need to carefully look at the larger context of the entire scriptures to find some meanings. For example, Daniel tells us that a wicked man (who we commonly refer to as the Antichrist) will successfully persecute God's people for "time, times and half a time" (Dan. 7:25). That phrase would never be clear to us without its being interpreted to mean 1260 days (or 3 ½ years) in Revelation 12:6, 14. And so, while Daniel does give to us information about the Antichrist, we would not get a fuller and clearer picture of him without the writings of Paul (e.g. 2 Thes. 2:3-9) and John (e.g. Rev. 13:1-10). A note of caution at this point. When comparing scripture with scripture, we must be as sure as we can be that the two different scriptures are talking about the same thing. Sometimes we fall into the trap of illegitimately taking a thought from one passage and imposing it on another separate passage. For example, Jesus (in Matt. 24:40-41) spoke of two men in the field and two women at the grinding mill, and said that one would be taken and the other would be left. Quite often this is used as a passage illustrating the rapture event. But is it? Jesus' discourse related to the 2nd Coming, not the rapture. So perhaps one should be careful in comparing that particular scripture with rapture passages such as 1 Thessalonians 4.

Fourth, we must interpret in light of possible time intervals. When the prophets proclaimed God's message they frequently were unaware that there was going to be an interval of time between prophetic fulfillments.

> In such passages, the sacred writer, as he foresaw these events in his day, viewed them in the distance of time like peaks of a mountain range, without realizing that valleys of time lay between them. This is especially true concerning events in the first and second advents of Christ.[20]

---

20 Leon Wood, *The Bible and Future Events*, (Grand Rapids: Zondervan, 1973), 24.

This phenomenon is found a number of times in the prophets and reveals gaps in prophetic fulfillment. For example, Daniel 9:24-27 contains a time gap that is critical to a proper interpretation of that prophecy. Daniel would never have guessed that several thousand years existed in those verses. Also, it is unlikely that Daniel understood that there would be a long time span between the appearance of the fourth "terrible beast" and the growing of the ten horns on the head of that same beast (Dan. 7:7, 23-24). It is, of course, only in the progress of history and God's revelation that we can see such intervals of time between prophetic fulfillments.

A Basic Outline of the Book of Daniel

I. INTRODUCTION TO DANIEL, Daniel 1:21

II. THE TIMES OF THE GENTILES, Daniel 2:1-7:28

    A. THE DREAM OF THE GREAT STATUE, Daniel 2:1-49

    B. THE GOLDEN IMAGE AND FURNACE OF FIRE, Daniel 3:1-30

    C. THE DREAM OF THE GREAT TREE, Daniel 4:1-37

    D. THE FEAST AND THE WRITING ON THE WALL, Daniel 5:1-31

    E. THE DECREE AND THE DEN OF LIONS, Daniel 6:1-28

    F. THE VISION OF THE FOUR BEASTS, Daniel 7:1-28

III. ISRAEL AND THE GENTILE NATIONS, Daniel 8:1-12:13

    A. THE VISION OF THE RAM AND THE GOAT, Daniel 8:1-27

    B. THE VISION OF THE SEVENTY WEEKS, Daniel 9:1-27

    C. THE FINAL VISION OF DANIEL, Daniel 10:1-12:13

QUESTIONS TO CONSIDER

1. Define a "two world view" and give some examples of how such a view might be evidenced in the life of a twenty-first century believer living in North America.

2. Discuss some specific ways that having a "two world view" might help us live authentic Christian lives and avoid being "one world" believers.

3. What value does the Book of Daniel have that makes it worth spending our time studying it?

4. Broadly speaking, what are the two positions that interpreters take regarding the author and the date of writing for this book? What difference does it make, if any, which position you hold?

5. Explain the principles that should be employed when interpreting the Book of Daniel.

6. Explain what life was like historically and spiritually when Daniel was a young boy.

CHAPTER ONE

COMING TO BABYLON

Preview: When Nebuchadnezzar took Jerusalem, he selected young men of Judah to be deported to Babylon. These young men, which included Daniel, were to be trained in order to serve in the Babylonian Government. The Babylonians appeared to be in control, but in reality, God sovereignly superintended the entire situation working in and through His devoted young servants.

The godly in the Kingdom of Judah would not have been overly surprised by the events of 605 BC. The arrival of the armies of Babylon, and the subsequent fall of Jerusalem, had repeatedly been foretold by the prophets. Because of the depth of idolatry and the amazing depravity brought in many years earlier by King Manasseh, judgment of the Kingdom of Judah was a certainty (cf. 2 Kgs. 23:26; 24:3; Jer. 15:1-4). But even after Manasseh died, the people embraced these evil ways and never really relinquished them in their hearts. Jeremiah had boldly prophesied concerning the end of Judah, making it abundantly clear that the Lord was going to side with the Babylonians in the coming conflict (cf. Jer. 20:4-6; 21:1-10; 32:1-5, 26-29; 34:1-3). And too, the prophet Habakkuk, in his dialogues with the Lord, was informed by the Lord that indeed the Babylonians were going to be His instrument for the discipline of Judah (cf. Hab. 1:5-11). These messages that were delivered by the prophets were firmly rooted back in the Law of Moses. There the consequences for Israel's disobedience were spelled out in great detail. In the Law it was revealed that there would be certain levels of discipline. If Israel did not respond to these disciplines of God then they would experience the final consequence of disobedience, which was military defeat and being taken into captivity by foreign nations (cf. Lev. 26:27-33; Deut. 28:25, 64-65). So, in the year 605 BC, this final discipline of God on Judah came, and the godly in Judah would have known this judgment was coming.

THE HISTORICAL SETTING (Dan. 1:1-2)

1:1 The book of Daniel has numerous chronological statements and the book begins with one of these. It states that the coming of Nebuchednezzar to Jerusalem took place in the "third year of the reign of Jehoiakim king of Judah." This seems to be a clear and uncomplicated expression concerning events in 605 BC. However, this clear statement by Daniel is apparently contradicted by Jeremiah who says that Nebuchadnezzar's coming was in the fourth year of Jehoiachim's reign (cf. Jer. 25:1). Critics have seized upon this difference to discredit the historical accuracy of the book of Daniel. One such critic observed that the author of Daniel was "fuzzy on the details" and that it was clear that his "forte is narrative art, not historical detail."[21]

However, there have been a variety of responses by scholars who would defend the accuracy and dependability of Daniel on this point. For example, C.F. Keil concluded that Daniel and Jeremiah were actually looking at two different phases of the same event. Jeremiah was looking at Nebuchadnezzar's arrival at Jerusalem while Daniel was focused on Nebuchadnezzar's departure from Babylon. Keil suggested that the statement in Daniel 1:1 that Nebuchadnezzar "came to" Jerusalem can legitimately be translated that he "marched to" Jerusalem. He believed that this made good sense since Daniel wrote this while in Babylon which was the point of departure for the Babylonian army.[22] While we can certainly commend this interpretation as

---

21 W. Sibley Towner, *Daniel*, (Louisville: John Knox, 1984), 22.
22 Carl F. Keil, *Biblical Commentary on the Book of Daniel*, (Grand Rapids: Eerdmans, n.d.) 62-63.

a positive desire to solve a difficult problem and uphold the integrity of the Word, a better and more accurate position reflects the more recent scholarship of Edwin Thiele.[23]

In dealing with the apparent contradictory chronological notations in the Old Testament, Thiele observed two critical factors that students of the Bible must be aware of. First, the scribes within Judah and Israel, as well as the scribes in foreign nations, could use two different starting points for the calendar year: one in the Spring of the year (Nisan) and the other in the Fall (Tishri). This immediately opens up the possibility of the same event being attributed to two different years, depending on which scribe was telling the story.

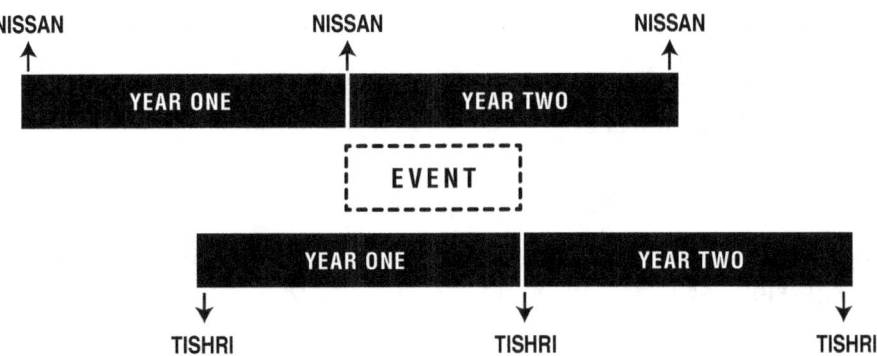

In this present case, Daniel apparently was using Tishri (Sept/Oct) reckoning while Jeremiah was using Nisan (March/April) reckoning for the beginning of Jehoiakim's reign as Judah's king. Any event that occurred between the spring and the fall could easily have a one year difference because these two different starting times were employed. Nebuchadnezzar's coming to Jerusalem took place in the summer of 605 BC and so would be reckoned as the fourth year of Jehoiakim in the Nisan calendar and the third year according to Tishri reckoning. So the problem can be solved quite easily.

---

23 Edwin R. Thiele, *A chronology of the Hebrew Kings*, (Grand Rapids: Zondervan, 1977) 14-22.

But Thiele noted a second critical factor in the matter of the dating of events in the Old Testament that had to do with the idea of the "accession year." He observed that it was the custom of some when a king began his reign, to call the year in which he came to the throne his "accession year"; that is, the year he acceded, or came, to the throne. This "accession year" could be a few days or many months depending on when the new year began on the calendar. His "first year" was then considered to be the first full twelve-month period following the beginning of a new year on the calendar. The other possible method employed by scribes was the non-accession year system that called the year that he came to the throne his "first year." This would be true even if the "first year" only comprised a few weeks or many months before the start of the next calendar year. The first full year of twelve months would be viewed as the king's second year. This use of the accession year and non-accession year systems also could account for a one-year discrepancy in describing the identical event.

1	2	3	4
ACCESSION YEAR	1	2	3

Therefore, when these two factors are observed, the apparent discrepancy is dealt with and there is no contradiction here between Daniel and Jeremiah. In fact, Thiele and others have demonstrated that most of the so-called discrepancies in the chronology of the Old Testament are solved when these variables in the dating methods are noted.

In this first verse, it should also be noted that Nebuchadnezzar is called "the king of Babylon". Technically at this point in time Nabopollasar, his father, was the king. Nabopollasar died in August of 605 with the result that Nebuchadnezzar cut short his western campaign and returned to Babylon and was crowned as king in September of 605. Again, an apparent historical blunder is used by critics to discredit Daniel. But, aside from the probability that he was already a co-regent with his father, the term would be easily understood as a common figure of speech. "The proleptic use of such a title is so common (e.g. in the statement "King David as a boy was a shepherd") that this does not cause a serious problem."[24] It is common in ordinary conversation to assign a position to a person earlier than the actual time when they held it. If we should say, "when President Bush was a young boy", we are not saying that George W. Bush was president of the United States when he was a young boy. We have assigned the title "president" to him at a point in time when he had not actually become president. This ordinary linguistic device is all that Daniel was doing here.

1:2 As prophets had previously warned Judah, the Lord did indeed align Himself with the Babylonians with the result that Judah fell into the hands of this foreign army. This statement reveals that God is absolutely sovereign over the affairs of men and of nations. This is not a testimonial to the superiority of the armies of Babylon, but of the sovereignty of the God of Israel. He does what He wishes in this universe of His. Judah now became the vassal state of Babylon and Judah's national independence was gone. A totally new period had now begun for the people of Israel and this period of dependence on the gentile nations would last until the time the Messiah would come to earth and personally reign over Israel. The "times of the gentiles" had commenced.

At this point in time, Nebuchadnezzar found it necessary to hurry back to Babylon because news had reached him that his father, Nabopollasar, had died. It was unwise to leave the throne empty for long even if you were the heir apparent. There was always a cousin or uncle or "friend" who would gladly seize the throne. With the need to get to Babylon quickly, the treasures and hostages of Nebuchadnezzar would come later by a longer route, according to Flavius Josephus.

---

24 John F. Walvoord, *Daniel: The Key to Prophetic Revelation*, (Chicago: Moody, 1971), 32.

> ...having settled affairs of Egypt and the other countries, as also those that contained the captive Jews...and having committed the conveyance of them to Babylon to certain of his friends, together with the gross of his army and the rest of their ammunition and provisions, he went himself hastily, accompanied with a few others, over the desert, and came to Babylon.[25]

But Nebuchadnezzar did not rush back to Babylon so hurriedly that he did not give careful thought to what needed to be done. First, he took *some* of the treasure from the Jerusalem temple. A century earlier Isaiah had said that "the days are coming when all that is in your house, and all that your fathers have laid up in store to this day shall be carried to Babylon; nothing shall be left" (Isa. 39:6). Eventually Nebuchadnezzar would remove all the temple treasure, but 605 BC was just the first installment. He shrewdly took some but not all of the vessels. By taking some he pointedly showed that his gods were more powerful than Israel's God, but by leaving many for continued use in the Jerusalem temple, he defused a situation that could lead to rebellion. Nebuchadnezzar would take the temple vessels and place them in the temples of his gods, which would include Marduk and Nebo. These temples were, of course, located back in Babylon, which is referred to here as the land of Shinar. "Shinar" was southern area of Mesopotamia of which Babylon was a part and the term is used in the Old Testament to refer to a place of false religion (cf. Zech. 5:11). The taking of temple treasure was not simply a means of increasing wealth but this action was a graphic way of proclaiming the superiority of these gods. Nebuchadnezzar wanted it to be clear that the gods of Babylon were superior to all other gods, including Israel's God. However, over the next years, the Lord God of Israel would work wonderfully to change the thinking and theology of Nebuchadnezzar on this matter.

---

[25] Flavius Josephus, *The Antiquities of the Jews*, trans. by Wm. Whiston, (Grand Rapids: Kregel, 1978), 224

The second matter Nebuchadnezzar attended to had to do with the throne of Judah. He chose to leave Jehoiakim the king on the throne of Judah. According to 2 Chronicles 36:6, Jehoiakim was actually bound with "bronze chains" for transportation back to Babylon. But this plan changed apparently due to the need of the moment to hurriedly return to Babylon. Nebuchadnezzar let him remain on the throne after extracting a promise of loyalty from the king of Judah, and a commitment to pay large sums of tribute money. These promises would be broken after a few short years. There was a third matter that Nebuchadnezzar addressed before he left for Babylon.

THE SELECTION OF THE TRAINEES (Dan. 1:3-7)

1:3 The third matter addressed by Nebuchadnezzar is discussed in some detail in the text. He decided to have young men from Judah taken back to Babylon. These young men from royal and noble families would act as a deterrent to any rebellion in Judah. It was less likely that these nobles would encourage an uprising if their sons were just a sword's length from their captors. Furthermore, as they were trained in the language and ways of Babylon, they would be able to make an effective contribution to the government of Babylon. Along with the taking of temple treasure, this taking of trainee/hostages was also a fulfillment of a word given a century earlier by Isaiah the prophet. Isaiah said to King Hezekiah: "And some of your sons who shall issue from you, whom you shall beget, shall be taken away; and they shall become officials in the palace of the king of Babylon." (Isa. 39:7). The man in charge of selecting and transporting these young men from Judah to Babylon was a man named Ashpenaz, who is said to be the "chief of his officials." The term "official" (Heb. *saris*) is commonly translated as "eunuch"; that is, a castrated male. This word is used concerning those youths spoken of by Isaiah the prophet (cf. 2 Kgs 20:18) which has interesting implications for Daniel and his three friends. Were they made eunuchs by the Babylonians? While that is a possibility, this word came to simply have the meaning "court official" without physical castration being required. Merrill Unger notes that the word came to signify "important servants". "We must remember that both the Hebrew and Greek terms were sometimes applied to those filling important posts, without regard to corporeal mutilation."[26] That they did not experience castration could well be supported by the next verse which tells us that Daniel and his friends had "no defect" in them.

1:4 There were clear guidelines that Ashpenaz was to use in the selecting of the hostage/trainees. First, as we have seen, they were to be taken from the royal family or from the nobility of Judah. It is quite possible, therefore, that Daniel and his friends were descendants of King Hezekiah, or at the very least they were from the upper level of society. They had to be true Israelites. Second, they were to be young men. It is generally understood that later on the Persians began the education of hostages at around the age of 14.[27] It is speculated that they probably adopted this practice from the Babylonians. Therefore, it is most likely that Daniel and his friends were somewhere around 15 years old when taken captive. And the fact that Daniel lived through the entire seventy year captivity period, and beyond, would support his youthfulness at the very beginning of the captivity.

In addition to these two qualifications, Ashpenaz had four other requirements by which he was to select the young men. First, they had to have "no defect"; that is, they had to be outwardly perfect with no physical deformities. This word was used for animals that could be used for acceptable sacrifices to the Lord. So we can conclude that Daniel and his friends were free from any physical abnormalities. Second, they had to be good looking. It is well known that only the beautiful people were allowed in the courts of the kings. Homely folks need not try and enter. "A beautiful form was, according to Eastern concepts, most closely connected with excellence of mind and spirit, and this was even considered as a sign of a favorable disposition on

---

26 Merrill F. Unger, *Unger's Bible Dictionary*, (Chicago: Moody, 1962), 328.
27 Leon Wood, *A Commentary on Daniel*, (Grand Rapids: Zondervan, 1973), 33.

the part of the gods."²⁸ Daniel, as well as the other youths, would have been a handsome young man. Third, all of them had to be intelligent and capable of learning. The four words used here describe someone who is well-versed in wisdom but also capable of learning and mastering knowledge. We do not know what testing Ashpenaz used to determine this, but he undoubtedly carefully carried out the orders of the King. Those taken were mentally sharp. And fourth, they had to evidence maturity, having poise that enabled them to carry themselves well in the court of a king. Presumably young men of this background would have already had exposure to palaces and the courts of kings and would easily qualify on this point.

These young men were chosen so that they could be taught "the literature and language of the Chaldeans." At that time, Aramaic was the language of normal communication and one that Daniel may well have known. Their training, therefore, was probably not to learn Aramaic but rather Akkadian.

> …the native language of the Babylonians was Akkadian, a Semitic language like Hebrew, but with an extremely complex writing system. It was written in syllabic cuneiform, with the additional complexity that it often utilized the ancient language of the region, Sumerian, in its technical literature. It is likely that our text has Akkadian specifically in mind in terms of the special training that Daniel and his friends were about to receive.²⁹

This training would enable them to delve into the "wisdom of Babylon" which included the arts of divination and astrology as well as mathematics, natural history, the chronicles of the empire and many other areas of study. It is interesting to observe that none of this wisdom would do any good when dreams from the Lord God needed to be interpreted or when handwriting on walls needed to be understood. It is also instructive to observe that

---

28 Harry Bultema, *Commentary on Daniel*, (Grand Rapids: Kregel, 1988), 39.
29 Tremper Longman III, *Daniel: The NIV Application Commentary*, (Grand Rapids: Zondervan, 1999), 49.

Daniel gave himself fully to the task and ended up "graduating" at the head of the class. He knew and practiced what the Apostle Paul would later tell Christians, that "whatever you do, do all to the glory of God" (1 Cor. 11:31).

1:5 This education was to take place over three years. It is evident that the subject matter would take some time to master. Actually, the training would not be three full years (i.e. 36 months) but portions of three different years. This is seen by the fact that Daniel and his friends would be involved in the interpretation of Nebuchadnezzar's statue vision that occurred in the second year of his reign (2:1). The three years would include part of the King's "accession year", his first full year and then part of his second year. During this time of study the trainees would be provided fine food and drink from the kitchen of the King himself. Free tuition, room and board was provided for all of these trainees.

1:6 Up to this point the text has not actually given us the names of these young men taken from Judah. We are now introduced to Daniel, Hananiah, Mishael and Azariah. It is clear that they are not the only ones taken from Judah's royalty and nobility. But apparently the other young men did not remain loyal to the Lord God.

> Naturally, countless young men had been taken from Judah to Babylon. They were all young men who had the sign of the covenant on them. But once they were in Babylon, we neither hear nor see them again. Did they, after their arrival in Babylon, become Babylonians? We do not know, but it would not surprise us. The attraction of the world was strong in Babylon, especially to a young mind. In any case, God did not count them worthy to be named in His Word.[30]

But Daniel and his three friends would honor their God and He in turn would honor them. God honors those who honor Him. This great spiritual law is recorded in 1 Samuel 2:30 and is in force today just as it was back then. Those men and women who chose to honor the Lord in the way

---
30 Bultema, 43.

they live are guaranteed that the Lord will honor them. The Lord does not say how He will do this but is clear that He will do so.

1:7 It was a common practice to change the names of individuals being brought into the court. It was a way of indicating new ownership and a new destiny and was designed to hurry along assimilation into the new culture. We observe this in our country, as often immigrants will "Americanize" their names. And we recall that this is what took place in the experience of Joseph who had his named changed to Zaphenath-paneah (Gen. 41:45). Also, the names of deities were frequently contained in the individual's name, as it is here in the case of the four young men from Judah.

The Hebrew names of the four clearly reflect their relationship with the Lord God of Israel and probably indicate that they came from homes where there was a devotion to the Lord. Their names are changed to identify them with Babylonian deities in an attempt to develop new allegiances and new direction for their lives. The Hebrew names are fairly clear in their meaning, but the Babylonian names are not. There is considerable debate on the exact meaning of the Babylonian names. One possibility is that Daniel ("God is my judge") received the name Belteshazzar ("May Bel protect his life"); Hananiah ("Jehovah has been gracious") became Shadrach ("command of Marduk/Aku"); Mishael ("Who is as God?") became Meshach ("who is what Aku is?); and Azariah ("Jehovah has helped") became Abednego ("servant of Nebo"). Whether or not these are the exact meanings of the names is unclear. But what is clear is that these who were identified with the God of Israel are now being identified with the gods of Babylon. It is interesting that the four young men apparently did not make an issue of the name change, though we would assume that in their own apartment they called each other by their Hebrew names. They chose not to fight this battle probably because the Law did not expressly prohibit such things. They did not make this an issue, but they would make an issue of the food and drink. They showed great wisdom in knowing where to take a stand for the truth of God and where not to.

THE TEST OF FAITH (Dan. 1:8-16)

1:8 They chose to take a firm stand on the matter of the food and drink that was given to them and the other trainees. Having to live in Babylon was no doubt an inherently defiling experience for them (cf. Ezek. 4:13; Hos. 9:3-4). But there was something so clearly defiling about the "king's choice food" that Daniel and his three companions determined that they simply were not going to partake of it and were ready to sacrifice everything. Obviously if it was the "king's choice food" then we can be sure that there was nothing contaminated or polluted about it. The defilement here most likely was ceremonial. The diet being provided to them, of course, may regularly have included those animals that were defined as "unclean" in the Mosaic Law Code (cf. Lev. 11:1-47; Deut. 14:3-21) or that were not properly prepared (Lev. 3:17; 17:10-15; 19:26; Deut. 14:21). But this very real possibility does not account for their refusal to drink of the wine which was not prohibited in the Law.

The defiling issue here is apparently that of idolatry. Most in our culture do not see eating and drinking as an inherently religious issue (except in a few isolated situations like Lent) because the religious or spiritual life is compartmentalized away from most everything else. But among these people religion was not a separate compartment of life but was interwoven with everything in life. They would not have understood the concept of "separation of church and state." The preparation and eating of food involved religious ritual and was often mystically important. The killing of animals was a religious act and food was ritually offered to the household gods. Any food and drink brought to the King would certainly have been offered to his gods. C. F. Keil seems very close to the truth when he says that these pagans

> ...offered up in sacrifice to their gods a part of the food and drink, and thus consecrated their meals by a religious rite; whereby not only he who participated in such a meal participated in the worship of idols, but the meat and the wine as a whole were the meat

and the wine of an idol sacrifice, partaking of which, according to the sayings of the apostle (1 Cor. X.20f.) is the same as sacrificing to devils.[31]

So, for Daniel and his friends this was nothing less than an issue of faithfulness to the Law of God and to the God of the Law. And as with all people who make a mark for the Lord God in this world, a clear-cut decision had to be made. Those who do not determine to serve and follow the Lord rarely, if ever, do make such an impression for the Lord God. A loyal follower of Christ today cannot serve Him and someone or something else. Christ's demands on this matter are clear (cf. Lk 9:23; 14:25-35). That idolatry is an ever-present problem to the Christian of the twenty-first century is seen in the exhortations of the apostles to "flee idolatry" and to "guard yourselves from idols" (1 Cor. 10:14; 1 John 5:21). Daniel's determination was a necessary and courageous thing. But several important points should be noted. First, his determined choice was not an emotional decision, but a reasoned act based on his knowledge of the Word of God. No such decision could be made without having a good grip on the Scriptures. We are transformed by the renewing of our minds not by the stimulating of our emotions. Christians cannot make good and godly decisions without having some understanding of God's desires and standards. Unfortunately, many a decision has been made in an intensely emotional atmosphere that was devoid of a clear presentation of God's Word. A second point to note is that this decision by Daniel was not the end of the story. Decisions are very important in the spiritual life, but they are the beginning and not the end of the spiritual walk. Daniel made his mark for the Lord God because after this initial important decision he lived a life of personal devotion and discipline. There are perhaps many people in the church today who made a decision of some sort in the past to serve Jesus Christ, but who wrongly assumed that their decision would carry them throughout life. They think that their sincere decision will be sufficient.

---
[31] Keil, 80.

It is one thing to make such a determined choice and it is yet another to deal with those around us who are involved in our lives in some way. Daniel knew that the one in charge of him as a trainee must be involved, and so, he approached him to ask that some adjustments be made. In this Daniel revealed an amazing maturity for a 15-year-old.

1:9-10 Daniel's request was directed to one who was sympathetic to him personally. The chief of the officials was favorable towards Daniel showing kindness (Heb. *hesed*) and deep sympathy (Heb. *rahamim*). This internal working in the heart of Ashpenaz, the chief official was a work of the Spirit of God. Proverbs 16:7 declares that "when a man's ways are pleasing to the Lord, He makes even his enemies to be at peace with him." Daniel had honored the Lord and the Lord then honored Daniel as He had said He would do (cf. 1 Sam. 2:30).

Although the chief of the officials was clearly drawn to Daniel and was appreciative of him, his fear of the King prohibited him from granting Daniel's request. When Ashpenaz said that he would be in danger of losing his head, he was not speaking in exaggerated terms. As the events in chapter two and three will reveal, the King could arbitrarily choose to put men to death without being challenged. So, Ashpenaz could not afford to have Daniel's group looking malnourished or sickly in any way. The risk was simply too great.

1:11-13 Daniel, however, was not done with the matter and approached a lesser official with a proposal. This man (called the "melzar") was a steward appointed by Ashpenaz to directly handle matters pertaining to the hostage/trainees. Daniel understood that any change of the King's orders was risky business, and no one was about to jeopardize their lives to accommodate some Jewish boys. So, the proposal was for a short-term change of diet that could be evaluated before the steward was placed into any real danger. Ten days was a reasonable time. After ten days of eating vegetables Daniel and his colleagues could be examined and compared with all the others who stuck with the King's "choice food."

1:14-16 The test proved to be a smashing success as Daniel and friends were much healthier looking than the rest of the trainees. They were not just as healthy as the rest but were clearly much healthier ("fat of flesh"). And this became evident in the amazingly short time of a week and a half. This certainly is not a testimony to a superior diet, but to the working of God. Some are reluctant to call this a miracle, but why not? What took place was not the natural course of events but was God intervening on behalf of faithful men and doing something unusual and wonderful. With the success of the ten-day test the diet became standard for the entire period of training.

THE "EXAM" AND GRADUATION (Dan. 1:17-21)

1:17 Once again the direct working of God in this situation is expressed, revealing that it is God who is really in control of these events. God is the One who gave Daniel and his three friends exceptional understanding. These four were earlier seen as possessing great natural ability. But what is being given here is beyond what they possessed naturally and is another gift from God in order to prepare them to serve Him with excellence in the coming years in the administration of Babylon. God not only continued to honor these who had honored Him, but He was preparing them to do battle with those who only had the "appearance of wisdom".

An additional note is given here. In the sovereign workings of God, Daniel was given an ability to understand visions and dreams. His three companions were not given this ability. God is sovereign in His dealing with all of us who are His children. He gives spiritual gifts, natural abilities, a level intelligence, financial resources, good health and opportunities in differing measures to His children. He does so in order that His sovereign plans can be carried out in this world. Our responsibility is not to covet or compare ourselves with others, but to faithfully serve Him as stewards of all that He has graciously given to us (cf. 1 Cor. 4:1-7). So, Daniel alone was granted the ability to interpret dreams because that fit into God's plan. We would suggest that Daniel did interpret some dreams prior to the dream of Nebuchadnezzar in chapter 2. And as it turns out, Daniel's wisdom was apparently much greater than that of his friends. In fact, Daniel's wisdom would soon become proverbial among the Jewish captives in Babylon (cf. Ezek. 28:3). God's dealings are different with each of His children, as is reflected in Jesus' parable of the three servants in Matthew 25:15.

1:18-20 As this section opens, the three-year training program has been completed. The King himself interrogated all of the trainees. His questions probably included every discipline in which the young men had been taught. When the "exam" time was over the results were clear. Daniel, Hananiah, Mishael and Azariah were superior to all the rest. They were at the head of the graduating class. They were so very far ahead of the rest of the trainees. But that was not all. The statement that they were "ten times better" is most likely a figure of speech that emphasizes the fact of their superiority. But it should be noted that the comparison is not made with the other trainees but with the intellectual elite of Babylon. While this probably did not endear the four Jewish boys to the rest of the administration, it reveals how greatly impressed Nebuchadnezzar was with these four. And it would be just a very short time before Daniel's God-given wisdom would be known throughout Babylon (cf. Dan. 2:48). The result of the "exam" was that all four became part of the administration of Babylon. At this point in time they are probably holding lesser positions in the government. But that would soon change.

1:21 This introductory chapter ends with a time notation. It states that Daniel, who was taken captive in the very first year of the Babylonian captivity, continued until the first year of the Persian administration. Some have said this contradicts the statement in Daniel 10:1 where the final vision of Daniel is dated in the third year of the Persians. However, such criticism misses the basic purpose of the statement which is simply to let us know that Daniel lived throughout the Babylonian captivity. "The passage does not say or necessarily imply that Daniel did not continue after the first year of Cyrus---which, as a matter of fact, he did."[32] John Whitcomb observes that "we have here a chronological point of reference that does not demand a termination...Daniel is not telling us in the verse how far into the reign of Cyrus he lived; he is simply emphasizing God's amazing providence and grace in allowing him to live throughout the entire reigns" of all the kings of Babylon and well into the empire of the Persians.[33]

It must also be noted that the first year of Cyrus marked the beginning of the end of the Babylonian captivity of Daniel's people. A decree was issued in that year which allowed the people to return and rebuild the temple in Jerusalem (cf. Ezra 1:1-4). Daniel 1:21 is informing us that Daniel who saw the start of the Babylonian captivity also saw the end of it and the return of the people of Israel back to their land. The fact that Daniel had a vision two years later is simply not pertinent to the point being made.

QUESTIONS TO CONSIDER

1. What made it possible for the four young men to make such an impact for God in a very hostile environment? What can churches and families do to produce such people?

2. One of the key truths in this book is the sovereignty of God. How would you describe or define God's sovereignty? How did God's sovereignty and mans' efforts play out in the life of Daniel and his friends?

3. God honors those who honor Him (1 Sam. 2:30b). This is a spiritual law that is seen in the life of Daniel. What other biblical characters illustrate this law? In what ways have you seen this law at work in the experience of Christians today?

---

32 Walvoord, 42.
33 John C. Whitcomb, *Daniel*, (Chicago: Moody, 1985), 35.

44 | DANIEL

4. Do you think that Daniel's decision not to eat of the king's food was really necessary? What do you think might have happened if he had not made this decision? What makes for good spiritual decisions?

5. What place should "decisions" have in our lives? What real value do they have? Describe some key spiritual decisions you have made and relate the impact that they had on you and on those around you?

6. From the experiences of Daniel and his friends, what are some truths that we can learn regarding living/working in a hostile setting?

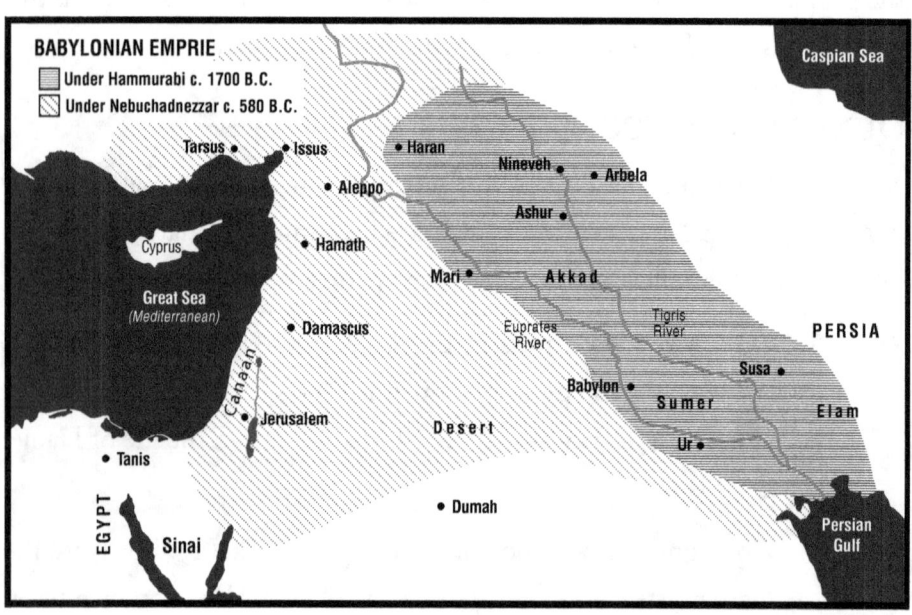

CHAPTER TWO

DREAMING OF EMPIRES

Preview: Early in his reign, King Nebuchadnezzar has a troubling dream of a great metallic statue. No one was able to interpret the dream until Daniel, enlightened by God, did so. The statue dream was the means by which God revealed the coming course of world history. The empires of this world would rise and fall but would finally and completely be brought to an end by the establishing of God's future, forever kingdom.

This is one of the more significant chapters in the Old Testament because it reveals something of the sovereign God's plans for this earth. It gives a basic outline of the rise and fall of major empires; an outline that will be developed in more detail in other visions in this book of Daniel. Since the other prophetic portions in this book are based on this first vision, some time and space needs to be given to it. Having a basic grip on this chapter is really essential to understanding that which is to come in Daniel. But this chapter also demonstrates to all who would see that there is none like the God of Israel who alone reveals mysteries and who alone dictates the course of events on this earth. Interestingly, God will give this key dream, not to Daniel, but to a pagan king.

DREAMING A DREAM (Dan. 2:1-3)

2:1 Again a chronological notation is given. This incident of Nebuchadnezzar's dream of the great metallic statue took place in the second year of his reign, which would be in the year 603 B.C. This date would seem to pose a problem since in the account given in chapter one, Daniel had already graduated after "three years" of training and had entered the king's service; and yet, this is said to be Nebuchadnezzar's second year. But it is not a significant matter when we remember the concept of the "accession year" (See pages 23-25 for comments on chronological matters). The dream of Nebuchadnezzar probably took place shortly after Daniel's entrance into the king's service.

NEBUCHADNEZZAR	DANIEL
605 "Accession Year"	Taken captive; first year of training
604 First full year of reign	Second year of training
603 Second Year (The Dream)	Third year of training and "graduation"

The dream that the king dreamed that night burrowed deeply into his soul and would not leave him alone. The dream, or perhaps nightmare, so gripped him that he could not sleep. He was, no doubt, absolutely convinced that a message of great importance was being communicated to him by the gods and he absolutely had to know its meaning.

2:2-3 The king ordered an immediate appearance of the professionals who could relieve the King's concerns by making clear the meaning of the dream. The hope apparently was to come to an understanding by bringing in various experts who had different means of securing information. The group that was brought in is identified by four words: the magicians, the conjurers, the sorcerers and the Chaldeans. The "magicians" may well have been the scholars since the word "is the translation of a Hebrew word with a root meaning of stylus or pen…and hence could refer to a scholar rather than a magician in the ordinary sense."[34] Those designated as "conjurers" are

---
34 John F. Walvoord, *Daniel: The Key to Prophetic Interpretation* (Chicago: Moody, 1971), 47.

sometimes seen as astrologers who "were the men who by gazing into the eerie realm of the stars thought to discover true or imagined wisdom."[35] The "sorcerers" were those who were in contact with the spirit world and were seen as capable of gathering information from that source. And in this context the word "Chaldeans" is apparently speaking of the powerful priestly class that had emerged in Babylon. They dealt in magical lore and were allegedly able to interpret dreams. They would have come into the king's presence that night armed with their dream interpretation books

> These experts in dreams worked on the principle that dreams and their sequels followed an empirical law which, given sufficient date, could be established. The dream manuals…consist accordingly of historical dreams and the events that followed them, arranged systematically for easy reference. Since these books had to try to cover every possible eventuality they became inordinately long; only the expert could find his way through them, and even he had to know the dream to begin with before he could search for the nearest possible parallel.[36]

These men were not ignorant but were well educated and were considered to be the wisest of men in Babylon. They were considered the best of the best. But all of their training would do them no good in this situation (cf. Dan. 2:27).

SEEKING AN ANSWER (Dan. 2:4-13)

2:4 One might speculate that there must have been some uneasiness among these wise men of Babylon as they were summoned in the night before an obviously agitated monarch. The influential Chaldeans were apparently the spokesmen for the entire group. (Here begins the Aramaic section of Daniel). After the usual and necessary greeting, the Chaldeans ask the king to share the content of the dream, so they can get to the task of interpreting it.

---

35 Harry Bultema, *Commentary on Daniel* (Grand Rapids: Kregel, 1988), 57.
36 Joyce G. Baldwin, *Daniel: An Introduction and Commentary* (Downers Grove: InterVarsity, 1978), 87.

2:5-6 The king's response to their query is quite harsh, quite unexpected and against normal protocol in such situations. Normally protocol "required the king to inform the professional interpreters of the content of his dream."[37] So they were no doubt taken back by what they heard. The King James Version reads that Nebuchadnezzar said, "the thing is gone from me". This has led some to understand his statement to mean that the king had forgotten his dream, or at least it was so unclear to him so as to keep him from helping out the scholars.[38] However, the New American Standard reads that he declared, "the command from me is firm". This would mean that Nebuchadnezzar had not forgotten his dream and was absolutely not budging on what he was requiring of these men. His requirement was twofold. First, they were to give the content of the dream itself, and then second, they were to give the dream's interpretation.

The idea that Nebuchadnezzar had not forgotten his dream seems the better interpretation in light of the context. First, it accounts for the settled anger of the king in regard to the men who stood before him. It is clear that Nebuchadnezzar had no patience with these wise men and this points to the likelihood that they had been less than honest in the past with his father Nabopollasar and, perhaps, with himself. He would not have been so hostile towards them if he had simply forgotten his dream and if he saw them as trusted, reliable men. Second, this was not simply blind rage but a test of the integrity and the ability of these men. They claimed to have great powers, secret knowledge and contact with the spirit world. This was a defining test for such men and, if they could produce, would validate their exalted claims. We must remember that this dream and its interpretation were so very important to the king and he wanted to take no chances when it came to understanding what the gods were trying to tell him. Third, it is improbable psychologically that Nebuchadnezzar would have forgotten a

---

[37] Tremper Longman III, *Daniel: The NIV Application Commentary* (Grand Rapids: Zondervan, 1999), 77.

[38] Arno C. Gaebelein, *Daniel*, (Grand Rapids: Kregel, 1968), 20-22.

dream that was of "extraordinary splendor" and "awesome" (cf. Dan. 2:31). As Whitcomb observes, "we must assume that when God gives special dreams to men they will be clear, startling, and unforgettable."[39] This seemed to be the experience of others like the Midianite soldier (Judg. 7:13) and Elihu (Job 33:15). And Pharaoh's experience of remembering vividly his dreams after waking up suddenly because his troubling dreams does seem to be very much like Nebuchadnezzar's experience (Gen. 41:1-8). And a fourth reason for saying that Nebuchadnezzar had not forgotten his dream has to do the phrase "the command from me *is firm*". The word 'azda' most likely should read "the word is assured from me" which translated means "the thing (command) is fully resolved upon by me."[40] While the meaning of this word is not absolutely certain, it seems to be focusing on the resolve of the king and not that the dream has somehow vanished from his mind. And finally, the statement at the end of 2:9 points to Nebuchadnezzar being fully aware of the content of his own dream.

The stakes could not be any higher. Failure to fulfill the two-fold demand would mean death for all of them. Furthermore, their failure would result in their houses being turned into garbage dumps or manure piles, which was a means of heaping dishonor and contempt on individuals. On the other hand, successful interpretation of the dream would bring with it wealth and status. They would either be heroes or goats (dead ones at that).

2:7-9 With so much on the line and their backs to the proverbial wall, the Chaldeans boldly request from the king once again to give them the content of the dream. The response from the king brings no encouragement to them. He again restates his unbending two-fold requirement as well as adding his observation about their motives in the matter. He declares that they know the seriousness of the situation they are in and are hoping beyond hope that given time the situation and the consequences will somehow change. One

---

39 John C. Whitcomb, *Daniel*, (Chicago: Moody, 1985), 40.
40 Ibid.

suspects that the king has observed their methods before and is giving them absolutely no room to maneuver. And the king is quite clear that no time will be granted; it is "put up or shut up" time. They were to get on with the business of giving both the dream and the interpretation. He knows the dream and wants to be assured that their abilities are all that they have proclaimed. He must hear the dream's content and then he will "know that you can declare to me its interpretation" (Dan. 2:9). With this impasse the final desperate statement of the Chaldeans is uttered, and the stage is completely set in preparation for the entrance of Daniel.

2:10-13 The Chaldean's revealed the bankruptcy of their wisdom and their sources. As their pride crumbled and fear gripped them, they complained that the king was being totally unreasonable and appealed to history to illustrate that no one else had made such an absurd demand. They pointed out that the king's demand was really difficult ("rare") and that when it is all said, only the gods could fulfill this requirement. This, of course, raises the question in our minds about how intimate they were with these gods of theirs. Their attempts at intimidating the king or making him feel guilty did no good at all. The king apparently had confirmed in his own mind his suspicions about these men. The king's simmering anger became white hot and he exploded in rage against these pseudo-wise men. He saw them as worse than worthless and ordered their execution. (Later, Daniel sees this event as a demonstration of the absolute sovereignty of King Nebuchadnezzar in Dan. 5:19). And since these wise men were apparently the best of the bunch, he ordered that all wise men of Babylon were to be executed immediately. The phrase "of Babylon" could refer to the city or to the whole empire. This order probably focused on the city itself and not on the whole empire of Babylon. Of course, most of the wise men "of Babylon" probably lived in or near the capital city.

FACING AN EXECUTION (Dan. 2:14-16)

2:14-15 The rage of the king fueled the actions of Arioch, the captain of the kings' bodyguard, which seems to be the highest office in the kingdom. Arioch wasted no time in obeying the command. He began immediately to round up and kill Babylonian wise men. The word used here implies that the process of execution had already begun by the time Daniel was arrested.

> A beginning was made with the slaughter of the sages. For this is the meaning of the words, that the wise men should be slain. The Dutch translation agrees with the Greek and the Latin: the wise men began to be killed, and this undoubtedly renders the participle *mithkatlin* correctly. The reason some translators and expositors wish to read this differently seems to be based on verses 14 and 24, but incorrectly so. These verses only show that the execution was stopped before all the wise men were killed. In this contested verse it is not stated they were actually all killed but only that at the command of the king the killing had already commenced. The wise men standing before the king were killed first of all, of course.[41]

Since Daniel and his three friends fell into the category of wise men, it was only a matter of time before Arioch and the soldiers arrived at Daniel's front door. When he was informed of his fate, Daniel reacted not with anger or panic but with amazing calm and wisdom. Daniel inquired as to why this harsh decree was being carried out so quickly. The fact that Arioch took time to explain it all to Daniel suggests that Daniel was much respected by Arioch and, possibly, that Arioch himself thought the decree was an overreaction on the part of the king. We should note here that one of the results of God's wisdom in a person is to bring a wonderful stability to that individual (cf. Col. 1:9-11). Any believer can be so characterized.

Daniel needed wisdom for this terrible trial and wisdom was granted to him. We should note that any child of God can have God's wisdom in

---
[41] Bultema, 72.

the midst of trials and in hard times. There is God's promise that when we need wisdom for trials and difficult times that He can supply what is needed. This presupposes, of course, that the believer has been faithfully pursuing wisdom during his life as it is found in the Scriptures. The Spirit can then take the wisdom stored away and marry it successfully with the current crisis. The Spirit does not work in a vacuum, which accounts for the inability of some believers to handle with calm and wisdom the trials that come into their lives. The Spirit had much to work with in the young man Daniel who gives much evidence of being a man of the Book. The wisdom and calm confidence with which Daniel interacted with Arioch apparently put the executions temporarily on hold for a few hours. Many of the wise men of Babylon would owe their lives to Daniel.

2:16 There is undoubtedly much more that was said between verses 15 and 16, but verse 16 finds Daniel entering into the king's presence, which seems a risky thing to do. There are a number of reasons why Nebuchadnezzar might have allowed Daniel (a certified wise man) to have an audience with him besides the possibility that he had cooled down considerably. First, Daniel (a recent graduate) was not part of the older group of wise men of whom Nebuchadnezzar was highly suspicious and had little tolerance. And it is likely that Daniel was highly esteemed by the king since he had already proven himself to be "ten times better" than the group that had failed so miserably that night (cf. Dan. 1:20). Second, Nebuchadnezzar knew that killing all the wise men would not bring him any closer to the one thing he really wanted, and that was to have his dream interpreted. And here he has been informed that there is someone who holds out hope to him of getting that critical knowledge. Daniel had come to him with the confidence that he could fulfill the king's two-fold requirement. He only needed some time to pray to his God who could, in fact, give him the needed information. And the anxious king granted him his request though we would assume that he was given a clear time limit.

SEEKING THE LORD (Dan. 2:17-24)

2:17-18 After his appearance before the king, Daniel returned to his house. The fact that the verse states that Daniel "went to his house" indicates that he himself went to see the king. It was a personal audience before the king and it was not that Arioch or someone else represented Daniel before the king.

Daniel informs his praying friends of all the events and conversations and they immediately seek together the only One who can reveal and interpret mysteries. Blessed is the believer who has close friends who know how to pray. So often when faced with difficult times in life believers will immediately seek to talk with individual after individual and not go quickly to the Lord. The four young men shared the information and then quickly went to prayer, rightly praying that the Lord would spare them since they were innocent of any wrong doing. They also needed to know the "mystery" (which is a divine truth that is beyond human ability to find out or comprehend). Mysteries are only discovered by divine revelation and in this case the "mystery" refers to the content of the king's dream.

2:19-23 God quickly and graciously answered their prayers and to Daniel is given a "replay" of Nebuchadnezzar's dream. We would think that Daniel received the same exact dream but one with the divine audio commentary attached. Daniel's immediate response was not to hurriedly run to the king, but to give praise to the King of kings.

The praise of Daniel reflects a wonderful working knowledge of the Scriptures. His praise focuses on the wisdom of God and the sovereign power of God. This dream of Nebuchadnezzar has already revealed that the wise men of Babylon are not really wise and that the powerful king of Babylon is not so mighty. God's sovereign power is seen in the fact that He controls "the times and the epochs"; by which we understand that He is the one who structures all history generally as well as the sequence of events. It is the Lord God of Israel who controls the events on this planet and not men, angels or circumstances.

This sovereign power is further evidenced by the fact that God alone decides who will rule and when they will rule. This is something Daniel fully appreciated, and that truth brought great calm to him. Believers today need to remember that for His own purposes God sets up leaders and takes them down. He might do it through death or the ballot, but He is the sovereign Lord over men and nations. In his dream, Nebuchadnezzar will begin to learn that it is the God of Israel who is sovereign, as He sets up empires and removes them. Later, in his second God-given dream (chapter 4), the king will learn in a most personal way that God, not Nebuchadnezzar, is sovereign, and that He chooses who will rule.

God is also the source of all true wisdom. While men can have knowledge and have great intelligence, they can never really grasp the wisdom that is so critical for living well in time and preparing for eternity. The wise men of Babylon were not the recipients of God's wisdom and thus were unable to deal with real life in real time. To Daniel was granted these "profound and hidden things" (Dan. 2:22) and this enabled him to not only deal with the current crisis but to represent the Lord God so well in this world. We cannot forget the Apostle Paul's powerful presentation on the wisdom of God versus the wisdom of men in his letter to the Corinthians (1 Cor. 1:18-31). The unbeliever can certainly be highly intelligent and brilliant in his own way. But he cannot solve the real problems of life and deal with the issues that really count in life, death and eternity; that is because all the treasures of wisdom and knowledge are bound up in the Person of Jesus Christ (cf. Col. 2:3). It is only possible to be truly wise by coming to know the source of all wisdom, Jesus Christ. The starting point of wisdom is seeing God correctly and all that implies ("the fear of the Lord is the beginning of wisdom". Prov. 9:10). This does not mean that all believers will automatically live wisely. But it does mean they have the potential for doing so if they immerse themselves in the Word of God. Solomon reminds us that the source of all wisdom is the Lord, but if we are to receive it, we are to carry on a disciplined search for it like one who hunts for treasure (Prov. 2:1-8)

Daniel's praise concluded with his personal praise to God for graciously answering their prayers and giving them the knowledge of the king's dream. This whole song of praise reflects Daniel's feel for the Psalms. He has not heard from the king what his dream contains, but there is no doubt in Daniel's mind that God has revealed it all to him. Real wisdom and real power have indeed been given to Daniel by the Lord (Dan. 2:23).

2:24 After taking time to thank the Lord for answered prayer, Daniel finds Arioch and tells him to stop carrying out the king's command since he is now able to fulfill the king's two-fold command given to the wise men. Daniel's specific request to leave the wise men alone indicates that Daniel was like the Lord in that he does not delight in judgment. Even though these men were idolaters and promoters of false doctrine, there was hope that some might eventually turn to the true God of Israel.

HONORING THE LORD (Dan. 2:25-30)

2:25 One can imagine that Arioch was happy to be relieved of his bloody task. But we can also imagine that he realized that he had better have some good reasons for ceasing to carry out the king's orders. This apparently is behind his hurried entrance into the king's presence along with his inflated description of his role in the matter of getting the king's dream interpreted. Visions of fame and fortune are dancing in Arioch's head. His statement seems to indicate that the king and Daniel have never met. But not only had Daniel been quizzed at the recent graduation (Dan. 1:19), he had made his earlier request for time with his commitment to give the king the interpretation (Dan. 2:16). Arioch's brief speech is simply emphasizing his "deep personal concern" in finding a solution to the king's problem and his "key role" in finding this young Jewish man. As Keil observes, "Arioch did not need to take any special notice of the fact that Daniel had already (vs. 16) spoken with the king concerning it, even if he had knowledge of it."[42]

---

42 C.F. Keil, *Daniel*, (Grand Rapids: Eerdmans, nd), 99.

2:26 Nebuchadnezzar has one track that he is on and the embellished speech of Arioch does not derail him. He simply wants to know if Daniel really can give the dream and give the interpretation to the dream. Nothing else matters to this desperate king.

2:27-30 What follows sounds very much like the events that took place in Egypt a millennium earlier when Joseph appeared before a troubled Pharaoh. We wonder if Daniel had reviewed the story in Genesis 41 before coming to see Nebuchadnezzar! As with Joseph, Daniel begins by making it as clear as can be that the ability to deal with these kinds of mysteries is totally a God-given ability. Both Joseph and Daniel took no credit for correctly interpreting the dreams, but deflected all honor to the God of Israel. Daniel was truly a godly man, seeing both God and himself correctly. He deliberately shows that the so-called wise men of Babylon were terribly deficient in true wisdom and thus their inability to reveal these things.

After Daniel's focus on the God of Israel as the only one who can reveal these great secrets, he gives a general statement about the scope and nature of the revelatory dream received by Nebuchadnezzar. Daniel states that these things will take place in the "latter days" (Dan. 2:28); that is, in the future (Dan. 2:29).

> … 'the latter days' in the prophetic literature of the Old Testament refers to the future of God's dealings with mankind as to be consummated and concluded historically in the time of the Messiah…It is not true that Messianic times alone are denominated thus. Many events of what is now Old Testament history are placed 'in the latter days' (as e.g. the tribal divisions of Israel in Canaan. Cf. Gen. 49:1ff.), but the reach is always beyond those time to Messiah's times. And let it never be forgotten that the Old Testament prophecies of Messiah always have in view the consummation of things in what we now know as Messiah's second advent. The importance of this fact cannot be overemphasized in relation to the interpretation of the second chapter of Daniel.[43]

---

43 Robert Culver, *Daniel and the Latter Days*, (Chicago: Moody, 1954), 106.

This author goes on to say that there is no reason for us to think that Daniel is using this term "latter days" in any other way than the usual way with the result that we are to expect that Daniel 2 will contain eschatological prediction.[44]

Daniel in effect declares the same thing as he tells the king that the dream pertains to things in the future. With these introductory matters declared Daniel is now ready to divulge the dream and Nebuchadnezzar is anxious to hear.

REVEALING THE DREAM (Dan. 2:31-35)

2:31 There was an infinite number of possible subjects for Nebuchadnezzar's dream and it was, of course, mathematically impossible to be able to guess the right subject. So, when Daniel said that the dream was about a "single great statue", it must have been an electrifying moment for the king. Daniel was clearly on target. The statue was not some insignificant icon to be put on the dashboard of one's chariot. It was immense in its size and the way the metals reflected light made it unusually brilliant. As the king stood before it in his vision, he was apparently dwarfed by its size and blinded by its brightness. It was truly an awesome sight.

2:32-33 Quickly and precisely Daniel spoke of the component parts of the metallic statue. It had a head made of gold; chest and arms of silver; stomach and thighs of bronze; legs that were made of iron; and finally, feet composed of a mixture of iron and clay (pottery). The metals that made up the statue clearly decline in value. Though we might speculate, it is not exactly clear what this declining value might mean. That these kingdoms deteriorate in quality and are of less and less value is clearly from the divine perspective.

2:34-35 What occurred next in the dream may have contributed greatly to the troubling of the soul of the king. He saw this magnificent statue toppled and crushed by a stone. This awe-inspiring image was suddenly reduced to

---
44 Ibid. 108.

rubble. The stone struck the immense metallic statue on its feet and then completely ground it to powder. It was so reduced to dust that a wind was able to blow every last bit of it away. Then with all parts of the statue totally removed the stone that forcibly hit the statue grew and grew until it dominated the entire earth.

Before the interpretation by Daniel is observed there are several significant points that should be emphasized concerning the stone. First, it is said to be a stone that was "cut out without hands". In other words, the stone was not sculptured by human hands, which would point to it being of divine origin. This will be confirmed later in the interpretation. Second, the divine stone hits the statue on its feet, not on its head or stomach. The divine activity that is being observed occurs in relation to the bottom part of the statue. Third, it is not until the *entire statue completely disappears* that the stone grows to fill the entire earth. This sequence is critical to observe and adhere to. Some dismiss this as unimportant to the story of chapter 2. But God is in charge of both the seasons and the chronology of events (Dan. 2:21). According to the vision, the statue and the stone do not co-exist except for that brief moment when the stone is obliterating the statue. And fourth, all metallic elements of the statue are brought to a final end when the stone strikes the statue on its feet. The significance of this will be dealt with later.

INTERPRETING THE DREAM (Dan. 2:36-45)

2:36-38 It is apparent that the king is speechless because he does not interrupt or comment on what Daniel has said. However, he will have a great deal to say when Daniel is finished (Dan. 2:46-49). He can now, of course, trust everything Daniel has to say in relation to the interpretation of the dream. Daniel now launches into the interpretation given to him by the Lord several hours earlier. It would seem that the "we" (Dan. 2:36) is more than the simple humility of Daniel but was to remind the king that this was not Daniel's wisdom or interpretation that he was now going to hear. Daniel first identifies the head of gold on the statue as Nebuchadnezzar himself. The interpretation is very precise and is not some sort of abstraction. But more than the king is in view here. The kingdom of Babylon is also in view as it is personified in its ruling king.[45] There is the dual idea in this book of the king and the kingdom (as in the horns on the various animals in chapters 7 and 8). Note also that Daniel will say that after Nebuchadnezzar will arise "another kingdom" (Dan. 2:39). But the king must surely have been delighted with being identified by the valued gold on the statue even if it was apparent that his kingdom would not last forever.

The king is told rather bluntly that it is the God of Israel who has given him his power and position in the world. Several times he is informed that he is ruling at the pleasure of Israel's God. And this power and prestige granted to the king by God is immense and amazing. Nebuchadnezzar is called "the king of kings" and it is said that he rules over the beasts and the birds as well as all men. This is not saying that Nebuchadnezzar ruled over Australia, Greenland and Brazil. These are expressions of the absolute dominion given to the king by God and that his was indeed a "world-kingdom".[46] He had received his sovereign power from God and "stood at the head of all nations and reigned over the whole known world."[47] These explanations given by Daniel reflect both Jeremiah and Ezekiel.

Jeremiah, who wrote some six years before this dream, spoke of this king: "And now I have given all these lands into the hand of Nebuchadnezzar king of Babylon, My servant, and I have given him also the wild animals of the field to serve him. And all the nations shall serve him…" (Jer. 27:6, 7a). Several years later, he would again write concerning Nebuchadnezzar: "For thus says the Lord of hosts, the God of Israel, I have put a yoke of iron on the neck of all these nations, that they may serve Nebuchadnezzar

---

45 Edward J. Young, *The Prophecies of Daniel*, (Grand Rapids: Eerdmans, 1949) 73.
46 Keil, 104.
47 Bultema, 88.

king of Babylon; and they shall serve him. And I have also given him the beasts of the field" (Jer. 28:14).

And the prophet Ezekiel, who wrote this particular prophecy about 15 years after the great statue vision used the same phrase "king of kings:" "For thus says the Lord God, Behold I will bring upon Tyre from the north Nebuchadnezzar, king of Babylon, king of kings, with horses, chariots, cavalry and a great army" (Ezek. 26:7).

2:39 With little explanation, Daniel simply states that following Babylon will come two other empires. The second empire is expressly said to be "inferior" in some way to Babylon. The empire that would follow Babylon is that of Medo-Persia, but it was not inferior in the size of its empire. Rather it is inferior in the sense that it lacked the inner unity of Babylon. It was made up of two separate peoples who contended with each other for supremacy and this created a fundamental weakness in that empire.[48] The third empire is only said to follow the second, but it is noted that it will extend its power "over all the earth." This kingdom is to be identified as the Grecian empire. Both of these empires will be discussed further in chapters 7, 8 and 11 of the book of Daniel.

2:40 The fourth empire is, however, discussed in some detail at this point. In history the Roman Empire followed the Grecian Empire and so it is to be identified as the iron part of the statue, as well as the iron/clay mixture.

It is at this point that a central issue needs to be dealt with; that of the identification of the various parts of the metallic statue. There have been two primary approaches to understanding the four kingdoms of Daniel. The first one (the "Roman" view) is the one that historically has been held by conservative interpreters: that the four kingdoms of Daniel are (1) Babylon, (2) Medo-Persia, (3) Greece and (4) Rome. The second view (the "Greek" view) presents the four kingdoms of Daniel as (1) Babylon, (2) Media, (3) Persia and (4) Greece. This second view has historically been the view of

---
48 Keil, 106.

those who do not acknowledge predictive prophecy and who give a late date to the book of Daniel. Rome is left out because they just do not admit that such a thing could be predicted. However, it should be noted that a few in the conservative camp have embraced this second view.

GREEK VIEW	Babylonian Empire	Median Empire	Persian Empire	Grecian Empire
ROMAN VIEW	Babylonian Empire	Medo-Persian Empire	Grecian Empire	Roman Empire
	1	2	3	4

There is little doubt that the "Greek view" is generally motivated by a bias against the idea of predictive prophecy. One writer states that "…human beings are unable accurately to predict future events centuries in advance and to say that Daniel could do so…is to fly in the face of the certainty of human nature."[49] But if it turns out that Rome was the fourth empire, then even a late date for Daniel would not eliminate the problem of supernatural prophecy since there are a number of prophecies related to the years after 165 B.C. Those who hold to the book of Daniel being written around 165 B.C. always link that idea with the "Greek view" of the empires thus eliminating Rome from the discussion. However, their interpretations of the various animals, horns and other specific points become badly garbled since nothing really fits well with the "Greek" scheme of things. There is usually a retreat into obscurity at this juncture with statements that Daniel is really not "precise history", or that the vision is just an allegory and was never intended to be "actual sequential history", but rather is simply about the wonderful theme of a God who is sovereign. Their view is that the last part of the statue (the feet/toes) is "almost universally taken to be a reference to the Hellenistic period" since it was likely "a composition of

---
[49] W.S. Towner, *Daniel*, (Lousville: John Knox, 1984), 115.

the Hellenistic period."[50] It certainly is a universal view, but only among those with a bias against predictive prophecy. They insist that Media is a separate kingdom from Persia and it alone follows Babylon. As far as the text of Daniel is concerned, this conclusion is based largely on Daniel 5:31 where "Darius the Mede" is said to rule after the fall of Babylon.

Fortunately, there is a much better way to view this portion of God's Word and that is to let the text of scripture speak for itself. The "Roman view" of the four kingdoms is by far the best since it allows the reader to approach the language of the text normally and has a much easier time relating it to actual history. Several supporting points can be made for the "Roman view"; the view that sees Media and Persia (the arms and chest of silver) as one united kingdom and not two distinct kingdoms. First, on the very night of the fall of Babylon, Daniel tells the Babylonian king that his kingdom is coming to an end and will be given to the "Medes and the Persians" (Dan. 5:28). Clearly Daniel is saying that there are two elements to this coming kingdom and not just one. Second, the king of this second empire ruled according to the "law of the Medes and Persians" (Dan. 6:8, 12, 15). Certainly, that is a rather odd statement if two entities were not involved in his kingdom. Also, this king is referred to as Darius the Mede and is connected in some way with Cyrus the Persian (Dan. 6:25, 28; 9:1 and 10:1). (This matter of "Darius the Mede" and "Cyrus the Persian" will be dealt with in connection with chapter 6.) They were, in one way or another, on the stage at the same point in time in history, which simply does not allow for some Median empire to come and go being followed later by a distinctly different empire of Persia. One author holding to the second view makes an interesting admission. He states that the Median Empire "hardly ever existed in actual historical fact" and yet it "equals the upper torso of silver".[51] Strange indeed that an almost non-existent empire would command such a notable place on the great

---

50 Daniel L. Smith-Christopher, *Daniel: The New Interpreter's Bible* (Nashville: Abington, 1996), 55.
51 Towner, 36.

metallic statue. But that is just one illustration of the "Greek" view's descent in interpretational obscurity. What purpose would there be in dragging a non-existent empire into a prominent place except to throw everyone into a state of confusion. Alfred Edersheim confirms that no independent Median empire existed after the end of the Babylonian kingdom in 539 B.C.

"Media regained its independence during the reign of Asurbanipal (668-626 B.C.) … But the independence of Media did not long continue. Astyages, the successor of Kyaxares, was dethroned by Cyrus (in 558 B.C.), and his kingdom incorporated with Persia."[52]

Also, in his well-known work on the Persian empire, A. T. Olmstead details the various fragile alliances that existed between Babylon, Media, Persia and others and how this led to the end of an independent Median kingdom. He reveals that at one point Cyrus of Persia rose up against the Medes who were for a short time dominant over him. The Medes sent an army against Cyrus, but that army defected to Cyrus. A short while later another army led by the Median king himself (Astyages) came against Cyrus, but the soldiers mutinied, seized their king and handed him over to Cyrus. Olmstead's next statement is quite significant.

Media ceased to be an independent nation and became the first satrapy, Mada. Nevertheless, the close relationship between Persians and Medes was never forgotten … Medes were honored equally with Persians; they were employed in high office and were chosen to lead Persian armies. Foreigners spoke regularly of the Medes and the Persians…"[53]

Historically, then, we can see why the Medes and Persians are so closely linked together but also, we see that Media came to an end as an independent nation years before the end of the Babylonian empire. The silver arms and chest of the statue simply cannot be legitimately identified as an independent Median kingdom.

---

52 Alfred Edersheim, *Old Testament Biblical History*, (Peabody: Hendrickson, 1995), 964.
53 A.T. Olmstead, *History of the Persian Empire* (Chicago: University of Chicago, 1959) 34-39.

A third point to support the first view (the "Roman view") is that the scripture text states plainly that the empire of Greece would replace the empire of "Media and Persia" (Dan. 8:20) and not simply replace the empire of Persia. Once again, the empire is seen as one realm but with two distinct parts. Fourth, both peoples (Medes and Persians) are seen as terminating Babylon, even though it is the Persian empire that is primarily seen bringing down and replacing the Babylonian empire (cf. 2 Chron. 36:20 and Isa. 13:17-19 with 44:28; 45:1). It will be seen later in the book of Daniel that the Persian Empire became the dominant part of the second empire and so the empire is sometimes spoken of simply as the Persian Empire. Fifth, the second view (the "Greek view") throws the rest of the prophetic chapters of Daniel into absolute chaos. For example, it is futile to try and fit the Persian Empire (the third empire in that view) into the description of the four-headed four-winged leopard (Dan. 7:6) and the goat with the large horn (Dan. 8:5, 21). And sixth, the two silver arms on the statue seem to make the point that there would be two parts to the second empire. While this is not conclusive, it certainly allows for such a possibility.

The Fourth Empire is, therefore, Rome. The Jews who lived under Rome saw the iron part of Daniel's statue as Rome and this is one reason why they felt they (i.e. the Messiah) would eventually conquer the Romans. And in the vision of Nebuchadnezzar, Rome is seen as a powerful and destructive empire as it crushes all others. The power and cruelty of this empire is confirmed by the corresponding vision in chapter 7.

The main objection raised against Rome being the fourth kingdom has to do with the present age we are now in. Are we now living in the "iron" phase of the metallic statue? Or did Rome come to an end at some time in the past? The passage, at this point, does seem unclear. But there is a good reason why that is so.

What is the relationship of the iron part of the statue and the present age? If it is true that Rome I (the iron phase) came to end sometime in history, and if Rome II (the iron-clay phase) has yet to come, then there is a gap in time located here. Dr. John Walvoord observes that such a phenomenon is seen in the Scriptures.

> Probably the best solution to the problem is the familiar teaching that Daniel's prophecy actually passes over the present age, the period between the first and second coming of Christ or, more precisely, the period between Pentecost and the rapture of the church. There is nothing unusual about such a solution, as Old Testament prophecies often lump together predictions concerning the first and second coming of Christ without regard for the millennia that lay between (Luke 4:17-19; cf. Isa. 61:1-2).[54]

His point is well taken. There is no question that the prophets did not see or understand the two separate comings of the Messiah and did not include that kind of distinction in their prophecies. None of them would ever have imagined that a time span of two thousand years would exist between Messiah riding on a donkey into Jerusalem and bringing peace to the nations (cf. Zech. 9:9-10), or between a light shining on the gentiles and the rod of oppression being broken (cf. Isa. 9:1-5). They simply did not see any expanse of time there and so it is left out. There are "gaps" in time in the scriptures because of this reality.

There is another possibility that should be considered. Some argue that there really are no gaps seen on the statue and that to put one there is to manipulate the interpretation. In answer to this objection, it is proposed by some that Rome (the iron phase) really never did go out of existence.

> There is a real and important sense in which all the "West", or European civilization, is a continuation of the old Roman world…Constantinople, the eastern capital of the empire, held out against all attackers until it fell to the Turks in 1453. The "Holy Roman Empire" continued in name in the western part

---
54 Walvoord, 72.

of the empire until abolished in 1806 by Napoleon. The "West", however, continues to be Roman. Our literature (including our grammar) as well as our law, and even our popular religion are borrowed from Rome.[55]

Even if one might disagree with some of his details, his basic point has validity. It is true that Rome continues on in its culture and institutions in the western nations. This position has some merit to it.

What must be remembered in this discussion is that any seeming uncertainty in these Old Testament prophets was because when the Messiah did finally come He could either be received or be rejected by Israel. What the covenant people Israel did regarding their Messiah was determinative in the course of events for Israel as well as for the gentile nations. This is a wonderful illustration of the sovereign predestining work of God coupled with the ability of man to make choices. While man ultimately cannot thwart the great purposes of God, mans' choices are significant and do have consequences. And such was the case when that generation of Israelites rejected their own messiah, Jesus.

The fork in the road came when Jesus of Nazareth presented himself to Israel as their messiah. If they had repented, believed and embraced Him as Messiah then there would have been no gap at all between the iron and iron/clay. The iron phase would have quickly and seamlessly flowed into the iron and clay phase. But if they rejected Him then some length of time

---
55 Robert Culver, *The Histories and Prophecies of Daniel*, (Winona Lake: BMH Books, 1980), 36.

would have existed between the iron and the iron/clay. This is so because He Himself declared judgment on that generation of Israel who rejected Him and declared that Israel would not see Him, their Messiah, again until they repented (cf. Matt. 23:36-39). This required, at the minimum, that one generation had to die off and the next generation become believers in Him. Some length of time would then have existed between the phases. And, as it turns out, that believing generation of Israelites has not yet come into existence, unless of course the present generation turns out to be *the* generation!

2:41-43 After a brief reference to the legs of iron the focus now is on the feet and the toes of the statue, which are made up of a composition of iron and pottery. This composition tells us that there is some continuity with the iron legs, and yet, there is something very different about the feet and toes. There is a kind of superficial unity to this final phase but clearly a basic disunity. The two elements are part of one entity but simply do not blend in with one another. It has the element of great strength (iron), and yet, it is subject to sudden destruction because of the "clay" (pottery). It seems to be much like a solid china plate that shatters easily when dropped on the hard floor.

The explanation for this mixture is found in Daniel 2:43 where it is said that "they will combine with one another in (or with) the seed of men." This phrase has spawned many interpretations especially that of intermarriage. But in interpreting this it must be noted that these two elements of iron and clay must carry with them the same basic content as the other metals on the statue. In other words, the gold, silver and bronze represented the cultures and peoples of the first three empires. So, it is entirely consistent to think that the iron and clay stands for people and cultures. The apparent problem with the feet and toes is that the various nationalities, cultures, philosophies, forms of government and races are not going to mix well together in the final phase of man's rule. No doubt these various elements will be forced into one grand empire by those who lead, but they are kept in union by external forces only.

They simply do not blend into a cohesive unit. So, while there will be great strength, there is also a very fragile aspect to this second phase of the fourth empire of Rome. The significant diversity within this kingdom (Rome II) will prevent it from having real unity and will lead to its destruction.

2:44-45 These verses bring to a climax the vision and its interpretation. These verses declare with certainty and clarity that God is going to establish His kingdom and that this will be a kingdom that will last forever. Unlike the kingdoms of man that rise and fall, the kingdom of God, once established, will never be taken over by anyone else nor will it disintegrate into oblivion. But if it is a kingdom that will last forever, why do some say that the Messiah's kingdom will last 1,000 years (the position of Premillennialism)? First, it must be emphasized that, in these verses, Daniel is simply declaring that once God's kingdom is established it will never be set aside by anyone or anything. Unlike man's kingdoms that will terminate, God's kingdom will never be brought to an end. But the future, forever kingdom of God does have two distinct phases to it: (1) the 1,000 year reign of Christ on this present earth (Rev. 20:1-6), and (2) the eternal phase of God's rule on the new earth (Rev. 21:1). These are two distinct aspects of the future kingdom of God. The Apostle Paul speaks of the transition between the two phases of God's future, forever kingdom in 1 Corinthians 15:23-28. He teaches there that at the end of the first phase (the millennium) Jesus "delivers up the kingdom to the God and Father" because Jesus has finally and totally subjected all of His foes (the last one being death). Then the eternal phase of the kingdom begins.

> The first phase is the Millennium, in which the Messiah reigns on this present earth in order to fulfill completely the covenant promises given primarily to Israel. The second phase is the eternal state, in which God reigns over a new heaven and new earth that is free from all opposition to His rule, as it was at the very beginning when the universe was created. In one sense the eter-

nal kingdom of God is a restoration of paradise lost. Referring to these as two phases of a future 'forever' kingdom is an attempt to emphasize some differences that exist while making clear that once Jesus Christ returns at His second coming no created being will ever again establish a kingdom and rule anywhere in the universe.[56]

THE FUTURE, FOREVER KINGDOM OF GOD
(The Stone/Mountain)

PHASE I	PHASE II
Christ rules on this PRESENT earth	The Trinity rules on the NEW earth

Daniel states that God is going to set up His forever kingdom sometime in the future, **"in the days of those kings"**. The kings being referred to are the last ones described in the vision; that is, the ten toes on the statue. These ten kings exist together at the same time and are not seen as succeeding one another (cf. also Rev. 17:12-13 and Dan. 7:24). So, the kingdom that God would establish would have a starting point sometime in the future at the time that those ten kings/kingdom existed. It is significant to note that this is clearly a phase of the "kingdom of God" that was not in existence when the dream of Nebuchadnezzar took place. It is important to remember that the term "kingdom of God" basically means the sovereign rule of God over His creation. In the Scriptures there are over 200 references to God's kingdom and we learn from these references that there are significant distinctions that must be observed. There are a number of different aspects to the kingdom.[57] The "stone/mountain" aspect of God's kingdom is looking at the Messiah's kingdom which was not yet in existence in Daniel 2.

---

56 Paul Benware, *Understanding End Times Prophecy*, (Chicago: Moody, 1995), 143.
57 Ibid. 135-145.

In connection with the establishing of God's eternal kingdom, the kingdoms of man are "crushed" and cease to exist. In case we have not grasped the truth yet, Daniel again names all the elements of the statue and says these will be destroyed by the stone. This interpretation naturally coincides exactly with the dream itself (Dan. 2:35). In Daniel 2:35, Daniel said that the various parts of the statue were crushed "all at the same time." What we learn from this is that elements from one destroyed kingdom continued on into the next kingdom. For example, even though Babylon fell in October of 539 B.C. to the Medes and Persians, there were elements of the Babylonian empire that continued on past 539 B.C. Things like philosophies, religions, governmental structures or cultural observations would continue to be seen. And so, it was throughout the kingdoms of man. But when God's kingdom will be set up there will be no carry over from man's kingdoms into God's kingdom. This same truth will be seen in Daniel's vision of the four beasts in Daniel 7 and will be looked at there.

Nearly all expositors are in agreement that the stone is a reference to the Messiah, and the Scriptures would certainly declare that to be the case as it frequently uses that symbol (cf. Gen 49:24; Ps. 118:22; Isa. 28:16; 1 Pet. 2:4-8; Matt. 21:44). The stone was **"cut out of the mountain without hands"**; a phrase that looks at the divine origin of this kingdom. Man has not sculpted this stone or fashioned it in any way nor is it the product of his planning. He has had nothing to do with it all. Man simply will have nothing to do with the establishing of God's kingdom. This would seem to cripple a basic tenet of "post-millennialism" which teaches that believers will have a key role in preparing the world for Christ's return.

This stone came from the mountain (Dan. 2:45) and will become a great mountain (Dan. 2:35) that will fill the whole earth. The word "mountain" is used symbolically and when used symbolically is "always a symbol of a king, kingdom, or throne."[58] (e.g. Isa. 2:2; Mic. 4:1-3). In the context of

---
58 Arnold Fruchtenbaum, *The Footsteps of the Messiah*, (Tustin: Ariel Ministries, 2003), 24.

the vision, the mountain does indeed refer to a kingdom; in this case, God's kingdom. So, in this vision, there is a progression of kingdoms on this earth until finally the kingdom of God is established. God's kingdom, unlike those of man, will never end.

The crucial question at this point is "when does the kingdom of God commence"? Did it begin with Christ's first coming or will it begin at His second coming? Is this looking at the church (a spiritual kingdom of God) destroying the powers of the world, or is it viewing the Messiah's destruction of these kingdoms (the millennial/Messianic kingdom) at His return? The view of amillennialism is that this kingdom began at the first coming of Christ and is looking at the church in this present age. It is the position of dispensational premillennialism that the kingdom is the Messianic kingdom that will commence at the second coming.

Concerning the kingdom of stone, one amillennial writer says,

> It shall, in fact, be a force that will be operative in the overthrow of all the kingdoms that the world produces…The Kingdom of God does that in part by the overthrow of the ancient and entrenched wrongs that are characteristic of all the world powers…Though thus engaged in continually overthrowing what the world constructs, such effort shall not wear out God's kingdom; but it shall stand forever….the Christian Church broke the power of pagan Rome.…Christianity was in a sense God's judgment upon sinful Rome.[59]

Though perhaps expressed differently, every conservative amillennial writer would concur that the Church presently represents the "stone kingdom" and is in some way fulfilling this prophecy found in Daniel 2. They see the stone as "rolling" over the statue and gradually bringing the kingdoms of man to an end. It is an ongoing process. The following represents the amillennial position.

---

59 H.C. Leupold, *Exposition of Daniel*, (Minneapolis: Augsburg, 1949), 121-125.

But if the normal understanding of words and expressions are taken, the text of Daniel does not give much support to the amillennial interpretation. The interpretation given by Daniel does, however, give strong support for the Dispensational Premillennial approach, which is illustrated below.

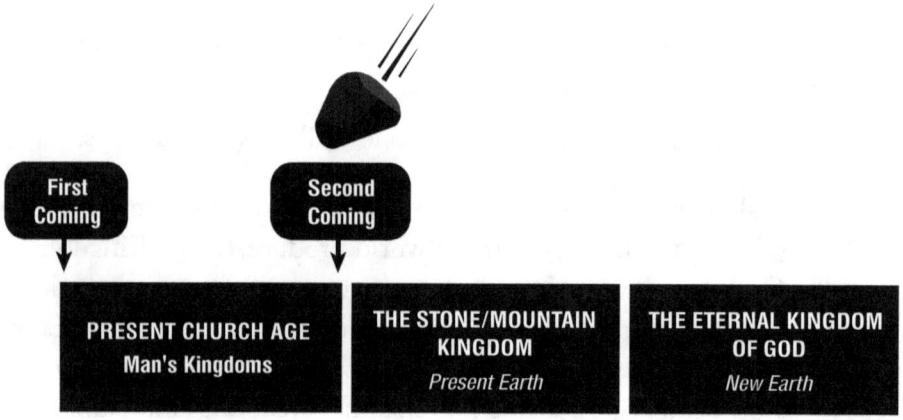

The following points need to be weighed carefully in determining the meaning of the dream.

(1) The destruction of the statue is sudden and violent and is neither tranquil nor gradual. The vision tells the story clearly. The stone collides with great force against the statue and topples it with one blow. This is not a gentle, time consuming process at all but a catastrophic hitting of the statue that quickly destroys it. A quiet, imperceptible victory of a spiritual kingdom is simply not what is portrayed here. Dr. James M. Boice, who is not a dispensationalist, notes that "although it is true that the church of Christ has expanded to fill the whole world in some sense, it has not destroyed the world's kingdoms, which is what the dream demands."⁶⁰ If God did want to tell us that the kingdoms of man would be brought to their end suddenly and violently, then how better could He do that in this dream?

(2) The Stone Kingdom only comes into existence after it has totally and completely destroyed the kingdoms of man. There is a distinct chronological order in the vision. It is <u>after</u> the statue is totally pulverized and turned into chaff and blown completely away that the stone kingdom fills the whole earth. The vision emphasizes the absolute and total removal from the scene of all parts of the statue prior to the emergence of the stone kingdom. "Not a trace of them was found" are the words of Daniel. The parallel existence of God's kingdoms and man's kingdoms on this earth is not allowed by the vision. To see them as somehow co-existing is to ignore the plain message that the vision is communicating. Only loyalty to a theological system would prevent one from accepting the vision at face value.

(3) The kingdom of iron was not destroyed at the first coming. When the Lord Jesus came into this world he did not destroy violently the Roman Empire or any other kingdom. Many of the Jews were hoping, of course, that He might do that, but He did not fulfill their expectations (e.g. Luke 19:11; Acts 1:6). If Israel had accepted Jesus Messiah, then the period of Tribulation would have come immediately and there would have been a sudden, complete destruction of man's kingdoms. It did not happen that way because of Israel's unbelief, so to try and detail what would have taken place is quite pointless.

(4) The kingdom of iron and clay was not in existence at the first coming. God's kingdom is to be established at the time when the ten kings/kingdoms of iron and clay are in existence. There was no such division of the Roman Empire at that point in time, which surely leads us to conclude that God's kingdom therefore could not have come into existence at the time of the first coming.

---

60 James M. Boice, *Daniel*, (Grand Rapids: Baker, 2003), 39.

(5) All of the kingdoms in the vision are political/physical kingdoms. It must not be overlooked that all the kingdoms on the great statue were political entities and the Church of Jesus Christ is not a political entity. To make one of the kingdoms a spiritual kingdom while the others are political would be somewhat inconsistent. The text ought to let us know that such a change was to be noted. The Messiah's kingdom, while the most spiritual time the earth has ever seen, has very clear physical and political aspects to it.[61] That aspect of the kingdom of God fits into the dream with no difficulties.

So, the interpretation sets forth the order of world governments that will be brought to an end when the Messiah comes and establishes the future, forever kingdom of God.

REAPING THE REWARDS (Dan. 2:46-49)

Daniel's relating of the dream and then giving such a precise interpretation of it had a powerful effect on King Nebuchadnezzar. The king's response was extreme to most westerners, but it was a way of expressing honor to a worthy individual. In the king's mind, Daniel was deserving of his praise and gratitude as one who represented well his God. The conversation that follows makes it clear that Daniel was seen as an excellent representative of his God, but he himself is not seen as deity.

What is quite significant at this point is the changing attitude of Nebuchadnezzar towards the Lord God of Israel. Previously, the king would

---

61 John F. Walvoord, *The Millennial Kingdom*, (Findlay: Dunham, 1963), 295-323.

have viewed the Lord as a lesser deity without much power or influence. After all, Israel's God could not even defend His own territory or His people. The fact that Nebuchadnezzar had taken some of the sacred vessel from the Jerusalem temple without a whimper out of this God was proof to the king that Israel's God was certainly a third-rate deity. But the Lord is kind and patient with foolish men and begins the process of changing the king's view of the Lord God of Israel. The great king is headed for a theological education that few ever receive with the result that he, I believe, comes to faith in the true God.

The king did seem to suffer from the "peril of the pendulum." He would swing wildly in his responses to situations and then swing back with equal force. When the evening began he was ready to kill Daniel and everyone else within the wise man category. Now he swings to the other end and bestows on Daniel significant reward. First, he gave Daniel great gifts. These great gifts were certainly not discount coupons for the nearby cafeteria. Surely, we are looking at considerable wealth coming Daniel's way. Whatever was Daniel's economic situation previously, he has now been elevated to entirely new bracket. Second, he is made governor of the province of Babylon. This was undoubtedly one of the most significant political positions for a man to have. There were dozens of provinces (like our states) but certainly "Babylon" was a rich political prize for anyone. And third, Daniel was elevated to be president over the wise men of Babylon. There was probably no resentment within that group since Daniel had saved the lives of many of them. So, seventeen-year-old Daniel is now wealthy, politically powerful and very influential in the court of the king. When Daniel got out of bed that morning he had no idea that he would go to bed that night as one of the greatest men in the kingdom of Babylon. God really does not need much time to do great things! And He really does not need the political maneuvering of men to accomplish things of significance. And at Daniel's request, King Nebuchadnezzar elevated the three friends of Daniel to positions of significance in his kingdom.

Daniel honored the Lord and the Lord in turn honored Daniel. And Daniel will now do something that believers often fail to do. He will pass the test of prosperity. Although he seems to be living in the lap of luxury and power, his relationship with the Lord his God does not at all diminish. In times of adversity, believers usually have their greatest spiritual growth spurts and greatest spiritual moments. At those moments we clearly see our need for the Lord's grace and provision in our lives. But most of us do not do nearly as well when enjoying times of prosperity (cf. Deut. 8:10-11). Daniel, however, will live consistently well for the Lord during the years ahead of him even though he is prospering as few ever do.

QUESTIONS TO CONSIDER

1. How is it possible for believers today to have the boldness that Daniel demonstrated in his life? Can you suggest ways in which this boldness might be seen?

2. How does a person become truly wise? What place does studying and "IQ" have in becoming wise?

3. In a democratic society where voting determines who is put in leadership positions, how does the idea of God raising up and taking down kings fit in? What significance, if any, does the voter have?

4. What caused Daniel and his friends not to fall apart but to confidently pray in a time of crisis? How can we mature in our own prayer lives to come to that place of confident praying?

5. What part does group praying have in our lives? What value does group prayer have? Can you think of a time when praying with others was particularly helpful or significant?

6. Nebuchadnezzar paid "homage" to Daniel. How can we courteously receive people's praise or admiration and yet deflect glory to Christ?

CHAPTER THREE

EDUCATING A KING

Preview: King Nebuchadnezzar had a terribly deficient view of the Lord. He saw the Lord as a lesser deity who was not at all on the same level with his gods. This grave theological error began to be corrected when the ability of the Lord to reveal mysteries became apparent in the interpretation of the statue dream. In God's gracious continuing effort to educate the king, He will use a fiery furnace and the faithfulness of three men to impact his erroneous thinking.

Although God had entered into a special covenant relationship with the people of Israel, He never abandoned the gentiles. At the very first giving of the Abrahamic covenant, God said that through Abraham "all the families of the earth" would be blessed (Gen. 12:3). It is obvious that God loves gentiles too. And so, we are not surprised to find cases in the Old Testament (e.g. Jonah, Ruth and Rahab) where the Lord went to considerable lengths to bring gentiles to Himself. The Apostle Paul noted that God is rich in kindness, mercy and love (Rom. 2:4; Eph. 2:4-5) and that His truth will lead people to His salvation. And this has been the experience of each of us who have been led into a saving knowledge of Jesus Christ whether we are Jews or gentiles. And these next two chapters in the book of Daniel point to the kindness and patience of God that led a proud, polytheistic monarch to a genuine knowledge of Himself. The key to the story of chapter 3 is found in the challenge thrown down by King Nebuchadnezzar when he said (Dan. 3:15) "what god is there who can deliver you out of my hands?" This is the account of that God and that deliverance.

The third chapter of Daniel contains an historical record of an actual event. And while it does not tell us anything related to prophecy, it does illustrate for us that which will take place in the future when the Antichrist will be established as an object of worship and the demand is mdade that all on the earth worship "the image of the beast" (cf. Rev. 13:3, 4 14-18). The believers of that future day will face the same kind of severe consequences for their refusal to worship as did Shadrach, Meshach and Abed-nego. Some may also be supernaturally delivered while most will not be delivered from physical death.

ESTABLISHING A NEW RELIGION (Dan. 3:1-7)

Unlike the first two chapters of Daniel, there is no chronological notation at the opening of this third chapter. The Septuagint (LXX), however, does place the date for this event in the eighteenth year of Nebuchadnezzar (c 587 B.C.), which would be some fifteen years after the great statue vision of chapter two. While the accuracy of this date is debated, it is clear that this event of the erecting of this great statue for worship took place sometime after the dream of Nebuchadnezzar in chapter 2. The evidence for this is found in Daniel 3:12 and 3:30 where reference is made to Shadrach, Meshach and Abed-nego being part of the administration in the province of Babylon; positions given them after Daniel had successfully interpreted the dream of Nebuchadnezzar (cf. Dan. 2:49). Also, it is likely that the "inspiration" for this statue came from his dream of the great metallic statue. And the constructing of this great statue for worship appears to have taken place sometime before the last days of the king's reign and the events of chapter 4.

3:1 The King created a great statue that was to be an object of worship. The statue was some 90 feet high and 9 feet wide at the base and was made of gold. Most all scholars agree that the statue was undoubtedly not of solid gold but was plated with gold. "The image was probably not made of solid gold but rather was *gold-plated.* If it were solid, it would have contained 5,467 cubic feet of gold...It is highly improbable that even the mighty Nebuchadnezzar could have managed such a display."[62]

Putting gold or silver on statues was commonly done. Isaiah mentions idols that are plated with gold (Dan. 40:19) as does Jeremiah who describes the process of plating wood with gold and silver (Dan. 10:3-9). Even the sacred "golden altar" of incense in the Tabernacle was made of wood and was overlaid with gold (cf. Exo. 37:25-26; 39:38). So probably it is best to understand this statue as simply being overlaid with gold.

And it is most likely that the height for the statue included a base that the image stood upon, or else the statue would have been a grotesquely long and narrow individual. But with a base, standing 90 feet tall on the plain of Dura would have made it visible for some 10 to 12 miles away. It is called the plain of Dura "in the province of Babylon." Bultema notes that this descriptive phrase has some importance to it: "It has recently come to light that there were two additional Duras. Daniel knew this very well and so made a careful distinction. A Palestinian Jew in the time of Antiochus could not possibly have given the details mentioned in this chapter."[63]

Was the statue an image of the King, or was it one of Nebuchadnezzar's gods? It is not possible from the text to be dogmatic. Actually, it does not make a great deal of difference since the real issue here is whether or not these Jewish men will forsake the Lord and His Law and enter into idolatry. "Even if this was Nebuchadnezzar's statue, falling prostrate before it would imply acknowledgment of his god, as Nebuchadnezzar's falling prostrate before Daniel (Dan. 2:46 – the same words) implied acknowledgment of Daniel's God."[64]

---

[62] John C. Whitcomb, *Daniel*, (Chicago: Moody, 1985), 54.
[63] Harry Bultema, *Commentary on Daniel*, (Grand Rapids: Kregel, 1988), 105.
[64] John E. Goldingay, *Daniel: Word Biblical Commentary*, (Nashville: Nelson, 1989), 70.

3:2-3 We cannot be sure of the King's motive in creating this gold-plated statue and demanding that all worship it. But since the list given in this verse is of political positions found in the Babylonian empire, it would seem that the King is attempting to bring about a unity in the midst of the diverse elements of his empire (note Dan. 3:7). Religion has often been used as a means of reinforcing the power of the state and of unifying people. On this occasion, the forcing of this display of oneness seems to have been important to political unity as well as a demonstration of loyalty to the king. As we noted earlier, in the story of the King's provisions for the trainees in chapter one, the idea of "the separation of church and state" would have been foreign to the thinking of these ancient peoples. The gods and the government were very much intertwined. And so, professing worship of the gods (or in this case of the gold-plated statue god) was also professing loyalty to the king and his kingdom. Not to worship was both sacrilege and would be seen as treason.

There are eight positions of leadership listed in verses two and three. Even after considerable investigation and analysis scholars still cannot be exactly sure which officials mentioned here are being referenced. However, we can be sure that every part of the empire, with its diversity of peoples, religions and cultures, was represented adequately at this dedication ceremony. All the important civil, judicial, military and influential men of the empire were probably there to demonstrate their allegiance to King Nebuchadnezzar. The evidence from antiquity is that these kinds of elaborate festivals were often celebrated at the dedication of some new building or statue. And now, after preparation and anticipation, the moment had come.

3:4-7 The protocol for this event was clear and had probably been made clear to all these dignitaries well in advance of the day of dedication. When the musical fanfare took place, then all present in the plain of Dura were to fall down to worship the golden statue. The instruments being used are listed in Daniel 3:5, but are also repeated in Daniel 3:7, 3:10 and 3:15 along with "all kinds of music". This repetition of the instrument list, which seems a little overdone to us, was a literary device to raise the level of tension in the story. "This list emphasizes the 'pomp' surrounding the ceremony and heightens the tension, focusing on the moment of obedience or disobedience."[65] And when the band played the special number for that special occasion, the people obediently fell down in an act of worship. They were no doubt encouraged to do so by the clause that was added which stated that death in a furnace of fire awaited any and all who might choose not to worship the golden statue (cf. Jer. 29:22). (Some scholars have suggested that the furnace of fire in the plain of Dura was there because it probably had been used in connection with the construction of the golden statue.) This tool for "evangelism" did the trick and all became "converts" to this new religion. This evangelistic tool has been used with great external success throughout history and is evidenced in groups today. We should also remember that generally for polytheistic people it was not a great issue to add another god to their worship experiences.

As we saw in the introductory material to this commentary on Daniel, the list of musical instruments contains three Greek words. Normally this would be passed over without much interest if it had not been for the liberal attempt to use the presence of these words as a proof for a late date for the book of Daniel. But as we noted earlier (see page 8), the presence of these Greek words does not require the writing of the Book of Daniel sometime after the conquest of the world by Alexander the Great and the subsequent spread of Greek culture (c. 333 B.C.). This has been the loud declaration of liberal theologians who are insistent on a Daniel being written very late (around 165 BC). Rather the presence of these three Greek words simply reflects an interchange between cultures and an assimilation of nations conquered by the Babylonians. For example, there was a wide distribution of pottery, musical instruments and mercenaries long before the incident of

---

65 Tremper Longman III, *Daniel: The NIV Application Commentary* (Grand Rapids: Zondervan, 1999), 99.

the golden statue. Also, Greek artisans were apparently employed during the reign of King Nebuchadnezzar, under the title of Ionians.[66]

> We do know that he personally had high regard for the Greeks, for he not only had some Greek mercenaries in his army as early as 605 B.C., but also used Ionic capitals on rows of yellow columns on the decorated façade of his throne room in Babylon. Thus, to say that he could not have had Greek musical instruments or even Greek musicians in his orchestra is to deny the obvious.[67]

All of this demonstrates that the liberals' attempt to make Daniel a second century B.C. writer of fiction instead of a sixth century B.C. prophet of God has no basis.

REFUSING TO WORSHIP (Dan. 3:8-12)

The service of dedication seemed to go well until it was learned that not all present had bowed down before the statue. This information was brought to King Nebuchadnezzar by several men who are identified as "Chaldeans." "Chaldeans" were earlier identified as the powerful, priestly class in Babylon (Dan. 2:2-3). It is, however, unlikely that these bringing the information here to the King are the same individuals who appeared in chapter two. Many of those died that night and furthermore many years have most likely gone by since that night when Daniel's ability to interpret the King's dream saved a number of the Chaldeans from certain death. Clearly though, these particular Chaldeans are not friends of the Jews and reflects an abiding dislike for these foreigners. This same sentiment will be seen when Daniel, the Jew, is manipulated into a den of lions (cf. Dan. 6:13). But this is not at all surprising, since from the beginning Satan has had a hatred for the seed of Abraham through whom the Messiah would come.

---

66 T.C. Mitchell and R. Joyce, *The Musical Instruments in Nebuchadnezzar's Orchestra: Notes on Some Problems in the Book of Daniel*, (London: Tyndale Press, 1965), 19-27.

67 John C. Whitcomb, *Daniel*, (Chicago: Moody, 1985), 56.

These Chaldean accusers purposely made this a personal issue for the King and appealed to his very large ego. They reminded him that it was the King himself who had issued these commands and, as a result, these Jews "have disregarded you" (Dan. 3:12). The King's honor is at stake here and in spite of the fact that the King had placed these men personally into their governmental positions, these men must be executed as required in the original decree.

These Chaldeans were not, however, really correct in their conclusions. The three Jewish men were not disloyal to Nebuchadnezzar personally. It was simply that they had a higher loyalty to the Lord their God. Believers have through the ages had to deal with the tension of their "dual citizenship"; being citizens of God's kingdom while being citizens of an earthly kingdom. And normally, believers are to live in submission to the laws of the earthly kingdom (cf. Rom. 13:1-7) unless those laws conflict with the laws of God's kingdom. And then in those cases their higher loyalty is to the Lord (cf. Acts 4:18-20). It is this higher loyalty that is in focus here.

The fact that only three Jews are mentioned by name in the story raises the question as to the whereabouts of Daniel. The text of Scripture simply does not tell us of Daniel's relationship with this incident, and so, it is somewhat fruitless to spend a great deal of time discussing the matter. It is, however, highly unlikely that Daniel would have bowed down to the statue. And while it is true that he too was a sinner and capable of idolatry, the Book of Daniel reveals him to be a genuine man of God before and after this event. It is probably best to assume that Daniel had either spoken clearly to Nebuchadnezzar about his position before the day of dedication, or he was simply elsewhere doing the King's business. The testimony of scripture is that Daniel was one of the most extraordinary men of God in the history of the world (cf. Ezek. 14:14, 20).

APPEARING BEFORE THE KING (Dan. 3:13-18)

The rhetoric of the Chaldeans had the desired effect. Nebuchadnezzar was absolutely furious with these men who had refused to bow before his statue of gold. But what he did next was unexpected since the original decree gave no "wiggle room" for a lack of compliance. He decided to give them another opportunity to obey him and bow before the statue by having a personal ceremony just for them. The King wanted to know if their action was a deliberate one or if by mistake they had simply neglected to obey his clear command. It is obvious that he wanted to save these excellent servants of his from the furnace of fire, and yet, he was angry with them for putting him in this unnecessary position of taking their lives; something he will do if they do not respond correctly this time around (Dan. 3:14-15). All that they need to do is to quickly bow down and it would all be over, and everyone could go on with life. And, after all, did not God understand unusual situations? (Did they recall the account in 2 Kgs. 5:18-19 where Elisha did not condemn bowing before a false god?)

Compromise in truth and in life is so common among believers today that (while we admire these three Jews) we see them as being a little extreme. Wouldn't it be better to just quickly bow down (basically unnoticed by the multitude) and be able to continue being an influence for God in this pagan kingdom? Why throw away their God-given positions when a second or two of necessary compromise would allow them to continue serving God in the kingdom? Didn't God know their hearts? But these three young men were men of the Book and knew that just a little compromise of God's Word can be absolutely deadly. Being broadminded and tolerant back then were not seen as the great virtues as they are so often seen today. There is no such thing as a "little idolatry." (cf. Exo. 20:2-6; 34:13-14; 1 Cor. 10:21-22).

The temptation to compromise must have been unusually great as the men stood before the King Nebuchadnezzar. "Having been brought to the very jaws of death by their initial steadfastness, the very goodness of the king in offering them a second chance…must have strongly impelled the confessors to abandon their intransigent position."[68]

The three respond with a calm assurance declaring their absolute faith in their God who is quite capable of delivering them. God's power was clear to them, but His will was a little less clear. At this moment they did not know for certain how things would come out, but they seemed to suspect that God might perform a miracle on this occasion. After all, the King has challenged the ability of their God to deliver them from his great power. The words of the three men seem to indicate that they did not believe they would die that day. King Nebuchadnezzar's words were similar to Pharaoh's belligerent words prior to the mighty miracles of God, which came on Egypt in the days of Moses (cf. Exo. 5:2). They seemed to sense that God was again going to do something truly awesome. But in either case their stance had "defeated" the King. Death was preferable to idolatry. Miracles (which are the temporary suspension of natural law) are rarely performed by God, who is the One that set these very natural laws in place. However, He does on occasion perform miracles when great glory will come to Him and His purposes are clearly advanced. The three Jewish men told the King that there was no need to discuss the matter of bowing before the golden statue with him (Dan. 3:16) since their minds were completely settled on their course of action. They were not being arrogant or disrespectful, but simply declaring the truth with grace, as the Apostle Paul would later exhort all of us to do (cf. 2 Tim. 2:24-26). On this occasion, these men evidenced one of the most significant truths of the spiritual life; that is, that they feared the Lord. The Bible and history testify that when a person fears God they will not fear men. But when they fear men it is because they do not fear God.

---

68 Robert Culver, *The Histories and Prophecies of Daniel* (Winona Lake: BMH, 1980), 52.

FACING THE FURNACE (Dan. 3:19-23)

Whatever kind feelings the King may have had for these three Jews disappeared totally in light of their bold, calm defiance of him. The smoldering anger of the King exploded into burning rage. But once again the Lord will use the anger of men to bring great glory to Himself. The King irrationally ordered the nearby furnace to be heated many times hotter, perhaps by adding oil to it (Seven times hotter should be simply taken as a figure of speech and not an exact measurement of temperature. cf. Dan. 1:20). It would seem that if he wanted to inflict the maximum harm to these Jewish rebels that he might cool the furnace down in order to roast them slowly. Apparently expecting resistance from the three men, the King ordered certain strong, capable soldiers to carry out the execution. In their obedience to the king, these soldiers lost their lives due to the extreme heat and flames of the furnace. There can be no doubt that the fiery furnace did not lack the power to execute men. The three men were thrown in the furnace from the top and landed bound by ropes in the heart of the flames. They were thrown in fully clothed, which was unusual. The text is emphasizing that the rage of the King required an immediate execution. The furnace apparently had an opening in the top where those being executed entered the furnace and had a viewing window in the side, which allowed observation of the executions.

> But in the matter of ancient smelting furnaces, it was probably a kind of silo constructed of brick and built into a mound or hillside with draft openings at the lower end at ground level with a flue opening at the top. Presumable entrance for the victims of this manner of execution was made at the top through which the flames and smoke were belching.[69]

---

69 bid., 56.

EXPERIENCING A RESCUE (Dan. 3:24-27)

As the King watched the three men tumble into the furnace he soon became amazed by two things. First, the men were very much alive and were walking around in the furnace, and second, he observed a fourth individual in the furnace also walking around. Neither of these things made sense to him. He was amazed and perplexed by what he saw and so he confirmed with the officials who were there observing the execution that indeed only three men were pushed into the furnace. Just three went in. Even in the midst of the roaring flames of the furnace, Nebuchadnezzar noted that there was something distinctive about the fourth individual. He perhaps observed a kind of glory or illumination surrounding the fourth individual, and so declared him to be "like a son of the gods" (Dan. 3:25). We, of course, need to remember that Nebuchadnezzar was not a biblical theologian and certainly had taken no course in Christology. We can surmise that he is not declaring the fourth individual to be the Second Person of the Tri-unity. Moments later he will make a statement indicating that this one was an angel (Dan. 3:28). It is apparent that the King is simply saying that the fourth individual is a heavenly being. It may be that this is an appearance of the pre-incarnate Christ, but there is simply not enough information to come to a clear conclusion. And Nebuchadnezzar is certainly not capable of making such theological distinctions. The author of the chapter does not say that "the angel of the Lord" was sent to deliver the three men. And later on, an angel will be sent to deliver Daniel from the teeth of the lions (Dan. 6:22). So most likely it is an angelic deliverance that is being recorded.

Nebuchadnezzar then issued an order to Shadrach, Meshach and Abed-nego that they could obey. He ordered them to come out of the furnace. It is doubtful that anyone was willing to go in after them. As all the many government officials gathered around the three men they were amazed at the complete deliverance of the men by the God of Israel. The men showed no evidence that they had spent the last few minutes in the flaming fires of the execution chamber. They did not have any burns on their bodies or anything like singed eyebrows and they did not even smell of smoke. Without doubt the question "what god is there who can deliver you out of my hand?" (Dan. 3:15), had been answered.

The Lord God chose on this occasion to work a miracle. Miracles are primarily to glorify God by instructing people about His character and His ways. And on that day in the plain of Dura, a miracle took place and God was honored and something of His greatness was revealed to the many officials from all over the empire. Daniel's contemporary, Ezekiel, recorded a word from God, which might provide a background for this miracle at Dura. The nation of Israel had failed the Lord badly resulting in their captivity in Babylon. They were to be a light to the gentile nations but instead they dishonored God in front of the nations. God was determined to vindicate Himself in the eyes of the nations who, if they thought of Him at all, thought poorly of Him.

> When they came to the nations where they went, they profaned My holy name, because it was said of them, "these are the people of the Lord; yet they have come out of His land. But I had concern for My holy name, which the house of Israel had profaned among the nations where they went…And I will vindicate the holiness of My great name which has been profaned among the nations…Then the nations will know that I am the Lord, declares the Lord. (Ezek. 36:20, 21, 23)

While these words will ultimately be fulfilled in the last days, God did not wait until the end of times to show His greatness to the entire Babylonian empire. When the officials who were there that day returned to their own cities and provinces, they had an incredible story to tell about a God who can deliver.

When the three Jewish men stood boldly for the Lord, refusing to bow before the King's idol, they did not know for sure what the outcome would be. The will of God for them was not absolutely clear. In this case, miraculous deliverance was the will of God for them. He chose to do something that was so incredible that all would sit up and take notice that a powerful miracle of deliverance had been done. But we must never forget that God's will is very individualistic. What the Lord does for one of His children does not dictate what He will do for another. The difference in His dealings does not reflect a greater love for one child, nor does it necessarily mean a greater godliness in a child of God. For example, God chose to let godly James die but delivered godly Peter (cf. Acts 12:1-11). Why didn't God send the angel who released Peter from prison to do the same for James? Or, why was it the Lord's will to allow John to live a long life while Peter's life would be "prematurely" terminated (John 21:21-22)? The Lord is the Good Shepherd of His sheep and He leads according to His absolute wisdom, sovereignty and goodness. If the three had died in the furnace that day, it would have been the good and perfect will of God. But they did not die in the furnace because deliverance was the best thing for them and the best thing for pagans around them and it brought the greatest glory to the Lord God of Israel.

MOVING TOWARDS THE LORD (Dan. 3:28-30)

To his credit, the King held no grudge against the three Jews. While eating a large helping of "humble pie", he issued a decree that the death penalty would be assigned to anyone who showed disrespect for the God of Israel. We must not make too much of this decree and assume that the Lord God of Israel has now been established as the God of Babylon or that Nebuchadnezzar had, at this point, become a believer. The King is simply acknowledging again that he terribly underestimated the power of this God. The Lord God was not some third-rate deity but must be seen as one of the greatest of the gods. Nebuchadnezzar's theological thinking is continuing to undergo a radical change.

The King also promoted Shadrach, Meshach and Abed-nego (Dan. 3:30). Undoubtedly this simple statement manifested itself in many ways.

These three men are another example of the great spiritual law that God honors those who honor Him (1 Sam. 2:30b). This was a great moment in the lives of these three godly men and it is the last time that they are mentioned in the Book of Daniel.

QUESTIONS TO CONSIDER

1. How would you define "idolatry"? How would you explain the concept of idolatry to a young child?

2. We are probably not tempted to bow in worship before a statue of gold, but believers in the church are still vulnerable to idolatry (Note what Paul and John say to believers. 1 Cor. 10:14; 1 John 5:21). What kinds of idolatry do evangelical believers today get snared in? Are there any areas in life that have become idols to you in the past (or present)?

3. Theological compromise is what seems to characterize churches and Christian schools today. What the three Hebrews did would likely be seen as "extreme" in the church of today. But what are some of the consequences of theological compromise? How are these consequences seen in the vitality of Christian living in our American culture?

4. God's will is always aligned with His Word, and yet, His will is also tailored to the individual, as is seen in the lives of the Jewish men in this chapter. Why is this reality important as we face times of personal difficulty? What often happens to us when we compare the way God deals with us and with others? Can you give a present-day example of ways that God has dealt differently with His children?

5. We sense that the 3 Hebrews believed that God just might deliver them from the furnace of fire. What might have given this kind

of confidence and boldness? If persecution came our way, where would our strength come from to face such adversity?

6. The last decades have seen the greatest number ever of Christian martyrs. Why do you think God allows so many of His children to die such terrible deaths? Why do you think this comes to some of God's children and not others?

CHAPTER FOUR

SAVING A KING

Preview: Nebuchadnezzar had another dream which needed interpretation. This one came some 50 years after his dream of the great metallic statue. In this vision, which was of a large tree, Nebuchadnezzar finally learned that there is no God like Jehovah. Daniel once again played a crucial role in the life of this powerful Babylonian monarch. The end result is a king who is dramatically changed. This is not the same man who was seen in chapter one.

PRAISING THE LORD (Dan. 4:1-3)

King Nebuchadnezzar's initial view of the Lord God of Israel was that He was a rather weak lesser god; that Israel's God did not match up with his gods. But the Lord patiently and graciously worked with this king, using faithful men, to change his understanding. Nebuchadnezzar soon realized that this God could reveal dreams and now more recently discovered that He alone could deliver from an execution chamber. We would assume that over the years Daniel shared truths about the true God with this monarch. Seeing God correctly is essential for salvation, but seeing oneself correctly is also essential. Nebuchadnezzar needed to see his own sinfulness and this fourth chapter records a great dream of the King and its powerful effect on him spiritually. It is the firm conviction of this writer that Nebuchadnezzar came to genuine faith in the Savior God of Israel.

The words of Daniel are central to this chapter, as he explains the dream to Nebuchadnezzar. Daniel said that "the Most High is ruler over the realm of mankind and bestows it on whomever He wishes" (Dan. 4:25b). The absolute sovereignty of the God of Israel over the affairs of men is the great issue here. This is the story of two sovereigns, one in heaven and one on earth. The Sovereign of heaven will be seen to be in absolute control over the sovereign on earth. It is at the pleasure of the Lord God that men rule, and not because of their power, wisdom or abilities (cf. Dan. 2:20-21). James 4:6 reminds us of the truth that God resists the proud but that He gives needed grace to the humble. In this fourth chapter Nebuchadnezzar is a grand example of this truth (cf. Prov. 16:18).

The opening verses of this chapter logically belong at the end of the chapter since they record the conclusion of the story. But they (Dan. 4:1-3) are placed first and then we learn in the following verses what brought the King to these conclusions.

4:1 There is no indication of the date given here but it is most likely well into the reign of the King since it was a time when wars were over, and he was living peacefully in his prosperity (Dan. 4:4). It is very possible that this event is to be located in the last decade of his reign (572-562 B.C.). John Whitcomb's comments on the date are helpful.

> This must have occurred near that end of his long reign (605-562), for the great goal of his reign, the rebuilding of Babylon, was now accomplished (4:30). If his insanity continued for seven years ("seven times" suggests years in light of 7:25), and the dream was experienced twelve months before the insanity (4:29), then this year must have been 570/569 BC.[70]

He addresses this royal decree to all in his kingdom and pronounces the common blessing of "peace" on them.

4:2-3 He tells his subjects that he has felt compelled to give to them this royal testimony of the amazing workings of the Most High God in his personal life. The sovereignty and power of this God are given generally

---
70 John C. Whitcomb, *Daniel* (Chicago: Moody, 1985), 62.

in these verses, but greater detail is found at the end of the chapter (Dan. 4:34-37). This is not a general theological discourse but an intensely personal testimony of the transformation of his understanding about the Most High God, which came about through a painful personal experience.

DREAMING ANOTHER DREAM (Dan. 4:4-7)

4:4 The King had another overwhelming dream and again he needed to discover its meaning. The dream occurred during that time in life when he was living peacefully and was prospering. (The word "flourishing" comes from an Aramaic word "to grow green" and fits in nicely with the dream of a luxuriant tree). The King was technically at rest from war and from major construction projects, but there is no rest for a person when they are alienated from the true Savior God. The Lord graciously disturbed his rest in order that he might experience true rest.

4:5-7 The content of the dream once again brought a great deal of anxiety to the King and heightened his need to know. Once again those who allegedly could deal with such matters were called in, but once again the wisdom of the world comes up short, as it always does in matters of the soul. Apparently in telling this part of the story the King wanted his subjects to be aware of the inadequacies of the wisest of the wise men of Babylon.

CALLING ON DANIEL (Dan. 4:8-9)

We can only speculate as to why the King did not immediately call for Daniel when he awoke from his dream. It may simply be because Daniel was not close by and he urgently wanted to know the interpretation and so turned to those at hand. Others have suggested that Nebuchadnezzar intuitively sensed that this dream was very negative and preferred not to get the unvarnished truth too quickly. At any rate, Daniel finally appears to give the authoritative interpretation of the dream and once again the stark contrast between God's wisdom and man's wisdom is magnified. The King refers to Daniel in three ways. First, he calls him by his Babylonian name, which would be natural since this is the name by which the citizenry of Babylon would know Daniel. And since this was a document for public consumption in Babylon, it only makes sense to use Daniel's Babylonian name. Second, a strange description is given of Daniel, which was that "a spirit of the holy gods" was in him. This is strange because it appears to be a combination of theologies; the polytheism of Babylon and the concept of holiness related to Israel's God. Third, he is still holding the position of the chief of the magicians, which views him as the head of the Babylonian scholars. It is clear that the King has utmost confidence in this man, declaring that "no mystery baffles you" (Dan. 4:9).

REVEALING THE DREAM (Dan. 4:10-17)

4:10-12 The dream was of a large, luxuriant tree. The tree represented Nebuchadnezzar and his glorious and prosperous kingdom (cf. Dan. 4:22). Several features of this tree are mentioned, which accurately reflected the Babylonian empire of Nebuchadnezzar. First, it was in the "midst of the earth", which speaks of the central, dominate place that this empire occupied in the world. Second, it was a huge tree, which speaks of the fact that it was greater than all the other nations in the world. Third, it had full foliage and an abundant supply of fruit, which speaks of the prosperity of this empire. Fourth, animals and birds found sustenance and protection in the tree, which speaks of the protection and provision that was provided for many through this kingdom. It is interesting to note that at this time (around 570 B.C.) that Daniel's contemporary Ezekiel used the imagery of a tree in a similar way (cf. Ezek. 31:1-3, 5, 6, 10-12).

4:13-14 After this happy beginning the dream turns ominous as the tree is chopped down and all seems to come to a dismal end as animals flee, and the tree is stripped of fruit and foliage. In his dream, the King saw a "watcher" who gave the orders from heaven that the tree was to be chopped down. The word "watcher" emphasizes the alertness/wakefulness of someone on guard. This personage is further said to be "a holy one". This particular "watcher" is one who is holy, thus identifying this one as an angel from heaven (cf. Dan. 8:13; Zech. 14:5). The first dream (chapter 2) had brought honor to the King, but this one speaks of his disgrace. However, God's punishment of the King would be gracious and corrective rather than penal.

4:15-16 Apparently, in the midst of this discipline, there will be mercy, as the tree is not totally destroyed. The stump and roots will be left intact and a bronze/iron band will be placed around the tree, probably to act in preserving it from splitting and deteriorating and thus allowing for the possibility of future growth. In the second half of this verse a dramatic shift takes place in the dream as the subject changes from a tree to a man (with the behaviors of an animal). The mind of the individual here will be terribly changed and impaired by a supernatural act of the Most High God. The man (Nebuchadnezzar) will behave like an animal.

> Although his insanity was supernaturally imposed, it is not to be regarded as much different in its result from what might be expected if it had been produced by natural causes. The form of insanity in which men think of themselves as beasts and imitate the behavior of a beast is not without precedent ... A person in this stage of insanity in his inner consciousness remains somewhat unchanged, but his outer behavior is irrational.[71]

Nebuchadnezzar would soon apparently suffer from a mental disorder called "zoanthropy". This is a mental malady that causes a human being to believe that he is physically a member of some species of animal (from the Greek words *zoon* which means "animal" and *"anthropos"* which means "man"; thus an "animal man"). The King's disorder is sometimes referred to as "boanthropy" which is a type of mental illness where the afflicted person believes they are an ox, or a cow, or some other bovine.

---

71 John F. Walvoord, *Daniel: The Key to Prophetic Revelation* (Chicago: Moody, 1971) 109.

The length of this psychotic condition would last for "seven periods of time". Exactly how long is being referred to here? It is probably not seven hours or seven days since that brief a time would probably not get the point across to Nebuchadnezzar. It is most likely speaking of years like it does in Daniel 7:25, 11:13 and 12:7.

4:17 God's clear purpose for the insanity of the King is stated with utmost clarity in these words; "In order that the living may know that the Most High is ruler over the realm of mankind, and bestows it on whom He wishes." There is an important lesson for the proud King to learn and it is that God, not Nebuchadnezzar, controls the world and He alone sets men up and takes them down. The angels are not making the decree (which would be contrary to Scripture) but are declaring it and carrying it out. What an important truth for all human leaders to remember (in government and the church as well); that it is the Lord who is sovereign and rules and not men. With this purpose statement the dream is concluded, and Daniel will now give the interpretation.

INTERPRETING THE DREAM (Dan. 4:18-27)

With the telling of his dream, Nebuchadnezzar now turns to Daniel for the dream's interpretation. There is no doubt in the King's mind that Daniel will give him the exact meaning of this dream. But Daniel did not immediately respond to the King's request for the interpretation. Daniel was overwhelmed by the negative nature of the dream and was speechless for a period of time. Finally, Nebuchadnezzar pressed him for the interpretation, acknowledging that the dream was apparently filled with bad news for the King.

As Daniel began his interpretation, he seems to genuinely express his desire that the dream might apply to the King's enemies and not to the King himself. Daniel does indeed seem to have real concern for this Babylonian monarch. As we have already noted, the tree/man/animal is none other than Nebuchadnezzar (Dan. 4:22). Using the same words given in the recounting of the dream, Daniel informs the King that the time of reckoning is coming upon the proud King. Daniel does add the fact that this decree comes from the Most High (Dan. 4:24) and not simply from the holy watcher. This is a word from the Sovereign God Himself.

Daniel clearly declares to the King that he is going to become insane, but that the insanity will not be permanent. It will last for "seven periods of time" (probably 7 years) and by then it will accomplish God's purpose of humbling the proud king. God proclaimed judgment but at the same time promised restoration of the kingdom back to Nebuchadnezzar. As He often does, the God who is rich in mercy (Eph. 2:4) mixes in mercy with judgment and demonstrates His great grace to this king.

After interpreting the dream, Daniel appeals to Nebuchadnezzar and exhorts him to "break away now from your sins by doing righteousness…in case there may be a prolonging of your prosperity" (Dan. 4:27). Nebuchadnezzar had abused his power and had been involved in much that was evil. In giving this encouragement to repent, Daniel perhaps had Nineveh of old in mind. God had pronounced judgment on that evil city/empire but at the preaching of Jonah they repented, and God turned away His judgment (Jnh. 3:10). The prophet Jeremiah, who had such an impact on Daniel's life as a young boy, stated that if a nation turns from its evil then God will also turn from His intent to judge (cf. Jer. 18:7-8). The king and people of Nineveh had changed, and Daniel is probably hoping that Nebuchadnezzar will change also.

FULFILLING THE DREAM (Dan. 4:28-37)

4:28-33 It is not possible to know if the King took Daniel's exhortation to repent seriously. But since Daniel was so highly respected it would seem likely that it impacted him for some months. But the pride that had been the habit of life soon returned and just twelve months after the dream was given all of it came to pass (Dan. 4:28-29).

One day Nebuchadnezzar stood on a rooftop where he could see the impressive city of Babylon. The city was indeed magnificent, and he had a hand in it. The following provides an excellent summary of some of the grandeur of this ancient city that has been discerned from archeological efforts. And as impressive as this record is, it surely is a very partial record of the real magnificence of the city.

> The city was protected by a system of great double walls, the inner line extending twelve miles around. The double walls were each 25 feet thick, with 40 feet between, and a total of 360 towers 160 feet apart.
>
> Through the center of the city, for two-thirds of a mile, extended the great 70-feet-wide stove-paved Procession Street, having walls decorated with enameled bricks showing 120 lions and 575 dragons and bulls arranged in alternate rows…the figure of each animal stood out against a uniform background tinted blue…At the northern end of the Procession Street was the famous Ishtar Gate, 35 feet high, decorated with 557 animals in bright colors against a glazed blue background….
>
> The city was dominated by a seven-story ziggurat (step-pyramid), 288 feet high, known as the Tower of Babylon. Nearly 60 million fired bricks were used to construct this huge tower, and on top of it stood the Temple of Marduk…containing a solid gold statue of Marduk, which weighed 52,000 pounds.
>
> At the north end of the city, near the Ishtar Gate, was Nebuchadnezzar's palace. His throne room was 171 by 56 feet, having a 'triple gateway and a richly decorated façade of glazed bricks. Yellow columns whose superimposed Ionic capitals were crowned by palmettes were linked to each other by a garland of lotus buds. At the northeast angle of the palace are…the terraced 'hanging gardens' built by Nebuchadnezzar for Amytis, his Median wife, as a reminder of her homeland.[72]

---

[72] Whitcomb, 66.

Nebuchadnezzar was clearly impressed with himself and his accomplishments, leaving the Most High out of his thinking. When he spoke his proud words (Dan. 4:30), there immediately came words of judgment from heaven. And as predicted, Nebuchadnezzar entered into the realm of insanity. Pride, of course, really is a form of insanity and his external madness now reflects what was already in the man.

If indeed Nebuchadnezzar's insanity lasts for seven years, who is running the kingdom? Was there an attempt to take the throne during this time? We have no answers to these kinds of questions. The best guess is probably that Daniel played an important role in the operations of the kingdom. Perhaps Daniel, who understood that the insanity was temporary, communicated that fact to all who were in the palace. It may be that he took special care of the King and used his influence to protect him. We just do not know, but Daniel most likely played some role of significance during those years.

4:34-37 As predicted, the insanity of the King came to an end. It began suddenly, and it ended suddenly, which proves that this was without doubt the finger of God touching the man. The insanity did not end simply because he had done his time, like a prisoner completing a jail sentence. It came about because he looked heavenward. He "raised his eyes towards heaven", which means more than he happened to look up at the clouds one day. Rather, raising his eyes towards heaven speaks of his submission, worship and acknowledgment of the Most High God. God had been clear that his insanity would last "until" (Dan. 4:25) he came to his spiritual senses and humbled himself before the true God. That is what has now happened. He was cured of his insanity but more importantly he was cured of his pride. And now the humbled King of Babylon gives his personal testimony of what he had learned.

This God is eternal, unlike the deities of Babylon. This God is the absolute sovereign of the universe, unlike the gods of Babylon. This God is true and just, unlike the deities of Babylon. Furthermore, this God is very much involved in the affairs of nations and of individuals, as He had been with Nebuchadnezzar. He had done exactly what He had said He would in humbling and then restoring the King back to his kingdom.

After the return of his sanity, he declares that he was reestablished in his role as the powerful king. His counselors and men of influence, who had apparently remained loyal to him during those years, once again came to seek and support him.

According to the final verse of the chapter, the King expresses how he now lives and views the sovereign King of heaven. He had nothing but praise for this God who humbled him and restored him.

Was Nebuchadnezzar a spiritually saved individual? While many follow Calvin who believed this was just an outward humiliation and not an internal conversion, it would seem better to see this as a true conversion. We must not expect him to use our terminology in expressing his faith in the Lord. He has confessed his sin and now openly follows the King of heaven alone. He acknowledges His total sovereignty, thus ruling out the power and influence (and existence?) of all the gods of Babylon. He sees God as everlasting, truthful and just. His willingness to give such a public proclamation of such a personal nature points to something very real and genuine. Walvoord notes,

> His issuance of a decree somewhat humiliating to his pride and an abject recognition of the power of God whom he identifies as "King of heaven" (4:37) would give us some basis for believing that Nebuchadnezzar had a true conversion. Inasmuch as in all ages some men are saved without gaining completely the perspective of faith or being entirely correct in the content of their beliefs, it is entirely possible that Nebuchadnezzar will be numbered among the saints.[73]

---

[73] Walvoord, 112.

CHAPTER	EVENT	VIEW OF GOD
1	Judah is conquered by King Nebuchadnezzar and he takes temple treasure and some hostages from Jerusalem.	Israel's God exists but he is a lesser, local deity who was even unable to defend Israel.
2	Nebuchadnezzar had a dream of a large metallic statue. No one can interpret.	Dream interpreted and his view changes. Israel's God is greater than first thought. He can do what other gods cannot.
3	The king tried to destroy 3 Jewish men in a fiery furnace for not worshipping his idol.	The 3 refused to worship but are delivered by God. Israel's God is seen as one of the greatest gods. He can deliver where no other gods can.
4	Nebuchadnezzar had a dream of a great tree which foretold his insanity.	The king "bows his knee" to the God of Israel and acknowledges Him as the only sovereign God.

It does seem that this event is the climax of the King's spiritual pilgrimage, and the God who loves gentiles too does indeed bring this gentile monarch to Himself. God used faithful Jewish men over a lifetime to communicate truth about the one true God to the proud polytheist. I expect to see Nebuchadnezzar in the court of the King of Heaven.

QUESTIONS TO CONSIDER

1. There is some debate whether or not Nebuchadnezzar became a saved individual. As a gentile, what did he need to believe in order to be saved? What must people today believe in order to be saved?

2. Daniel 4 places great emphasis on the sovereignty of God. In terms that would be understandable to a 10-year-old, define the sovereignty of God. If God is sovereign, does mankind have a

"free will"? What difference does it make to us today if God is sovereign or not?

3. Take a look at Isaiah 40:9-26. What are three or four truths that stand out to you concerning the power and sovereignty of God? If we really believe these truths, what difference would it make in our view of the world?

4. How might the truth of God being sovereign in the affairs of mankind affect our view of what is going on in our world? It should impact the way we view Washington DC, Moscow, Tehran and the great cities of the world, but how?

5. Nebuchadnezzar was living the "good life", living in splendor and luxury, but his prosperity seemed to hinder his spiritual vision. Why is prosperity so dangerous to the spiritual life of people (cf. Matt. 19:23-24; Luke 16:13; Rev. 3:17)? To keep a vibrant spiritual life in times of prosperity, what needed steps must be taken by a believer?

6. In a culture which lives for money, material possessions and pleasures, what should a godly believer do in resisting a wrong emphasis on these matters. Note Paul's words in 1 Timothy 4:4-5; 6:6-19.

CHAPTER FIVE

ENDING AN EMPIRE

Preview: About 25 years have gone by since the end of Chapter 4, and there is a different king in Babylon by the name of Belshazzar. As the Babylonian Empire is in the process of disintegrating, King Belshazzar puts on a feast during which he purposely defies the Lord God of Israel. This willful act brings immediate judgement; a judgement that is foretold by a hand writing the message on a wall for all to see. Once again, God will be glorified, and His sovereignty declared by an unprecedented and dramatic event.

Many centuries before these days of Babylonian dominance and glory, the Lord revealed to Moses that He was a God who is "compassionate and gracious, slow to anger and abounding in lovingkindness and truth; who keeps lovingkindness for thousands, who forgives iniquity, transgression and sin…" But then the Lord revealed that "He will by no means leave the guilty unpunished" (Exo. 34:6-7). God is indeed gracious and kind to sinful people in ways we do not fathom. And each of us who have placed our trust in Jesus for salvation have personally experienced His kindness and grace. But when men refuse to repent and do not respond to the promptings of God to turn to Him, then eventually because of His holiness and justice, He will act in judgment. Nebuchadnezzar had sinned in many ways but had eventually turned to the Lord and experienced His mercy and grace. But that would not be the case with King Belshazzar, as this chapter in Daniel reveals. This chapter again reveals the sovereignty of the Lord God, but this time it is seen in His powerful act of judgment on those who will not repent. It graphically shows how the Sovereign Lord can quickly humble those who believe themselves to be powerful. It again reminds us that wise individuals walk humbly before their God.

THE WICKEDNESS OF KING BELSHAZZAR (Dan. 5:1-4)

5:1 The chapter does not begin with a chronological indicator, but we know from the last verse of the chapter that this event took place on the night of October 12, 539 B.C., the night that the Babylonian empire was finally taken over by the empire of the Medes and Persians. The end of Babylon appears to happen quickly, but in fact the empire had been losing territory and power for a decade prior to the night of Belshazzar's feast. Before proceeding into the account here in this chapter it would be good to briefly relate what took place in those years between chapters 4 and 5 of Daniel.

> **BETWEEN DANIEL 4 AND DANIEL 5**
> Nebuchadnezzar had died in the year 562 B.C. and was succeeded to the throne by his son Amel-Marduk (referred to as Evil-merodach in 2 Kings 25:27 and Jeremiah 52:31-34). Although he treated Jehoiachin the exiled King of Judah with favor, this son of Nebuchadnezzar ruled badly, apparently having none of the strength and abilities of his father and grandfather. His reign was short (562-560 B.C.) and he was assassinated by his brother-in-law, Neriglissar. Neriglissar's reign was also short, but acceptable (560-556 B.C.) and he apparently died from natural causes; at least he was not assassinated. His son, Labashi-Marduk (aka Laborosoarchod) evidenced bad character and lasted only a few months in office when he was executed by a rival faction led by a Babylonian noble by the name of Nabonidus. Nabonidus reigned from 556 B.C. to the end of the Babylonia empire in 539 B.C. Since Nabonidus was away from Babylon much of the time he appointed his son Belshazzar as his co-regent. Nabonidus was known to be a loyal follower of the moon god Sin and this put him at odds with the powerful priests of Marduk in Babylon. Nabonidus came up with innovative religious practices, which increased the opposition to him by the priests in Babylon. This apparently was part of the reason for his residing much of the time away from Babylon. But he also went on a military expedition to Tema, deep into the heart of the Arabian peninsula, where after his victory he built a palace for himself and resided there for a period of ten years. With the empire crumbling, he returned to Babylon and reinstated some of the ancient religious festivals but the damage was done and the resentment against him (and apparently Belshazzar) was deep. After

this return to Babylon, Nabonidus faced Cyrus in battle, lost and fled, but was eventually captured and exiled by Cyrus.

During those years in Persia important events were taking place. In 558 B.C. the Median king Astyages was defeat by Cyrus the Persian and the Median kingdom became incorporated with Persia. By 550 B.C. Cyrus (the Great) had consolidated his power and ruled as the King of Persia. In the decade that followed, the Medo-Persia empire under Cyrus, began to chip away at the once large Babylonian empire as well as adding other large land areas to the kingdom. His victories enabled Cyrus to steadily add more and more warriors, which would eventually make an assault on Babylon itself possible. Nabonidus' various affronts to the gods of Babylon had alienated many powerful people in Babylon who were looking for a deliverer, even if such a one were a foreigner like Cyrus. In early October of 539 a number of Babylonian cities fell or surrendered to Cyrus. The city of Babylon appeared to be impenetrable and safe, but it fell quickly and easily. How? Greek historians Herodotus and Xenophon state that the river Euphrates, which ran under the wall and through the area between the two great walls of the city, was diverted into a reservoir allowing Persia troops to get under the first wall to the second wall. Then, the gates into the city itself were opened by Persian sympathizers (undoubtedly by those who despised Nabonidus and Belshazzar) and the Persians easily took the city.

It was not just the ebb and flow of armies and nations that dominated the 23 years between Daniel 4 and 5, but God was at work also. To His man Daniel, God revealed two important dreams concerning the rise and fall of gentile nations. Daniel 7 (the vision of the four beasts) and Daniel 8 (the vision of the ram and the goat) are both dated in the early years of Belshazzar's reign.[74]

According to the text of Daniel, King Belshazzar chose to put on a rather large feast, which involved well over a thousand people. For years the critics of the Book of Daniel (who retain a tenacious grip on their low view of Scripture) enthusiastically pointed out that there was no such person who ruled Babylon; that the last king of Babylon was Nabonidus, not Belshazzar. But over the years texts have been discovered and translated where the name Belshazzar is found again and again and identified as a co-ruler with his father Nabonidus who had, in fact, entrusted the kingship to him.

---

[74] Alfred Edersheim, *Bible History: Old Testament* (Peabody, Mass.: Hendrickson, 1995) VII, 964-973; A.T. Omstead, *History of the Persian Empire* (Chicago: Univ. of Chicago Press, 1959), 34-58; John F. Walvoord, *Daniel: The Key to Prophetic Revelation* (Chicago: Moody, 1971), 113 (quoting Flavius Josephus who quotes the historian Berosus); Leon Wood, *A Survey of Israel's History* (Grand Rapids: Zondervan, 1971), 382-383.

As a result, Belshazzar emerged from the shadows as a definite historical character. Today we have abundant textual witness to the fact that he was the son of Nabonidus. More than that, Belshazzar was coregent and actually in charge of Babylon during his father's ten year absence from the capital city, thus explaining the reference to him as king.[75]

So once again this is real history and not a figment of imagination and the man Daniel is again proven absolutely accurate in what he has declared to be historic reality.

A practical question now arises concerning this event of Belshazzar's feast. Why would Belshazzar choose at this time to have this lavish feast? Surely, he was well aware that his empire was evaporating and that Cyrus was close by. Only days before key cities had fallen to Cyrus and he certainly was knowledgeable of this. The text itself does not give us his reasons or motivations. But given the recorded events of that evening, the recent military loses and the ongoing antagonisms of the powerful priests and others, we can suggest some probable reasons.

First, we would suggest that this was to demonstrate to the priests and to the gods of Babylon that the King was a loyal follower of them, and second, the feast was designed to boost morale and temporarily put bad news out of mind. We will look first at the second suggested purpose. There is nothing that acts as a diversion (though always very temporary) like drunkenness and sensuality (so I am told). The fact that Belshazzar is said to be drinking wine "in the presence" of the guests is making the point that he was setting the tone for a night of drunkenness and revelry. And we are informed that present also were his wives and concubines (Dan. 5:2b). Several authors see this as clueing us in on the decadence of that "great feast" in the banquet hall of the king.

---

[75] Tremper Longman III, *Daniel: The NIV Application Commentary*, (Grand Rapids: Zondervan, 1999), 135.

> In the East it was not the custom for women to be present at carousals. But at this occasion there was a shameless trespassing of all morals and propriety.[76]
>
> It begins with a scene that can be read as one of ostentation, decadence, carousing, coarseness, wantonness, and self-indulgence, a scene that might have been designed to illustrate the wisdom literature's warnings about power, sex, and drink.[77]
>
> There would have been overeating; actual gorging with food. When capacity to eat was exhausted, emetics were sometimes taken to enable the revelers to disgorge their food and start in all over again. One by one they drank themselves to the floors and under the tables. Add to this feast of Belshazzar the overtones of sexuality provided by the presence of the wives and concubines…[78]

The prophet Habakkuk tells us that drunkenness and immorality often go together (Hab. 2:15). Whatever the details may be, this feast was clearly not characterized by clean fun and righteous behavior. Furthermore, since Babylon was thought to be "siege-proof" and, therefore, a false sense of security probably prevailed. A rousing good time was needed to demonstrate that they all had a lot of living to do.

5:2-4 Even if all of the above were worse than imagined, the real evil of this event is found in what Belshazzar did in relation to the sacred vessels that had been taken from the Jerusalem temple years earlier by Nebuchadnezzar. This is probably the main reason for the feast. He purposely took these sacred vessels, which had remained in storage in Babylonian temples, to use in his night of revelry. By using the Jewish Temple vessels, he made this a "faith" issue. He used them to drink toasts to the various gods of Babylon. Surely, he had enough cups of his own to toast the Babylonian deities. No doubt that he

---

76 Harry Bultema, *Commentary on Daniel*, (Grand Rapids: Kregel, 1988), 157.
77 John E. Goldingay, *Word Biblical Commentary: Daniel*, (Nashville: Nelson, 1989), 113.
78 Robert Culver, *The Histories and Prophecies of Daniel*, (Winona Lake; BMH Books, 1980), 76.

had an abundance of beautiful silver and gold chalices. But most likely he is purposely defiling these sacred cups from Israel's temple to demonstrate to the priests and power brokers of Babylon that he was a devoted follower of Marduk and the other gods. He was not like his father who had too much loyalty to the foreign moon god Sin; and he certainly was not like Nebuchadnezzar who had apostatized from Bel, Marduk and the rest to worship the God of Israel. Everything points to this being a purposeful, defiant act and not just a mistake. We would suggest that God's immediate judgment of it points to willfulness and not a careless mistake. And in his superstition and ignorance, he perhaps hoped that his public denunciation of Israel's God and demonstration of his loyalty to Babylon's gods would reverse the course of events and bail him out of the terrible situation that he, and the nation, were in. Daniel's censoring of the King (Dan. 5:22-23) reveals that Belshazzar was indeed sinning in the light of knowledge and that this was a prideful challenge to the Lord God of Israel. This defiant, sacrilege will now be immediately dealt with by the God who is "slow to anger" but who will judge those who remain unrepentant in their sin.

THE FINGER OF GOD (Dan. 5:5-9)

5:5 It is likely that the King was on a raised platform in that banquet hall where all could see him and see the detached hand that would appear and write. One writer sees the setting of the feast in the following way.

> The room in which Belshazzar probably sat was 56 feet wide and 173 feet long; at least archeologists have uncovered a throne room in the ruins of Nebuchadnezzar's palace with these dimensions. The center part of the long wall was covered with some kind of white plaster, surely the divine screen for this media event. The word for lampstand appears nowhere else, but most scholars consider it a reference to some kind of large chandelier containing many candles or torches. In other words, the handwriting appeared in a part of the room that was well illuminated.[79]

---

79 Kenneth Gangel, *Daniel: Holman Old Testament Commentary*, (Nashville; Homan, 2001), 133.

The escalating revelry was brought to a sudden halt by the appearance of a detached hand in the illuminated area. The text states that Belshazzar saw the "palm" of the hand, which would suggest that the hand appeared on the wall right above his head. The hand immediately began to write in the white plaster on the wall, and then apparently, it disappeared after doing so. The message remained for all to see and so that there would be no mistake about this message. God did not communicate this time to the Babylonian leader by means of a vision or a dream but with visible words. It is interesting to note that this is not the first time that the finger of God had written truth for men to read. The stone tablets of Sinai were the work of His finger (cf. Exo. 31:18) and, while not a written message, the magicians of Egypt recognized the finger of God when they saw it in the plagues on Egypt (Exo. 8:19).

5:6-7 Instant sobriety took place! The shock of this supernatural event overwhelmed the arrogant king who now was totally gripped by terror. The author tries to describe the radical physical response of the king to the appearance and writing of the hand. The color drained from his face and he shook uncontrollably. "He is in extreme distress, perhaps even implying by the last clause that he has lost control of his most basic bodily functions…"[80] In his shock and terror he screamed for any and all wise men to come and interpret the writing on the plaster wall. Evidently there were some attending the feast or, at least, they were nearby and so quickly appeared before the king. Belshazzar's intense desire to learn the meaning of the writing is seen in his offer of three rewards to the one who could successfully interpret the message. He offered a purple robe, which was the color and sign of royalty (cf. Esth. 8:15); a gold necklace, which communicated a high position in government or significant status (cf. Gen. 41:42); and the authority to be the third ruler in the kingdom. While some have debated the meaning of this Aramaic word translated "third", it is more than likely speaking of one who rules with two others. This reward

---
80 Longman, 138.

meant that the one who made sense of the writing would have an authority only after Belshazzar and Nabonidus in the empire. That was the highest position that this co-regent could offer.

5:8-9 For the third time in the book of Daniel, those who were called "wise men" were baffled by a message from the true God, which causes us to wonder why they kept these men on the payroll. The writing, which was in Aramaic (cf. Dan. 5:25-28), was right in front of them, and so we wonder why they were unable to give the meaning to the inscription on the wall. Aramaic was the language used in trade and diplomacy in the times of both the Assyrian and Babylonian empires. It was the undisputed "lingua franca" of the ancient Near East in Daniel's day.[81] This point will be dealt with a little later (in Dan. 5:25-28). When Belshazzar saw that the wise men were mystified by the writing he turned paler than before. This heightened fear within him then began to spread among the leaders who were in attendance. The God of Heaven views the proud defiance of the rulers of the nations and then "He will speak to them in His anger and terrify them in His fury" (Ps. 2:5). This He has now done, and the King has a right to be afraid because the time of judgment is rapidly coming. "Oh, what must it be for a sinner one day when he must meet the righteous Judge in person!"[82]

THE RETURN OF DANIEL (Dan. 5:10-16)

5:10-11 In the midst of the fear and chaos, which enveloped the banquet hall, the "queen" calmly walked in. Because of the bedlam coming from the feast, she either heard it herself or was informed about the ongoing chaos. At any rate, she enters the scene and gives wise counsel and becomes a stabilizing presence. But, at this point, there is a question that confronts the interpreter of the Bible. It is, "who is this queen"? Several possibilities have been set forth. First, it is the wife of Belshazzar. But this is probably

---

81 Steven Fassberg, *"Languages of the Bible," The Jewish Study Bible*, (New York: Oxford, 2004), 2067.
82 Bultema, 160.

not the case since we already have been told that Belshazzar's wives were already present at the feast and this "queen" has just now entered. Almost all scholars agree that this is most likely not Belshazzar's wife but actually the "queen mother." So a second proposal is that the "queen" being spoken of here is the aged wife of Nebuchadnezzar. But it is believed that she had actually died just a few years prior to this event and so should be ruled out. The third possibility is that she is Belshazzar's mother, the wife of Nabonidus (who may have been a daughter of Nebuchadnezzar). Some have objected that she would not have been in town since her husband was in exile. But Nabonidus had returned to Babylon recently from his ten-year stay in Tema. He had, to be sure, more recently fought with Cyrus and fled. But her presence in Babylon seems quite possible since Nabonidus would probably not have taken her into battle. And in view of the motherly way in which she spoke to Belshazzar, it would seem best to understand that this is Belshazzar's own mother, the queen.

She first calms her son and then confidently informs him that there is someone in the city of Babylon who is very capable of interpreting the handwriting. She indicates that he possesses a supernatural wisdom, an ability to discern, an ability that is God-given. And she speaks of Daniel in a similar way that Nebuchadnezzar had years earlier when he declared that a "spirit of the gods" was in Daniel (cf. Dan. 2:47; 4:8, 9). And if, in fact, she was a daughter of Nebuchadnezzar, she would have perhaps heard her father utter such words when she was a little girl.

In her conversation with Belshazzar, she speaks of "Nebuchadnezzar your father." This expression is used several times in this chapter (Dan. 5:2, 11, 18, 22) but does pose a problem since it is a fact that Nebuchadnezzar was not actually the father of Belshazzar. A number of options have been suggested by scholars, but with the lack of clear evidence one can only speculate. Perhaps the best suggested for now is that Nabonidus had married a daughter of Nebuchadnezzar, making Nebuchadnezzar the grandfather of Belshazzar.

Walvoord notes that there is no Hebrew or Chaldee word for "grandfather" and that a grandfather was not called "father's father" but simply "father."[83] And, in light of the queen mother's precise knowledge of Daniel, it would seem quite possible that she was indeed the daughter of Nebuchadnezzar, making Nebuchadnezzar the grandfather of Belshazzar.

She gives to the king fairly extensive information about Daniel's former positions in the kingdom as well as his unique, God-given abilities. It would seem that Belshazzar is lacking certain knowledge about Daniel. Perhaps her repeated use of "your father" in her discourse was a "silent rebuke that the man who was held in such great esteem by his famous ancestor had been forgotten by him."[84] Clearly Daniel was no longer in his former positions of influence indicating that he had likely been removed by a previous king. Although Daniel is no longer prominent in the life of government of Babylon, the queen mother seems to know where he is and urges Belshazzar to go and get him.

5:13-16 When Daniel arrived before the king, his identity was questioned by the king. Belshazzar referred to him as one of the exiles from Judah and not by his previous positions in the Babylonian empire. One senses a touch of distain in the king's voice.

To Daniel, Belshazzar repeats the testimonial of the queen mother, the failure of the alleged wise men and then the great reward that will be given to the one who can successfully interpret the godly graffiti that was still up on the wall.

THE INTERPRETATION BY DANIEL (Dan. 5:17-28)

5:17 When the eighty-year-old Daniel spoke to the king he did so firmly and truthfully. He made it clear that he would unravel the written mystery for the king and give him the unvarnished interpretation. He also

---

83 Walvoord, 118.
84 Bultema, 164.

made it clear that he was not swayed by any rewards of the king. Daniel was no "rent-a-prophet" who had a price tag attached to his service for the Lord his God. (May we march to the beat of his drum!)

5:18-23 For whatever reason Daniel does not begin with the normal salutation "O King, live forever" but rather immediately begins with a scathing rebuke of this arrogant king. Daniel rehearses the sovereign power, descent into insanity and the restoration of King Nebuchadnezzar. Using the names "Most High God" and "Lord of Heaven", which are echoes of Nebuchadnezzar's testimonial, he reminds Belshazzar that this God brought down the proud Nebuchadnezzar and then raised him up again after he came to recognize that the God of Israel is the only one who is truly sovereign (Dan. 5:21). He then rebuked the king for his flagrant irreverence of this Most High God; sacrilege that was willfully done in light of his knowing all these things about King Nebuchadnezzar (Dan. 5:22). And then in front of the king, and probably the powerful priests of Babylon, Daniel declared that their gods were no gods at all, reflecting the derisive words of Isaiah (Isa. 37:19; 44:10-17), Jeremiah (Jer. 10:1-5) and the Psalmist (Ps. 115:1-8). The king had foolishly brought irreversible judgment upon himself by mocking the God who created him and allowed him to keep breathing. We can only imagine the stunned silence in that great banquet hall as the aged Israelite rebuked the prideful, foolish king as well as the rest of them. What a courageous declaration he made in front of over a thousand people. But he was able to do so because he did not fear what men could do. He only feared the Lord God of Israel.

5:24-28 Without hesitation Daniel pointed out that the hand that wrote on the wall was sent directly from this same Most High God, Lord of Heaven. It is this God that he mocked publicly who is now communicating a message to him.

In Daniel 5:25, we are finally told what it was that the hand had written on that white plaster wall. The words written were the Aramaic words MENE (written twice) TEKEL and UPHARSIN. Now if the words are known Aramaic words, why were the wise men unable to read and interpret them? We cannot know for sure, of course, because the text does not tell us. However, it is very possible that if it were written in Aramaic script then only the consonants and not the vowels would have appeared. As one states, "the Babylonian wise men stumbled because the inscription was written in scripta continua and without vocalization."[85] So without vowels and the consonants running together, the wise men simply could not figure it out. It would be like one of us walking into a classroom and seeing "jump, jump, rock, green" on the chalkboard. We would know the English words but still could not give a meaning to them. We would be at even a greater loss to understand the writing if what we saw was "jmpjmprckgrn". If we saw such writing on the chalkboard we would not pay much attention it. However, if a detached hand wrote them on the chalkboard we would call upon every resource to figure it out.

So perhaps what Daniel observed on the wall was **mnhmnhtklprs** (except written from right to left). Daniel separated the letters and identified them as three different words with the first one being repeated. He interpreted them as passive participles. MENE appears twice, apparently for emphasis, and has the idea of "numbering". Daniel explained that God had allotted a certain time frame for the existence of the reign and the empire of Belshazzar and now time is up. Belshazzar's time was up because God had "weighed" (TEKEL) the king and his kingdom on His divine scales and found that they came up short. The righteous standard of God was on one side of the scale and Belshazzar and the Babylonians were on the other and they were sadly deficient. Daniel then interpreted the third word PERES (UPHARSIN). PERES means "divided". (Note: *upharsin* is the plural of *peres*, and has the "u" attached which is like the English conjunction "and"). The great empire of Babylon is now going to be divided up among the next empire of the Medes and Persians. Note that Daniel is quite clear that the dual kingdom of Media/Persia will be the weapon of God to destroy Babylon. In response to those

---

85 Longman, 142.

scholars who contend that it was the Medes who defeated Babylon (and are, thus, the second empire of Daniel's four empires), it is worth emphasizing that Daniel says it is a dual empire with an emphasis on the Persians, not the Medes. This is seen in what is certainly a play upon words. The consonants PRS could refer to PERES ("divided") or PARAS ("Persians"). So, Daniel quickly and accurately interpreted the writing of the detached hand and in so doing pronounced final judgment on Babylon.

We must not forget that God "weighs" all nations and men and all are found deficient. But thanks be to God for supplying what is missing through Jesus Christ. We who have trusted Christ have His righteousness placed on the scale so that now we are accepted in His sight. But men, or nations, who do not accept this provision, will face the judgment of God. One wonders how long it might be before the Lord God places our own country on His scales. No person or nation ever gets away with neglecting or rejecting the truth of God. It is a spiritually dangerous thing to walk away from God's truth. Revelation demands a response; a response that is positive.

THE END OF THE EMPIRE (Dan. 5:29-31)

5:29 Belshazzar was true to his word and rewarded Daniel with the authority of the third ruler in the empire and the insignias of that position. Daniel did not resist the bestowing of the rewards, which seems to be a reversal of his previous statement. He apparently believed it was the Lord's will for him, since in this way the Most High God would once again be exalted through His servants. And, in this case, it would place Daniel in a position where he would become a key leader in the coming Medo-Persian Empire.

Daniel, of course, was aware that all of Belshazzar's rewards would not last 24 hours and would be meaningless. Also, it may be that Daniel's initial remarks were simply emphasizing that the rewards had nothing whatsoever to do with his willingness to decipher the message on the wall.

5:30 As we observed at the beginning of this chapter, the Scriptures inform us that the Lord our God is slow to anger yet will judge if men do not turn to Him (cf. Exo. 34:6-7). We must never assume that God's judgments are always off in the distant future somewhere. God is holy and just and can chose not to prolong judgment. He can judge immediately. Just ask Belshazzar, Ananias, Sapphira, Uzzah and a number of others. The Psalmist declared that "the Lord preserves the faithful and fully recompenses the proud doer" (Ps. 31:23). The "proud doer" Belshazzar is now going to be paid.

5:31 In one simple sentence the record of the transfer of power from Babylon to Medo-Persia is given. No details of the military conquest are given since that is really a minor matter in the plan and program of God. Four kingdoms of man will rise and then fall prior to the coming of God's forever, future kingdom. Daniel has lived to see the end of the first of these empires (the gold part of the statue) and the emergence of the second empire (the silver part of the statue).

What is not so simple in this verse, however, is the identification of "Darius the Mede". This individual is again mentioned in 6:1, 9, 25, 28; 9:1; and 11:1. There has been an ongoing debate among scholars concerning this man. The following is a very brief summary of the matter.

WHO IS "DARIUS THE MEDE"?

There are three basic positions taken concerning the identification of the individual who Daniel refers to as "Darius the Mede." It is a complex study with limited information, but the positions and some of the evidence is mentioned here.

(1) Daniel is in error as there is no such person in history as Darius the Mede.

This view states that Darius the Mede is fictional since we know that Cyrus the Persian conquered Babylon. It is usually felt that the author of Daniel imported the later Persian king, Darius I, into the storyline.

"Darius the Mede is unhistorical. Darius was a famous Persian king (522-486 BCE)."[86]

"Nor was Babylon captured and its king slain by anyone named "Darius the Mede." This person never existed."[87]

It ought to be remembered that similar statements were made years ago related to Belshazzar being a fictional character.

(2) "Darius the Mede" is another name for Cyrus the Persian.

This view has been set forth by D. J. Wiseman.[88] He disputes the third view (see below) and suggests that there is a lack of historical evidence for that position in ancient documents. He supports his position by observing that: (1) Cyrus' age corresponds to that given in Daniel 5:31 when he was welcomed into the city of Babylon by the citizens there. (2) Near East kings often bore more than one name. Wiseman believes that Daniel 6:28 is an explanatory note stating that the text speaks of the reign of "Darius even (that is) "Cyrus the Persian." (3) He also argues that there was a complete intermingling of the Medes and Persians, which would account for the use of both titles. He argues that what ancient documents are available best support this position.

(3) "Darius the Mede" is an individual in history known as Gubaru.

John C. Whitcomb has presented the case for this third position.[89] He notes that Cyrus was away on eastern campaigns during this time and Darius the Mede was ruling for him in Babylon. Whitcomb notes that Darius "received the kingdom" (5:31), which he understands to denote delegated authority; a subordinate is receiving authority from a higher power. He also notes that Josephus says that Darius is a relative (uncle) of Cyrus as well as arguing that the actual conqueror of Babylon was not Cyrus. He believes that General Ugbaru took Bablyon, but died a month later being replaced by Gubaru.

From the conservative perspective #2 and #3 are good attempts at harmo-

---

86 Laurence M. Mills, *Daniel: The Jewish Study Bible*, (New York: Oxford, 2004), 1653.
87 W. Sibley Towner, *Daniel*, (Louisville: John Knox, 1984), 70.
88 D. J. Wiseman, *"Some Historical Problems in the Book of Daniel"*, Notes on Some Problems in the Book of Daniel, (London: Tyndale Press, 1965), 9-16.
89 John C. Whitcomb, *Darius the Mede*, (Phillipsburg: Presbyterian and Reformed, 1959), 14ff.

nizing Daniel's statements with what is known from history. It should be noted that others have attempted to show that "Darius the Mede" is yet another individual named Ugbaru who was the general who actually took Babylon. But we have no doubt that "Darius the Mede" is not Darius I since Darius I appears later as king of Persia and Daniel does not make historical blunders. Questions about whether names are dynastic titles or not is not yet clear. But the fact is that there is simply not enough documentary information at this point to solve the problem. The day may come when some cuneiform inscription is discovered and translated, which makes abundantly clear the identification of this key character in the book of Daniel.

QUESTIONS TO CONSIDER

1. What place does (should) the message of coming judgment have when we speak to people about their need to repent and trust Jesus Christ for salvation?

2. Does God judge in the present day, or is all judgment future? If it is in the present day, what does it look like? Is the death or injury of a person in an automobile accident His judgment? Is the gunning down of a drug dealing gang member His judgment? Is the death of a homosexual from AIDS God's judgment? Was the destruction of the World Trade Center on September 11th part of His judgment? Was Job's tragic experiences of loss the judgment of God? (cf. Rom. 1:18-2:4; John 5:22; 9:2-3; 12:31)

3. Are we allowed to judge others? If yes, how do we correctly do that? If not, are we then to simply ignore the sin and evil of others?

4. What is the sin of sacrilege that was manifested by Belshazzar? Can unbelievers (and believers) today be involved in it? How does holiness relate to it?

5. What can we learn about the spiritual life from Daniel's appearance at the feast? And what can we learn about representing God correctly before unbelievers?

6. What do you suppose a hand sent from God might write on the walls of the U.S. Congress? On the sanctuary wall of your local church? On the wall of your family room?

CHAPTER SIX

DEFYING A DECREE

Preview: Daniel has already been seen as a faithful follower of the sovereign God of Israel. Now, empires have changed, but the challenge to be faithful continues. Daniel once again occupies an important government position. But this time of prosperity and honor is short lived when enemies of Daniel are behind a royal decree which makes praying illegal for a 30-day period. Daniel prays anyway, faithfully seeking the Lord. His non-compliance with the royal decree brings judgment which, in turn, brings deliverance from the Lord. Again, the result is that the sovereign God is honored. And true to His Word, the Lord honors those who honor Him.

The story of Daniel entering and exiting the den of those ferocious lions is one of the most famous stories in the entire Bible. But the lions are actually only bit players in the drama and are not the focus of attention. Even the king is just playing a supporting role. It is faithful Daniel and his faithful God that take center stage.

THE NEW ADMINISTRATION (Dan. 6:1-3)

6:1 As Darius the Mede began his tenure as ruler over Babylon he found it necessary to provide some structure for his government and so he appointed three commissioners and 120 satraps. Scholars have observed that Darius I (Hystapes) is the one that actually organized the Persian Empire some years after the fall of Babylon. This has given rise to a chorus from critics that Daniel has again blundered historically by mixing up Darius I (Hystapes) with this other character Darius the Mede.

> But the historical figure alluded to in Daniel 6 must be Darius I, the usurper of the Persian throne after the death of Cambyses. Once again, however, it is undoubtedly fruitless to try to force the folklore of Daniel to fit what we know the actual circumstances of Persian history.[90]

Historically it is true that Darius I (Hystapes) divided up the Persian Empire into various provinces (satrapies). But what is in view in this passage is the structuring of the region of Babylonia alone. This seems to be supported by Daniel 9:1 where it is said that Darius "was made king over the kingdom of the Chaldeans." Whitcomb observes that the text of Daniel 6 does not expressly say that Darius set up provinces but rather that he established satraps over the area that he was ruling over. He notes that the term "satrap" was a "Persian official who could rule over a large province or over a small group of people."[91] Longman concurs in this view about what Darius is doing in this chapter: "Over him is Cyrus, the king of Persia, so we are to understand this story as concerned only with Babylonia. While it is true that at a later date Darius will divide the entire empire into twenty satrapies, the present division involved much smaller units."[92]

So, it appears that the governmental structure in this account is not over the entire Medo-Persian Empire that stretched from Egypt to India but just over the area of Babylonia.

6:2-3 The primary purpose of this new governmental structure was to insure that proper revenues were received without financial loss to the king's treasury. The reader is informed that Daniel, who is now in his early

---

90 Daniel L. Smith-Christopher, *Daniel: The New Interpreters Bible*, (Nashville: Abingdon, 1996), 88.
91 John C. Whitcomb, *Daniel*, (Chicago: Moody, 1985), 81.
92 Tremper Longman III, *Daniel: The NIV Application Commentary* (Grand Rapids: Zondervan, 1999), 159.

eighties, has been placed in one of the three significant positions of commissioner. The position is clearly a prestigious and important one. Why was the aged Daniel put into such a position? The text itself does not specifically say but we can hazard a guess. We should remember that Daniel was the third ruler of the previous empire (if only for a few hours), and so, he would have immediately been known as a "person of interest" to the conquering Medes and Persians. Normally being in a high-ranking position may have been fatal, but we would assume that Daniel's rebuke of Belshazzar, his amazing interpretation of the handwriting on the wall and his long tenure under Nebuchadnezzar would have been reported to the conquerors. A similar thing had happened to Daniel's spiritual mentor, Jeremiah the prophet (cf. Jer. 39 and 40) when Nebuchadnezzar and the Babylonians took Jerusalem. Their knowledge of Jeremiah's ministry resulted in Jeremiah being singled out for preferential treatment.

Within a short period of time, Daniel's excellence as a man and as a government official became apparent to Darius. It is at this point that the plot thickens dramatically. We would understand that the plot to destroy Daniel was only concocted when it became known that there was going to be an adjustment in the new governmental structure. And that adjustment would add a new position right under the king himself. This would make Daniel head over the three commissioners, and apparently, he would be the only one with direct access to the king. This was not good news to those in the administration who desired power and prominence in the kingdom and who also envied Daniel the Jew.

THE ENEMIES OF DANIEL (Dan. 6:4-5)

The sin of envy is such a pure evil because it not only wishes to take what belongs to another, but desires to destroy the person as well. The enemies of Daniel were envious men and embarked on a course that would steal Daniel's position and destroy Daniel as well. Initially they figured that Daniel was like so many men in high places (and probably like themselves) in that he skimmed a little money off the top for himself, falsified a few records here and there, took a few bribes and made some careless mistakes. So, they put his life under the microscope and examined everything about him and the way he did the king's business. Much to their deep disappointment, all efforts to dig up some neglect or corruption concerning Daniel failed. He was not only free from any corruption, but he did his work with excellence. The New Testament exhorts believers today to live this same way and by so doing represent well the Lord Jesus in this world (cf. Phil. 2:15; Acts 24:16). What an impact the Church would have today if those who were in it lived like Daniel did. But while the scrutiny of Daniel's life did not turn up anything bad, it did reveal that his religious life was markedly different from others. He was a Jew and he did not follow the Persians in their worship. This was the area of life that was the most promising in bringing Daniel down. And to this these enemies of Daniel gave their full attention.

Commentators debate whether or not the matter of anti-Semitism is to be seen in the events of this story. It is true, as some have pointed out, that these men just did not like him because he was a foreigner. In other words, Daniel could have been Syrian or Cyprian and it would not have made any difference to them. But while the fact that Daniel was not a Mede or a Persian undoubtedly bothered them, there is a deeper matter at issue here. Daniel was one who was in covenant relationship with God. He was a Jew and a key one at that in the purposes of the Lord God (cf. Dan. 6:13). These were crucial days in the program of God and behind evil men often is the Evil one. Satan, the ultimate anti-Semite, was not slumbering or on vacation during these days and one can see his hand in this matter. This first year of Darius was not only the setting of Daniel 6, but also the setting of Daniel 9 and Daniel 11. In Daniel 9, Daniel agonizes in prayer concerning Israel's condition. With time running out in the prophesied 70-year captivity period, God did not appear to be doing anything in bringing them back to the land of Israel. Daniel prayed pointing out that God's reputation was at stake in the matter because of His promise to return them to the land after 70 years. Now the last thing the Devil wanted to see was Israel back in their land since so many of God's covenant promises are dependent on Israel being back in the land. Would Satan not resist Israel's return by working against Daniel?

Also, this first year is when there was significant warfare in the angelic realm (Dan. 11:1) as God's predicted program transitions from the first kingdom of gold to the second kingdom of silver. Clearly evil angels under Satan's direction are involved in an attempt to thwart God's work. And anyone who does the work of God and promotes His will on earth will be a target of the Enemy. And of all men on the planet in the first year of Darius, none was more significant than Daniel the Jew. God is at work to accomplish His purposes through Israel, His covenant people.

THE PLOT TO ELIMINATE DANIEL (Dan. 6:6-9)

6:6-7 Without a doubt the conspirators had thought through every detail of the decree that they wished Darius to put into law. They had one person in mind when writing the decree and had sought to eliminate any loopholes. They did a pretty fair job, but as we shall see they did miss one point. The two commissioners and a group of the satraps came to the king with every intention of deceiving the king. The decree stated that no one would be allowed to make a petition, except to the king, for a thirty-day period. This, of course, has the idea of petitions in the religious realm, either to a god or to a priest. Normal requests of daily life were not the subject of the decree; so that little children could ask their mothers for a drink of water without fear of facing the lions. But what this decree did was to elevate Darius to a place of deity, or more likely a representative of deity. In any case, it would have been viewed as a significant test of loyalty to the new administration.

The conspirators stated that "all" of the commissioners and satraps were supporters of this decree, which was obviously a lie since Daniel never knew about it much less agreed to it. But Darius was led to believe that Daniel was indeed favorable to the decree. Now since they lied about the full support of the commissioners "it is highly probable that many if not most of the 120 satraps were likewise ignorant of this cunning plot."[93]

Decrees customarily had the penalty for violators clearly spelled out and Darius' decree followed that usual form. Anyone violating this decree would be cast into the den of lions. This form of punishment was quite different from the fiery furnaces of the Babylonians. Why the sudden change in the method of execution?

Many scholars are convinced that the avoidance of fire by the Medes and Persians as a means of execution had religious overtones to it. The Persians were Zoroastrians.

> Many scholars believe that Zoroaster taught not a monotheism, but a dualism, with two primordial uncreated Spirits, a Good Spirit…and an Evil Spirit…all things in creation belong either to one sphere or another; aligned with the Good Spirit are light, *fire*, summer, water, fertile land, health, growth, and domestic animals, especially the dog. Aligned with the Evil Spirit are darkness, night, winter, drought, infertile land, vermin, sickness and death.[94]

Fire played an important role in many of their religious rituals. There was a fire-god (named Atar) and fire was kindled and used in sacred rituals. Therefore, to use fire to kill would have been seen as a sacrilegious act, and so, another form of execution was devised. But clearly the end result would be the same, that of death.

6:8-9 Being persuaded that all of his leaders were behind the decree King Darius signed it making it an irrevocable law. Why would he sign such a decree? First, there was apparently considerable pressure exerted on him to

---

[93] Whitcomb, 82.
[94] Edwin M. Yamauchi, *Peoples of the Old Testament World*, (Grand Rapids: Baker, 1994), 123.

do so. The presence of this group of leaders would have produced pressure on the king. It was not just that there was a fair-sized group that approached the king, but these men were influential leaders in the kingdom (or they would not have been appointed to their positions). Also, the Medo-Persian kings did not have the same kind of sovereign authority as did a Nebuchadnezzar. They were influenced by the powerful nobility. Furthermore, the decree was most likely presented by the conspirators as a display of loyalty to the brand-new administration, which no doubt had to deal with various factions as well as dissidents in those early days of its existence. And it was, after all, just a thirty-day period that was being set aside giving all people in Babylonia a chance to show their loyalty to the new king. It probably seemed like a grand idea to Darius as well as flattering to his pride.

The written decree needed the royal seal and signature in order to make it an irrevocable law; that is, a law that not even the king could change. This "law of the Medes and Persians" is a phrase found in the Book of Esther (Esth. 1:19; 8:8) where it also speaks of royal edicts that could not be revoked even by the king himself. The idea of there being laws that cannot be changed are found outside of the Scriptures as well.[95]

These conspirators knew exactly what they were doing and they were counting on Daniel to be his usual disciplined, courageous self. By all indications, their evil scheme was well on its way to success. But the words of King David are appropriate here: "The wicked plots against the righteous, and gnashes at him with his teeth. The Lord laughs at him; for He sees his day is coming" (Ps. 37:12-13).

THE DECREE DEFIED (Dan. 6:10-13)

6:10 The King's decree did not deter Daniel from his pattern of prayer. He continued to seek His God and fellowship with Him. Daniel was not a political activist bent on acts of civil disobedience, but he was a godly man

---
95 Longman, 160.

whose life was characterized by righteous habits (cf. Ezek.14:14), and in this case these habits conflicted with the government. When he heard about the decree he did not run to the king to point out the unfairness of the decree or to protest in any way. Rather he did what he always did with great calm and focus. He reacted this way because he was a man who knew the Word of God and had embraced it into his own life. It is worth observing here that such an unflinching, stable approach to life is available to all believers, according to the Apostle Paul since it is the by-product of the wisdom of God (cf. Col. 1:9-12).

According to this verse, it was his habit to pray three times a day with his windows open to the west, facing Jerusalem. The fact that he faced Jerusalem when he prayed is based on 1 Kings 8 and it may be that he prayed according to the daily sacrificial schedule in the temple. This would seem to be verified by Daniel 9:21 where, on that occasion, Daniel was praying about the "time of the evening offering." It seems quite possible then that Daniel's pattern of prayer corresponded with the times of the offerings in the Jerusalem temple which he would have been familiar with while growing up. These times of worship would have been at sunrise, mid-morning and around 3 o'clock in the afternoon. The temple, of course, at this point in history was non-existent having been destroyed by Nebuchadnezzar. But years before God had promised King Solomon that He would put His name there forever. In 1 Kings 9:3, the Lord said, "I have heard your prayer and your supplication, which you have made before Me; I have consecrated this house which you have built by putting My name there *forever*, and My eyes and My heart will be there *perpetually*."

Daniel was not being superstitious when he faced Jerusalem during his times of praise and prayer. Rather it was based on the prayer of King Solomon at the dedication of the temple in Jerusalem. Solomon had prayed that when Israel did sin and ended up in captivity that God would hear their prayers of repentance *as they faced Jerusalem* and would forgive them and restore them.

> If they take thought in the land where they have been captive, and repent and make supplication to Thee in the land of those who have taken captive, saying, 'we have acted sinned…' if they return to Thee with all their heart and with all their soul in the land of their enemies who have taken them captive, and pray to Thee *toward their land* which Thou has given to their fathers, the city which Thou hast chosen, and the house which I have built for Thy name, then hear their prayer and their supplication in heaven Thy dwelling place, and maintain their cause, and forgive Thy people who have sinned against Thee. (1 Kings 8:47-49)

And we discover this very kind of impassioned prayer of confession and repentance is recorded in Daniel 9:3-19. It is helpful to remember that this great prayer of Daniel 9 is dated at the same time as this incident of the decree and the lion's den and suggests why Daniel, who was so deeply concerned about God's holy name and Israel's future, would not stop praying just because of some decree.

6:11 The wicked conspirators expected Daniel to be consistent in his worship and devotion to the Lord and they were not wrong. In the days when they were carefully watching Daniel and scrutinizing all that he did, they undoubtedly discovered that his religious exercises took place at home. This, of course, is why the entire group of conspirators showed up there and observed Daniel praying. We do not know how long into the thirty-day period they waited before they sprung their trap. But on one designated day they all came to observe the praying Daniel.

> In his house he had an upper room. Such a room was often built on a corner of the flat roof. People would occupy it when they wished to be alone. However, it was also used for all kinds of other purposes such as a lodging room, bedroom, sickroom or death chamber. Such a little upper room had an exit to the inside as well as one to the outside, which connected it to the street (see Judg. 3:20; 1 Kings 17:19; 2 Kings 4:10; Acts 1:13; 20:8).[96]

---

[96] Harry Bultema, *Commentary on Daniel,* (Grand Rapids: Kregel, 1988), 184.

With his windows opened and facing Jerusalem they could have observed his praying without entering the chamber itself.

6:12-13 Normally faithfulness to the Lord does not require being unfaithful to people. But in this situation, Daniel's faithfulness to the Lord required that he could not faithfully follow the decree of a man. After observing the praying Daniel, the enemies of Daniel quickly went to the king to share their shocking report and did their best to make it a personal matter against the king ("Daniel pays no attention to you"). In their speech, they rehearsed the content of the decree; noted that it was indeed a royal law and thus could not be changed; and that there was a trip to the lion's den for anyone who failed to comply. But before they mentioned Daniel by name, they cleverly got the king to verbally agree with the points that they had made. They had made their approach to the king very carefully because they knew that Daniel was one who was favored by the king.

THE ATTEMPT TO RESCUE (Dan. 6:14-15)

It is difficult to know at exactly what point in their speech Darius came to realize that he had been deceived. But the moment it dawned on him what was going on he "set his mind on delivering Daniel." Darius not only had a fondness for Daniel, but he had benefited from Daniel's leadership skills and personal integrity. He spent all day attempting to find a loophole in this law that he had signed. He probably sought the best legal minds he could find and likely talked to Daniel himself. But this law had been written with just one man in mind and the conspirators had carefully written it so that there would be no way to get around the law should they be able to entrap Daniel.

The conspirators observed the king's attempts to extricate Daniel from their deadly web, and so came again "by agreement" later that day. This word "by agreement" (NASB) has been used twice before in this chapter (Dan. 6:6, 11) and has the idea of "thronging" around the king. It carries with it the implication of a hostile crowd that has surged into the king's presence. We should suggest at this point that this throng probably does not consist of all 120 satraps. The conspirators had lied to Darius about "all" the commissioners being in favor of the decree and we can feel confident that "all" the satraps were not involved either. It is interesting to note that the earlier emphasis (Dan. 6:5, 6) is on "these men" and not on all of the satraps. "The words of the text do not by any means justify the supposition that the whole council of the state assembled."[97] Later on, when the conspirators are tossed into the lions' den it would be a pretty crowded place if all 120 and their families were down there. There was probably a select group who spearheaded the attack against Daniel.

The hostile throng pointedly reminded Darius that this was the "law of the Medes and Persians" that he was dealing with and it could not be broken. Even if he could somehow break such the royal law it would undermine his government and result in negative consequences. And, of course, if Darius the Mede is indeed a subordinate of Cyrus the Persian then he simply would not have the authority to do so.

THE NIGHT IN THE DEN (Dan. 6:16-24)

6:16-18 With all efforts ending up being fruitless, Darius was resigned to giving the order for Daniel to be arrested and placed into the den of lions. Amazingly, he addressed Daniel with the words that the Lord God would "Himself deliver you"! There is an expectation in his voice that such a deliverance might possibly occur. One can only imagine that Darius was not only deeply impressed with the man Daniel but that he had also heard accounts of the power of this God, including the fiery furnace incident.

After Daniel was placed into the den, it was sealed with the king's seal as well as seals of the nobles since this was the execution of one who had violated royal law. The seals, of course, did not physically secure the entrance but were there to ensure that no one would try and rescue Daniel.

---

97 C.F. Keil, *Biblical Commentary on the Book of Daniel* (Grand Rapids: Eerdmans, n.d.) 208.

It was not a good night for Darius as he could not sleep. In fact, the normal palace routine of food and entertainment had been set aside. There was no entertainment and Darius ate no food that night. Of course, Darius would have felt much better if he had only known that the lions were fasting that night too. And herein is the loophole in the carefully crafted decree. The decree declared that anyone who violated this royal law would be cast into the den of lions. It did not say that anyone who violated the decree would be killed. The assumption was that going into the lions' den equaled death. The decree was obviously written by those who did not know the sovereign power of Daniel's God, the creator of heaven, earth and lions.

6:19-24 In the early hours of the morning, a troubled Darius hurried to the den and in an anxious voice called out to Daniel. Darius perhaps only half believed the stories of the might and ability of Daniel's God, but still he hoped that it just might be true as is evidenced by the fact that he actually calls out to Daniel. He again states that Daniel "constantly serves" his God, which is an acknowledgement of Daniel's consistent, disciplined life. Daniel immediately answers, bringing relief to the troubled king. Daniel calmly and politely addressed the king with the courteous greeting "O king, live forever." Daniel is again amazingly calm in a moment of crisis (as in chapter 2), revealing that inner tranquility does not depend on the external circumstances. Daniel had found "grace to help in time of need" (Heb. 4:16).

Daniel informed the king that an angel of God came and kept the lions from doing any harm to him. This deliverance recalls the entrance of a fourth heavenly individual ("His angel") into the furnace of fire. This angel could have been the Lord Himself or it may have been Michael who has the job to protect the people of Israel (cf. Dan. 12:1). In any case, the lions were totally subdued, and Daniel enjoyed the night with the heavenly messenger. Daniel "had trusted in his God" (Dan. 6:23) and Hebrews 11:33 echoes that this deliverance did take place because of Daniel's faith in his God, who can and does deliver. Daniel was delivered not only because of his faith but because he had not sinned against God nor had he done anything harmful to the king. The deliverance was proof of his innocence. The Scriptures tell us that those who have this kind of loyalty to God and awesome reverence for God are recipients of a special commitment from the Lord (cf. Ps. 25:12-14; 33:18; 34:7-9; 85:9; 103:11-13; 111:5 and 147:11). And just as the three men had come out of the fiery furnace unscathed, so Daniel came out of the den of lions without a scratch on him.

Someone might suggest that the lions did not attack Daniel because they were not hungry, perhaps having been secretly fed or drugged by orders from Darius. But 6:24 states that when the enemies of Daniel were thrown into the den on orders of Darius, the lions attacked with great ferocity and destroyed those who had wished to destroy Daniel. The lions had a hearty appetite after their forced fast of the night before. Those key men who had plotted against Daniel were executed along with their families. While the Law of Moses forbade executing the families, "the condemning to death of the wives and children along with the men was in accordance with Persian custom, as is testified by Herodotus."[98]

THE GLORY BROUGHT TO GOD (6:25-28)

Once again, a man of courage and faith has brought great honor to God and the name of the Lord God was elevated among the unbelievers. As Daniel again honored God, He in turn honored Daniel as He said He would (Dan. 6:28 with cf. 1 Sam. 2:30b). The last verse of the chapter talks about "this Daniel" which accentuates this man; the very one they wanted to destroy, this same one now enjoys success.

The king wanted all people under his authority to be clear about the God of Daniel. First, this God is a living God, unlike the dead gods and idols that many worshipped. Second, He is eternal and did not have a beginning unlike the many so-called gods in the world. Third, He is sovereign and reigns

---
[98] Keil, 218.

without interruption, unlike the many gods around them whose fortunes rise and fall for various reasons. Fourth, He is a God who is powerful enough to intervene in the affairs of men and nations and rescue His followers. All those under Darius' authority are to show respect for Daniel's God. Darius is, of course, not attempting to start a state religion nor is he necessarily declaring his faith in the Lord God. He is at least declaring that Daniel's God is the greatest among the gods and must be reverenced.

QUESTIONS TO CONSIDER

1. How should we view powerful, ungodly political forces in our country? What if Christians should increasingly be the target of those forces? What can we learn from Daniel as he lived in the Babylonian and Persian empires?

2. If Daniel were alive today and were a schoolteacher, would he pray in the public school where he was teaching? If he were a judge would he hang a copy of the Ten Commandments in his courtroom? If he were a mayor would he put up a Nativity scene in front of city hall? How does 2 Corinthians 10:3-5 fit into this discussion?

3. Would it be good or bad if the United States were a "Christian nation" with the backing of the Federal government?

4. Daniel was clearly a man of faith. What is faith? Why is it that a person of faith pleases God so much (cf. Heb. 11)? What are some of the consequences of being a person of faith?

5. Daniel' quiet and calm spirit in the midst of a crisis provides a model for all believers. How was Daniel able to respond this way? Why do so many Christians become anxious and complaining when difficult times come? What can believers do to become more like Daniel?

6. What are some truths about God that are revealed in this chapter? What should be the impact of these on the believer as he/she lives life?

CHAPTER SEVEN

DREAMING OF BEASTS

Preview: Fifty years after interpreting Nebuchadnezzar's statue vision, Daniel is given a dream which parallels that revelation concerning the rise and fall of the four gentile world empires. The dreams do parallel one another but also have differences including additional information that is given to Daniel. Daniel sees the gentile empires as four strange beasts, all of which will be destroyed and then followed by God's future, forever kingdom which will be established by the "Son of Man."

The stories found in chapters 1-6 again and again reminded the reader that the Lord God is sovereign over men and nations. These accounts showed that He is all-powerful and that He takes care of His own in spite of the terrible threats and evil actions of powerful men. He, not men, is in control. Chapters 7-12 will again demonstrate that the Lord God is sovereign over men and nations and is control of heaven and earth. But this time it is revealed through four visions that Daniel receives. In these visions, God reveals to His servant Daniel that, according to His timing, He will establish and then He will remove mans' kingdoms from the earth and after that He will set up His own kingdom, which will never end.

A. THE SUMMARY OF THE VISION, Daniel 7:1-14

THE HISTORICAL INTRODUCTION (Dan. 7:1)

The reception of this vision by Daniel is set in the first year of King Belshazzar. This would put the revelation to Daniel in the year 553 B.C., which was the first year of the co-regency of Nabonidus and his son Belshazzar. Nabonidus had begun his reign in 555 B.C. and after about three years he began his self-imposed exile at the Arabian oasis of Tema, some five hundred miles from Babylon. When he departed to go to Tema he installed Belshazzar as regent in Babylon.[99]

So exactly half a century after outlining the course of world empires to King Nebuchadnezzar (in 603 B.C.), God now gives the same outline of world empires to His man Daniel and by repeating the prophecy declares the certainty that these events will surely come to pass. With the date for this vision being 553 B.C. it clearly falls chronologically between Daniel 4 and 5. So when Daniel received this dream of the four beasts Nebuchadnezzar had been dead for about nine years and it would be another fourteen years before the fall of Babylon at the feast of Belshazzar.

Daniel received his dream one night in bed and wrote down the principle parts ("summary") of that vision. That night he had a dream (singular) and visions (plural). The use of the singular emphasizes the unity of this revelation while the use of the plural focuses on the various parts in the unfolding of the revelation. Not all the details of the vision are given in verses 2-14, as additional points are noted in the interpretation (e.g. the fourth beast had bronze claws in Dan. 7:19).

---

[99] Bill T. Arnold, *"Babylonians"* in *Peoples of the Old Testament World*, ed. A. Hoerth, G. Mattingly, E. Yamauchi (Grand Rapids: Baker, 1994), 66.

THE EMERGENCE OF THE FOUR BEASTS (Dan. 7:2-8)

7:2-3 There were three things that Daniel first observed in his vision, which set the stage for the development of this revelation: (1) "four winds of heaven", (2) the "great sea", and (3) "four great beasts" who came out of the sea.

First, Daniel mentions the activity of "the four winds of heaven." This phrase, and forms of it, are used in both Old and New Testament and communicate two primary truths. The phrase is an expression of the *universality* of something, such as the worldwide dispersion of Israel, universal judgment or the worldwide activity of angels (cf. Jer. 49:36; Dan. 8:8; 11:4; Zech. 2:6; Mark 13:27). Jesus used this expression in this way to speak of the universality of Israel's regathering in the end times when He stated that Israel would be gathered "from the four winds" (cf. Matt. 24:31; Mark 13:27). Daniel himself will use the phrase in this way to speak of the four directions of the compass and thus the worldwide nature of the third kingdom (cf. Dan. 8:8; 11:4). This expression is used by Ezekiel "as a Semitic expression for the four corners of the earth, which definitely implies that Israel will be regathered from the four quarters of the globe."[100] But the expression also expresses *divine involvement or activity* especially through angelic beings (cf. Jer. 49:36; Ezek. 37:9; Zech. 6:5; Rev. 7:1). This wind does belong to and come from "heaven." We would agree with Keil when he states that "the wind is the most appropriate among all earthly things for symbolizing the Spirit of God, or the energy of the divine operation."[101] The word for "wind" (Heb. *ruah*) is also translated "spirit" and "breath", which beautifully allows for several blended meanings in any given verse. For example, in his famous "dry bones vision", Ezekiel used "breath" and "wind" blowing upon the lifeless bodies in the valley to speak of the life-giving work of the "Spirit" of God (cf. Ezek. 37:9, 14). It is also interesting to note how the Psalmist ties the "wind" and angels together in the carrying out of God's work in the world (cf. Ps. 104:4). So, when Daniel

---
100 Charles Feinberg, *The Prophecy of Ezekiel: The Glory of the Lord* (Chicago: Moody, 1970), 214.
101 C.F. Keil, *Jeremiah* (Grand Rapids: Eerdmans, 1967), 280.

speaks of "the four winds of heaven" he is telling us that what is to take place among the nations is going to be brought about by the working of God and that it is a worldwide activity, and not events isolated to some local area.

The second point of interest in the setting of Daniel's vision has to do with the "great sea." The beasts are said to come out of the sea (Dan. vs. 3), which is described as the "great" sea (Dan. vs. 2) apparently to inform us that the beasts do not come out of the Sea of Galilee, Bass Lake or some other smaller body of water but from the expansive oceans. Waters are often used of the gentile nations of the earth (e.g. Isa. 8:6-8; 57:20; Jer. 6:23; 46:7-8; 47:2 and Matt. 13:47-50). "The O.T. uses 'waters' as a symbol for 'peoples.'"[102] Often the waters are seen as roaring, raging, overflowing forces, which do harm to God's people. Isaiah 17:12-13 together with Revelation 17:1 and 15 are particularly helpful in identifying the "great sea" as that restless, loud and destructive mass of humanity known as the gentiles. These four beasts will arise out of the gentile nations.

The third item of interest will become a focal point of the vision and that is the four great beasts. We do not have to go far to understand the identity of the beasts because the heavenly interpreter declared that the four beasts represent four kings/kingdoms (Dan. 7:17, 23). These beasts are "great", which again is informing the reader that tribal groups and small nations are not being discussed here. So then, these four nations will arise out of the larger mass of gentiles (the great sea) and all of this will come about because of God's purposeful activity (the four winds stirring up the great sea). The four beasts now become the focus of the chapter.

7:4 The first beast to emerge out of the sea of gentile nations was said to look like a lion. But it was not the usual city zoo variety of lion because it had the wings of an eagle. The imagery of a lion is used in a number of ways in the Scriptures and one of those ways is to represent powerful, frightening, destructive nations (cf. Isa. 15:9; Jer. 49:19; 50:44; Hos. 5:14).

---

[102] A.T. Robertson, *Word Pictures in the New Testament* (Nashville: Broadman, 1933). 6:434.

These nations are savage and generate fear in the hearts of other peoples. One such lion-like nation was Babylon, according to the prophet Jeremiah (Jer. 4:7). Jeremiah used this imagery for Babylon in a message given during the days of King Josiah of Judah, several years before the Babylonians came upon Judah in 605 B.C. and took the nation captive. We wonder if Daniel, as a young boy living in Jerusalem, may have heard this message or at least may have been aware that his hero Jeremiah had declared the nation of Babylon to be lion-like.

This lion empire was unique in that it had wings attached to it that looked like the wings of eagles. Like the lion, the eagle was also used in the Old Testament as a reference to nations (cf. Deut. 28:49; Jer. 48:40; 49:22; Hos. 8:1). Eagles moved quickly, swooping down suddenly upon their prey and destroying it. It is their ability to swiftly and unexpectedly attack that is emphasized. And, as with the lion, this eagle imagery was used of Nebuchadnezzar and the Babylonians by one of Israel's prophets (cf. Ezek. 17:3, 7-12). This lion with eagle's wings would, therefore, represent the empire of Babylon. It may have been that Daniel immediately understood that the winged lion represented the Babylonian empire, since he could look out the window of his apartment and see that very statuary in the city. Winged lions were in front of the royal palaces in the city of Babylon and lined an important street that was used in processions. In Daniel's day, Nebuchadnezzar had constructed the famous Ishtar Gate which had winged lions on it.

The verse goes on to speak of a tremendous change that occurred in the lion with its eagle's wings. The beast experiences an amazing transformation. It is said that its "wings were plucked" and this was followed by it becoming more human-like and less beast-like. It was made to stand on two feet and it received a human heart (mind). The transformation that is revealed most likely looks at that great change that took place in King Nebuchadnezzar, which was documented in chapter 4. "It was probably the spiritual transformation God accomplished within that is here symbolized by the beast's nature being transformed into a human nature."[103]

At this point we ought to note that almost nothing is said about the first three beasts that come up out of the great sea. They are briefly described without any real attempt to identify them or to say much about them. The only information given about the first three beasts is that they are, in fact, empires (Dan. 7:17) and that each will be brought to an end (Dan. 7:12). Daniel's interest, and thus the focus of the chapter, is on the fourth beast and events pertaining to the fourth beast. While this is true, it is also true that information about the course of world empires was given some 50 years earlier by means of Nebuchanezzar's dream of the great metallic statue. There the four main parts of the statue were identified as the four nations of Babylon, Medo-Persia, Greece and Rome (see pages 53-59). We are to use the great outline of human history, found in chapter 2, to assist in our interpretation of this chapter and in the prophetic visions yet to come. The fourth beast will exist at the very end of human history because it will be annihilated completely by the Son of Man just before His kingdom is established (cf. Dan. 7:11, 13, 14, 25-27). This would mean that the fourth beast corresponds to the iron (iron/clay) part of the statue, which was identified as the Roman empire. Working backwards we would conclude that the first beast does indeed represent Babylon as is suggested by the imagery used by the prophets Jeremiah and Ezekiel. We would agree with Longman who states,

> As with the statue in chapter 2, we begin in the present. There the head of gold was explicitly identified as Nebuchadnezzar (i.e. the Babylonian empire). Here, in the waning years of that same empire, the most natural interpretation of the symbolism is that it stands for Babylonia. Perhaps the clearest key to this identification is the fact that the hybrid animal become human-like, reminiscent of Nebuchadnezzar's own experience as recorded in chapter 4.[104]

---

[103] John C. Whitcomb, *Daniel* (Chicago: Moody, 1985), 94.
[104] Tremper Longman III, *Daniel: The NIV Application Commentary* (Grand Rapids: Zondervan, 1999), 184.

In fact, there is general agreement among scholars that the first beast does represent the empire of Babylon. However, as we noted earlier in chapter 2, there is a clear lack of agreement concerning the other three empires.

7:5 The second beast that emerges out of the great sea is said to resemble a bear. There are very few references in the Old Testament to this animal (e.g. 1 Sam. 17:34-37; Amos 5:19). It is used of the actual animal on several occasions and used at other times to speak of someone's ferocious action when provoked (e.g. Hos. 13:8). However, unlike the use of the eagle and the lion, the bear is not used to represent a nation, except here in Daniel 7:5. Several brief statements are made regarding the bear. First, it is raised up on one side and, second, it has three ribs in its mouth. Being raised up on one side is not explained and would be very difficult to even guess at the meaning if it were not for the fuller description of this second empire in the next chapter of Daniel. There the Medo-Persian Empire is represented by a ram with two horns, which pictures those two nations. The horn representing Persia is much bigger than the other representing the Medes, giving the same picture of a lopsided animal (cf. Dan. 8:3, 20). It is, therefore, very possible that this is the point being made when it is stated that the bear is raised up on one side (lopsided). The second matter (that of the three ribs in the mouth of the bear) is generally thought to represent three nations that had been "eaten up" by the second empire. There is disagreement over which three nations are in view, but perhaps they represent Babylon, Lydia and Media (or Egypt or Assyria). The bear is then commanded to devour more besides the three ribs already consumed. This would look at the further conquests of the Medo-Persian Empire.

As noted above, there is agreement about identifying the first empire (the lion with eagle's wings) as that of Babylon. But the identification of the second empire is again the subject of debate between those who see it as representing the Median Empire[105] and those who see it as representing the

---

105 An alternate view is that the four empires were Assyria, Media, Medo-Persia and Greece. This is

Medo-Persian Empire. This issue was discussed in connection with the statue vision of Daniel 2 (cf. pages 55-59). It was concluded there that the second empire is that of the Medo-Persian Empire. This view is the "Roman view" of the four kingdoms, which agrees nicely with the details of the text. Walvoord correctly states that "recent discoveries have proved beyond question that the second empire was in fact the Medo-Persian empire."[106] He then notes that Cyrus the Persian arrived less than a month after the city of Babylon fell to Darius the Mede. Both peoples are therefore involved in the terminating of the Babylonian empire, as the prophets had foretold. And he observes that historically there simply was no independent Median Empire in existence at the time of Babylon's final end. Edwin Yamauchi concurs and says that there was no independent Median Empire at the time of Babylon's fall.

> The last king of an independent Median kingdom was Astyages (585-550). His daughter Mandana married a Persian, Cambyses I, and gave birth to the famous Cyrus the Great. Cyrus led the Persians in a successful revolt against his grandfather Astyages and the Medes in 550. Thereafter the Medes were to play a subordinate though an important role under the Persians in the Achemendid period (550 to 330).[107]

So, we cannot agree with those who say that the imagery at this point in the vision is too obscure and therefore must be understood mainly as a conflict between God and human evil.[108]

7:6 The third empire is said to be "like" a leopard, but with some very obvious differences from the usual leopard. This leopard had four wings and it also had four heads. In the Old Testament there are just a few references

---

suggested by John H. Walton, *"The Four Kingdoms of Daniel"*: Journal of the Evangelical Theological Society (March, 1986), 25-36.

106 John F. Walvoord, *Daniel: The Key to Prophetic Revelation* (Chicago: Moody, 1971), 155.

107 Edwin M. Yamauchi, *"Persians"* in *Peoples of the Old Testament Word*, ed. A. Hoerth, G. Mattingly, E. Yamauchi (Grand Rapids: Baker, 1994), 110.

108 Longman, 185.

to the leopard and none of them are used to symbolize some specific nation (aside from here in Dan. 7:6). The figure of a leopard was used by Jeremiah (Jer. 5:6) and Hosea (Hos. 13:7) as a symbol of swift judgment that was coming on Judah and on Israel. The leopard was apparently used in these pictures of coming judgment because the leopard would pounce suddenly on its victim. So, it would seem that the quickness of this empires movement is being pictured here. And this coupled with the four wings that it had speaks of its unusual speed. This fits well with the amazing speed of conquest under Alexander the Great, the leader of this third empire. In a very short span of ten years Alexander defeated the Persians and took over their empire and expanded it so that the Macedonian empire extended from Greece to India. This interpretation will be supported by the speed of movement of the third empire in Daniel 8 where it is pictured as a swift moving goat (Dan. 8:5).

The heavenly interpreter does not explain the four heads in this passage. But again, the next vision (chapter 8) gives some help. That vision indicates that the third empire would experience a four-fold division. And this is what did take place. When Alexander the Great died in 323 B.C. his empire was divided into four parts among four of his generals. "The four head obviously refer to intelligent direction of the beast and indicate, in contrast to the earlier beasts, which had only one head, that the third empire would have four governmental divisions with corresponding heads."[109] The four-winged, four-headed leopard perfectly pictures the Macedonian (Grecian) empire that conquered with lightning speed across the ancient world and then split into four divisions.

7:7-8 The fourth beast that came out of the "great sea" of the gentile nations did not resemble any known animal. Daniel did not say that it "looked like" some animal, but rather described it as being "different", "strong", "terrifying" and "dreadful." What particularly caught his attention were the ten horns on its head. While he thought about the ten horns he was amazed to

---
109 Walvoord, 157.

observe an eleventh horn growing in the midst of the ten horns on the beast's head. This eleventh horn, which had human characteristics, forcefully pulled up three of the ten horns.

This fourth beast was both horrifying to look at as well as terribly destructive in its actions. With its iron teeth it was able to rip and shred everything it could get a hold of. And that which was not pulverized by the iron teeth was crushed under the feet of this cruel, strong beast. But what nation is being spoken of here? Those who hold to the "Greek view" insist that the fourth beast represents the Greek empire, and that the "little horn" is Antiochus IV.[110] However, this view runs into insurmountable hurdles within the text itself causing interpretation to become vague and without much value to the reader. For example, John Goldingay holds to the fourth beast being Greece with the "little horn" being Antiochus IV. He suggests that the beast is probably a battle elephant because that animal, which crushes others under its feet, was known to be used by the Greeks and by Antiochus IV.[111] But then he is less than clear in explaining matters found in the text, such as why Daniel does not say that this beast was "like" an elephant; what iron teeth have to do with an elephant; what the ten horns stand for; and what is meant by the overpowering of the three horns. He suggests that the "10" horns may be symbolic but admits that the "3" horns seem to be literal.[112] In fact, this descent into obscurity is rather characteristic of the interpretation of those holding to the "Greek view." For illustration purposes several other examples of this phenomenon of obscurity in interpretation surrounding the fourth beast of Daniel 7:7-8 are given here. The defeat of the three horns is discussed by one author: "In other words, Antiochus came to the throne by murder and violence, though we know of only two "horns" which he uprooted, and neither "horn" was actually a predecessor king, as stipulated by verse

---

[110] W. Sibley Towner, *Daniel* (Louisville: John Knox, 1985), 95.
[111] John E. Goldingay, *Daniel* (Nashville: Nelson, 1989), 163.
[112] Ibid. 163-164.

24."[113] The meaning of the "ten" horns is evaluated by another: "The variety of opinions increases dramatically when one tries to figure out who the "ten horns" might refer to. Alexander and six of the Seleucids who followed? Or is "ten" simply to be reckoned as "many"? Does it matter?"[114]

The "Roman view", which sees the fourth beast as the Roman Empire, deals much more forthrightly with the text of Daniel. And it has a much better fit with the events that have taken place and that will take place. And, as we shall observe, the "Roman view" finds strong support from the Apostle John in the Book of Revelation.

The very first thing that needs to be emphasized is Daniel's description of this beast as being unlike the previous beasts (empires). This is so because this fourth empire is so very terrible, cruel and destructive. It went far beyond the other empires in the brutality of their conquests. What it does not devour it tramples underfoot. Historically, it was Rome that forced submission of all and brutalized the people that it conquered. Rome and Greece were notably different, as John Walvoord observes:

> The description of the beast to this point more obviously corresponds to the Roman Empire than that of the empire of Alexander the Great. Alexander conquered by the rapidity of his troop movements and seldom crushed the people whom he conquered. By contrast, the Roman Empire was ruthless in its destruction of civilizations and peoples, killing captives by the thousands and selling them into slavery by the hundreds of thousands. This hardly is descriptive of either Alexander or the four divisions of his empire which followed.[115]

The horns that appeared on the head of this fourth beast held a significant place in the vision. The horns of an animal represented its strength and

---

113 Towner, 95.
114 Daniel L. Smith-Christopher, *Daniel: The New Interpreters Bible* (Nashville: Abingdon, 1996), 102-103.
115 Walvoord, 161.

its power to conquer and the term "horn" is used in the vision to represent powerful kings and their strong kingdoms. "Frequently in the Old Testament the term *horn* is used to describe power, and thus, appropriately, powerful rulers (1 Kgs 22:11; Ps. 75:10; 132:17; Zech. 1:18)."[116] In this vision the beast had ten horns on its head, which the heavenly interpreter has declared to represent kings and kingdoms (cf. Dan. 7:17, 24). It should be observed that the ten horns were there at the same time and, therefore, the kings/kingdoms being spoken of are in existence at the same time. One does not follow another, which surely dampens enthusiasm for the position that these are successive rulers (as is interpreted by many holding the "Greek view"). And they remain in existence until the time that an eleventh horn grows up in the midst of them. So, at the end of human history, there will be eleven kings/nations together on the world stage.

There are several key scriptures, which help the interpreter understand the meaning of the horns found on the fourth beast. First, **Daniel 2:42-44** has already informed us that there will be ten kings (ten toes on the statue) that will exist in the end of human history. Like the ten horns on the fourth beast, these ten toes emerge out of the fourth part of the statue (the iron part). It is in the days of those kings (when all exist simultaneously) that the kingdoms of man will be destroyed and the future, forever kingdom of God will be established. So, to have these ten kingdoms represent something from the days of the Grecian Empire does not fit well at all with the text of Daniel. The kingdom of God, which will never be challenged or destroyed, was not established at the time of the demise of the Grecian empire.

Secondly, the Book of Revelation makes an interesting and important contribution to the understanding of the horns. Progressive revelation adds great clarity to the meaning and activity of the horns of Daniel. In **Revelation 17:3, 7, 12-16** the Apostle John gives several points of information about the horns. The one that is particularly helpful here is that at the time of the

---

116 Whitcomb, 96.

writing of Revelation by the Apostle John *these ten kings had not yet received their kingdom*. As of John's day, they had not yet come into existence, which categorically excludes them from being part of the Grecian empire. John also reinforces their simultaneous existence when he says that these ten horns are united in one purpose to serve the Beast (that is, the Antichrist) and to strengthen his kingdom. And in **Revelation 13:1-2**, John again identifies the ten horns as ten rulers (wearing their crowns) who are all in existence together and are part of the Beast.

The "little horn" came up after the ten horns were already in existence and this was of great interest to Daniel. If each of the ten horns represents a king and his kingdom, then it is required that the "little horn" represent an individual king and his kingdom. He must be a single individual who heads one nation, and not something else (such as head of the United Nations, as some have speculated). The "little horn" is said to have eyes and a mouth. These human characteristics are designed to emphasize something about this ruler; namely that he possesses notable intelligence and that he speaks persuasively (cf. Ezek. 1:18; 10:12; Zech. 3:9; 4:10 where eyes speak of intelligence and cf. Dan. 7:25; Rev. 13:5-6 and 2 Thes. 2:4 where his bold speech is emphasized or suggested). From later revelation it becomes clear that he is a man of great ability and known for his blasphemy against God. Also, in the vision, he is said to "subdue" three of the other horns (Dan. 7:24), which apparently catapults him into prominence and power on the world stage. This will be dealt with in the interpretation of the vision.

If the interpreter holds to the fourth beast and the eleven horns being the Roman Empire, then several possibilities exist on how it works out. Some amillennial interpreters, like Edward J. Young, spiritualize the "ten" horns and the "three" horns and, therefore, do not find it necessary to look for some historical fulfillment.[117] Other amillennial writers will either find historical fulfillment of some kind in the past and so do not need any future

---

117 Edward J. Young, *The Prophecy of Daniel* (Grand Rapids: Eerdmans, 1949), 275-294.

fulfillment or will see it finally fulfilled with the Second Coming of Christ. Those who hold to a premillennial position believe that there will be ten literal kings/kingdoms that will be in simultaneous existence at the end of the age along with the kingdom of Antichrist (the 11th). It is in the days of those kings that the Lord Jesus Christ will return to the earth, judge the wicked and establish His own kingdom.

THE NATIONS	STATUE VISION (CH. 2)	BEAST VISION (CH. 7)
Babylon	The Head of Gold	The Lion with Eagle's Wings
Medo-Persia	The Arms and Chest of Silver	The "Lopsided" Bear
Greece	The Belly and Thighs of Bronze	The Leopard with 4 Heads and 4 Wings
Rome (1)	The Legs of Iron	Dreadful, Strong, Terrifying Beast
Rome (2)	The Feet of Iron and Clay	The Ten Horns
God's Kingdom	The Stone/Mountain	The Kingdom of the "Son of Man"
The Antichrist	XXXXX	The Little Horn

THE HEAVENLY SCENE (Dan. 7:9-12)

7:9-10 At this point in the dream, there comes a dramatic shift, as he no longer is focused on frightening, ravaging beasts of the earth but rather gazes upon a truly awesome scene in heaven. He observes thrones being put in place and preparation taking place for coming judgment. Since the scene is now in heaven it is best to understand the text as saying that "thrones were set up"

(NASB) and not that thrones were "cast down" (KJV). Those following the KJV suggest that it is the thrones of the 10 kings that are being judged and cast down. But the "setting up" of thrones fits the context that follows; that is, preparation is being made for a time of judgment. The focus of the vision is on the individual who is identified as "the Ancient of Days." This One will take His seat on the throne in order to adjudicate things related to the earth.

It is most interesting, however, that not just one throne was set up for the occasion, but thrones (plural) were set up. It is helpful at this point to make the observation that the scene here in Daniel 7 is closely paralleled by the scene found in Revelation 4 and 5. In Revelation, the throne of God is seen surrounded by 24 thrones. On these thrones are seated 24 elders. The evidence from Revelation seems to point to these elders as being men and not angels. And the Scriptures are quite clear that believers will indeed be involved in heavenly courtroom settings in the future (e.g. 1 Cor. 6:2-3) and will be involved in the actual execution of some of Christ's judgments in the future (cf. Rev. 17:14; 19:4, 14-16, 19).

The phrase "Ancient of Days" is only found in Daniel 7:9, 13 and 22. In identifying the Ancient of Days, the scene from Revelation 4 is helpful in that it informs us that this Person is none other than God the Father. He is seen wearing pure white garments and His hair is also white. This description of Him is most likely communicating His holiness, eternality and wisdom (cf. Ezek. 1 and Rev. 1).

Fire is closely associated with His throne, as fire was observed by Daniel sparkling all around the throne and a river of fire flowing from it. Fire is commonly used in the Bible for the presence of God and the judgment of God (cf. Exo. 3:2; Ps. 18:8; 97:2-3; Rev. 1:14-15; Deut. 4:24; Heb. 12:29; Ezek. 1:4ff). The picture then is that of God mounting His throne for the purpose of an all-consuming time of judgment. This blazing throne was said to have wheels, which were also of fire. "In the East thrones quite often had wheels, so that these heavy golden chairs could be easily moved."[118]

---

[118] Harry Bultema, *Commentary on Daniel* (Grand Rapids: Kregel, 1988), 219.

Daniel observed several other things in this vision. He saw that the throne of the Ancient of Days was surrounded by a multitude of beings. In the scene in Revelation 4 and 5, angels were prominent, and it is most likely that this multitude in Daniel 7 represents the holy angels. So it would seem that both angels and redeemed men are around the throne of God. Also, Daniel observed that books were brought out and opened when the court sat in judgment. Books (scrolls) are mentioned a number of times in connection with the future evaluation of men. Obviously, God does not need books to jog His memory or to ensure that He does not forget some pertinent fact. Books are there is let us know of the certainty of the judgment (cf. Mal. 3:16; Isa. 65:6; Rev. 20:22). Judgment is for sure and it is fair, whether it be for rewarding or for punishing.

7:11 With the coming judgment prepared for, Daniel's attention returns to the earthly scene and the "little horn." The one thing that is emphasized is the mouth of the "little horn" with its terrible boastful words. Daniel speaks here of the "boastful words" of this "little horn" and later he will state that this evil one will "speak monstrous things against the God of gods" (Dan. 11:36). The Apostle John will later echo this characteristic of the Antichrist ("little horn"). "And there was given to him a mouth speaking arrogant words and blasphemies…and he open his mouth in blasphemies against God, to blaspheme His name and His tabernacle…" (Rev. 13:5-6).

John places this aggressive blasphemy in the last 3½ years of the tribulation period;[119] a period that closes with the judgment of this wicked individual. Daniel's vision would be in agreement with the timing given by John. In Daniel 7:11, the fourth beast is seen being burned up with the fire of judgment (no doubt coming from the throne of the Ancient of Days). It must be that if the fourth beast is killed and burned up completely that all

---

[119] The term "tribulation" is being used as it is popularly used in reference to the seven-year period of trouble that will close this age. More precisely the reference should be to the "Seventieth Week of Daniel" but that will not be discussed until we get to Daniel 9:24-27. It is understood that some hold to the "tribulation" as being just the last 3 ½ years of the "Seventieth Week."

eleven of the horns will also be consumed at that time. The verse declares that this final kingdom is completely and utterly destroyed with nothing being left of it. In the following interpretation it is clear that it is at this juncture that the kingdom of God is instituted.

7:12 This verse is basically parenthetical and answers the question "what about the other three beasts in the vision? What happens to them? The information given here is essentially the same as that found in Daniel 2:35, 45 (see page 64). The first three empires had their domination over other nations ended by the appearance of stronger empires. But when they did lose their dominion, they still continued to exist in many ways. For example, when Babylon came to end in October of 539 B.C. at the hands of the Medes and Persians, there were elements of Babylonian religion, philosophy, government, language and learning that continued on long past 539 B.C. Elements of old Babylon would be detected centuries later for those who had eyes to see. And so it was for the first three empires. This is why they (the lion, bear and leopard) are seen embodied in the last terrible beast in Revelation 13:2. So to each of the three, after their defeat, "an extension of life was granted to them for an appointed period of time" (Dan. 7:12).

But this was not to be the case with the fourth and final beast. It too would be deprived of its empire, but it would not experience "an extension of life" as Revelation 19:19-20; 20:10 makes abundantly clear. It would be totally destroyed (along with the remaining vestiges of the first three beasts)

and would vanish completely forever in order that God's kingdom could be instituted. The order of events is again preserved; that is, the kingdom of God comes only after the total and complete destruction of man's brutal empires. There is no co-existing of man's kingdom with God's kingdom.

THE APPEARANCE OF THE SON OF MAN (Dan. 7:13-14)

7:13 After the scene on earth and the annihilation of the beasts, once again Daniel's attention is riveted on heaven and the grand events that transpire there. And once again there exists a clear parallel with the later vision of the Apostle John in Revelation 5. This portion of the vision, and John's parallel vision, record the transference of ruling and judging authority to the "Son of Man". This vision complements the vision found in Daniel 2 where the "stone cut out without hands" destroyed completely the great statue and then ushered in the rule of God in the great everlasting kingdom of God.

Daniel first saw the "son of man" coming on the clouds of heaven. The "clouds of heaven" are used throughout scripture of the glory and the presence of deity (e.g. Exo. 13:21-22; 19:9, 16; 1 Kgs 8:10-11; Isa. 19:1; Jer. 4:13; Ezek. 10:4; Matt. 24:30; Acts 1:9, 11; 1 Thes. 4:17; Rev. 1:7). This One, who was coming in the clouds of heaven and into the place of the thrones, is being identified as deity, and yet, He is referred to as a "son of man". The "son of man" is clearly distinct from the horns and beasts in the earlier part of the vision.

"Son of man" was the favorite title that Jesus used of Himself in His earthly ministry. Perhaps He chose this identification because on one hand it linked Him to Daniel's messianic prophecies while on the other hand avoided the negative response from Israel's leaders had He specifically called Himself "Messiah." This was how He identified Himself before the High Priest the night before the crucifixion (Luke 22:69). Dozens of times in the gospel record He spoke of Himself this way and used it in reference to His future coming.

"And then the sign of the SON OF MAN will appear in the sky, and then all the tribes of the earth will mourn, and they will see the SON OF MAN coming on the clouds of the sky with power and great glory....For this reason you be ready too; for the SON OF MAN is coming at an hour when you do not think He will." (Matt. 24:30, 44) (cf. Matt. 11:19; 12:8; Mark 2:10; 9:31; Luke 9:56; 17:30; John 5:27; 6:53). It was a title that clearly pointed to the genuineness of His humanity. And yet, it communicated even more than that. It pointed to Him as the one who would solve the problem of man's sin and separation from God and the problem of the loss of ruling the planet which was usurped by Satan. This title is linked with the "seed of the woman" (Gen. 3:15). It was humanity which brought the terrible problem of sin into the world, but it would be humanity which was to bring about the solution to these monumental problems. Mankind brought sin, separation and loss into this world and it would be the "seed of the woman" (a human being) that would bring the complete and final solution to these matters. The "Son of man" would be the one to do all this. He is seen being presented before the Ancient of Days, which therefore makes Him distinct from the Ancient of Days.

7:14 The result of His appearing before the Ancient of Days was the granting of ruling authority. It needs to be noted that the ruling authority given does not refer to His rule as part of the Godhead but focuses particularly on His position as Messiah. It is in the first phase of the eternal kingdom (the Millennial/Messianic aspect) that the Son is preeminent. When the one-thousand-year Messianic kingdom is completed, then the Son will turn ruling authority back to the Father (cf. 1 Cor. 15:23-28). But this Messianic phase of the eternal kingdom of God is necessary to fulfill the covenant commitments made by God to Abraham and his descendants.

There are several observations that can be made from this verse. First, His rule is universal. It is said that "all" peoples and nations (men of "every" language) will be the subjects of His rule. All of these mentioned will worship ("serve") Him. The Bible is clear that one day every knee will bow before the rightful authority of Jesus Christ (e.g. Phil. 2:9-11). Second, this is a permanent kingdom since it will never end. Unlike all the kingdoms of man, which had termination points, this kingdom will last forever and will never be destroyed. And third, it is a rule and a kingdom that can only be described as "glorious." It will be magnificent and will be like none other before it. It ought to be noted that these realities do not now exist. Jesus is presently functioning as our great High Priest at the right hand of the Father and that His throne is established in connection with His second coming (cf. Matt. 19:28; 25:31). Those who hold that this present age is the "millennium" are forced to spiritualize the language of this and other texts. It simply is not accurate to say that Jesus is presently ruling over "all the peoples, nations and men of every language", all of whom have bowed the knee to Him. And it is difficult to see that the present state of affairs can be His "glorious" kingdom. In fact, Satan is still the "god of this world" and Jesus is obviously not going to engage in co-rulership with him. Even if one tries to limit Jesus' rule to just His church, it is hard to see that as "glorious" and over "all" peoples and nations. The theological idea that this present age is the rule of Messiah Jesus defies the plain, normal reading of literally dozens and dozens of Old Testament passages.

And in the upcoming interpretation given by the heavenly interpreter (Dan. 7:26-27), it is again seen that the future universal, permanent, glorious kingdom of God is not established until after the total removal of the fourth kingdom.

B. THE INTERPRETATION OF THE VISION, Daniel 7:15-28

DANIEL'S RESPONSE TO THE VISION (Dan. 7:15, 28)

The overpowering nature of these scenes affected Daniel mentally and emotionally. Not only were the beasts horribly real and the fiery scenes in heaven overwhelming but the implications of it all for Israel and the world imploded in the soul of Daniel. He could not dismiss the images from his mind (Dan. 7:15). And though he finally learned much of the significance of his vision from the heavenly interpreter, Daniel's mind remained agitated and overwhelmed (Dan. 7:28). The power of these visions impacted Daniel physically, mentally, emotionally and spiritually. Being a conduit for the revelations of God apparently is not an easy or casual matter.

THE GENERAL INTERPRETATION (Dan. 7:16-18)

7:16 Daniel did not intuitively understand the meaning of this vision and so asked one who was nearby. This one is commonly assumed to be an angel and probably one of those of the myriads surrounding the throne of the Ancient of Days. There seems to be no doubt on Daniel's part that this heavenly person could interpret the visions correctly giving "the exact meaning" of them.

7:17-18 The heavenly interpreter succinctly stated that each of the beasts in Daniel's vision represented a king (kingdom). The kings are seen as the founders and representative of four kingdoms. It is clear from his statement that these kingdoms will not be permanent, but will come to an end, being replaced by God's kingdom.

There is an intriguing point made by the heavenly interpreter. He states that the saints of God "will receive the kingdom." This statement points to a participation in ruling by the saints (same word used in Dan. 5:31). The saints (regenerate believers) are seen ruling in the future kingdom of God. It is the Son of Man who will rule and have dominion and yet the saints are also there ruling. The truth of this statement reaches back to Genesis 1 where Adam and Eve were made the king and the queen of the earth and were to rule and subdue the planet. Their sin brought an end to their "reign" and allowed Satan to become the ruler of this world (cf. 2 Cor. 4:4; John 12:31; 1 John 5:19). But with the victorious conquest of Messiah (Son of Man) ruling will once again return to mankind, first in the person of the God-man Jesus and then in those who will rule with Him. The faithful obedient believer is seen in a number of scriptures ruling with the Messiah in His kingdom (cf. 2 Tim. 11-12; Luke 19:17; Rev. 22:5).

We must note, however, that when Daniel spoke of the "saints" or holy people, he could only have been thinking of his people Israel, who were clearly distinguished from the unbelieving gentile nations. These holy people are also referred to in Daniel 7:22, 25 and 27, as well as in 8:24 and 12:7.

> To one versed in the Old Testament scriptures these can be understood in only one fashion---of the covenant nation Israel. Consider the evidence. The Hebrew adjective equivalent to the Aramaic *qaddish*, saint, is *qadosh*. In Exodus 19:6 it is used of Israel and of Israel alone in her peculiar relation to God as His covenant people. In Leviticus 20:7, 26 it is used in the same sense as Deuteronomy 7:6; 14:2, 21. The Hebrew noun *qodesh* is also equivalent to this Aramaic word, and is used of Israel and of Israel only in this special sense of describing a people peculiar to God...The whole point is that Daniel was referring to his own people when he used these terms, and whatever the New Testament may add does not contradict this simple fact.[120]

Daniel is not thinking of the Church when he refers to the saints. The term is consistently used in reference to the nation of Israel that sustained a covenant relationship with the true God. The point made above, by way of

---

[120] Robert Culver, *Daniel and the Latter Days* (Chicago: Moody, 1954), 133-134.

application, that faithful believers from the church age will also reign with Christ does not set aside the meaning of these texts. Israel does have a future as a nation. When they turn to the Lord in faith, which is the primary purpose of the tribulation ("Seventieth week"), the promises made to them nationally will be fulfilled. And so, Israel is the focus of Daniel's thinking here.

THE SPECIFIC INTERPRETATION (Dan. 7:19-27)

7:19-20 It is apparent that Daniel's interest lies with the fourth beast and particularly with its eleven horns. This is probably true because it is in connection with the end of the fourth empire, which ushers in the long awaited and desired kingdom of God. And this was of great interest to godly Daniel.

The heavenly interpreter seemed willing to explain the vision to Daniel and so Daniel inquired into some of the details concerning the beast and its horns. In the process of asking his questions, Daniel repeats many of the details that he had observed in his vision. Once again, this fourth beast is described as uniquely terrible and vicious. Once again it is stated that the "little horn" was responsible for the felling of three of the ten horns. However, this time an additional point is made; namely, that the "little horn" actually became larger than the other ten horns. Apparently, we are to understand that when the "little horn" first appears, he is in fact smaller. But in a short period of time he grows in size and power and actually dominates the other ten horns.

7:21-22 Another fact that was not previously mentioned was that the "little horn" would make war against the people of God and do so with great success. It is God's people Israel that are the target of this successful persecution, though this does not mean that believing gentiles will escape the wrath of the Antichrist. But the emphasis in this book of Daniel is on "Daniel's people" Israel as the objects of God's favor and the Enemy's disfavor (cf. Dan. 9:20, 24; 12:1). This triumph over the "saints" takes place after the "little horn" has grown to be the largest of the horns. The Apostle John also speaks of the

Antichrist's successful persecution of God's people and connects it with the second half of the period of tribulation (cf. Rev. 13:7-8). This individual will experience a brief time of notable triumph over God's people. But the time of victory for him will last only "until" (Dan. 7:22) God moves in judgment against him.

The text says that "judgment was passed in favor of the saints." The idea is not that the saints are given the role of judging (as some have thought), but that God executes judgment on their behalf. This is exactly what is seen in Revelation 17:14 and 19:11-21 as the Lord Jesus, to whom all judgment has been given (John 5:22), executes that final judgment on the Antichrist. And again, the chronological sequence remains the same. It is *following* the judgment of the last phase of the human kingdoms that the Lord and His saints will rule in His kingdom.

7:23-24 The angelic interpreter then states clearly that the fourth beast is the fourth empire. He once more stresses the brutality of the fourth empire by saying that it "devours" and "crushes" everything. He then reveals that just as the fourth empire is distinct from the other three, so the eleventh horn (the "little horn") is distinct from the other ten. The "little horn" (the Antichrist) arises after the ten horns, but while they are still in existence. He uproots three of the ten, which shows that all these horns are contemporaneous and, therefore, they are not ten successive kings (or kingdoms). These ten kings are in power at the very end of the age, which indicates that they are yet to appear on the stage of human history (cf. Rev. 13:1; 17:12). There is no need, therefore, to try and find fulfillment at some point in history. We would believe, therefore, that the vision is pointing into the future when the last phase of the fourth empire (Rome) will emerge and be dominated by the "little horn". We would not, therefore, agree with the statement that "to think of the ten horns and the little horn as future manifestations of the Roman Empire is bizarre."[121] The details of the vision

---

121 Longman, 190.

do indeed point to the future end times when the fourth empire and the Antichrist come to its end at the hands of the Son of Man to whom all judgment has been committed.

The "little horn" (the Antichrist) conquers three of the ten horns. The Antichrist forcibly brings these three kings under his authority. But what happens to the other seven kings (horns)? Nothing is said in the vision, but in light of other revelation it is most likely that the other seven simply acquiesce and submit to the Antichrist. This seems to be their position in Revelation 17:12-13 where all ten are clearly subservient to the Antichrist, since it is said that they "give their power and authority" to the Antichrist. So that after the conquering of the three kings (kingdoms) takes place, the Antichrist becomes the head of an eleven-nation confederacy of some sort. The prophecies of Daniel and Revelation would place the formation of such a confederacy in the days of the tribulation. It is quite possible that this conquering of the three nations is what the Apostle John is speaking about in Revelation 6:2. In that verse, the first seal judgment takes place and the rider on a white horse (commonly believed to be the Antichrist) goes forth and conquers. This particular conquering would be 3 ½ years before the Antichrist becomes ruler of the entire world. The first seal judgment takes place at the very beginning of the seven-year tribulation period. If in fact Revelation 6:2 is speaking of the same thing as Daniel 7:24, then the forming of this western confederacy of nations takes place only after the start of the tribulation. And if that is the case then the signing of the covenant between the Antichrist and Israel, which is the event that starts the tribulation (see discussion of Daniel 9:27), is between Israel and the Antichrist when he is the ruler of a single nation only. If he is the ruler of a single nation, then it is most likely that he emerges out of a nation that is fairly powerful; powerful enough to guarantee the security of Israel.

THE CAREER OF THE "LITTLE HORN" (ANTICHRIST)			
Leader of one nation	(2) The "LITTLE HORN" by means of conquest becomes the ruler of a confederacy of 11 western nations	(3) The "LITTLE HORN" with Satan's backing and power becomes the ruler of the entire world for 42 months	(4) Judged and destroyed by Jesus at the 2nd coming
THE 7 YEAR PERIOD OF THE TRIBULATION			

7:25 The heavenly interpreter next outlines three great evils that will characterize the Antichrist during those final days. First of all, he mentions the Antichrist's wicked words. Secondly, the Antichrist's persecution of the saints of God is revealed, and finally, his altering of God's times and laws. However, before these three issues are analyzed it should be noted that these three great evils will be manifested during the second half of the tribulation period (that is, the second half of the seventieth week of Dan. 9).

The verse states that the time frame involved for these evil activities is "time, times and half a time." The same expression will be used in Daniel 12:7 where the discussion is about Israel in the end times. The expression is normally understood to be a reference to a three-and-a-half year period; "time" equaling one year, "times" equaling two years and "half a time a time" equaling half a year. Even the critics take this expression to mean 3 ½ years, but generally apply it to the Grecian king Antiochus Epiphanes. This interpretation of the phrase as being 3 ½ years is confirmed as accurate by later revelation. The same expression is used in Revelation 12:14 where it is equated with a time-period of 1260 days (Rev. 12:6) for the persecution of the nation of Israel. The Apostle John had received this and other information on a scroll, the contents of which are found in Revelation 11-14. In that section there is a great emphasis on events that will occur in the last 3 ½ years of the tribulation. Revelation 11:2 speaks of "42 months"; 11:3 mentions "1260 days"; 13:5 makes reference to "42 months"; as well as the references in chapter 12 given above. We can, therefore, suggest with some certainty that the heavenly interpreter of Daniel's vision is discussing the final 3 ½ year period of the tribulation when Israel will be tested and the crescendo of the human kingdoms will come.

During the second half of the tribulation (the "Seventieth week") the Antichrist, who is empowered by Satan, will aggressively "speak out against the Most High." He will be arrogant, boastful and will speak "monstrous things" against God (cf. Dan. 7:8, 12; 11:36). We can only imagine the evil and deceit of the godless rhetoric of this man. This ultimate in blasphemy is closely linked with the setting up of the "abomination of desolation" in the Jerusalem temple. We should observe that "blasphemy" is not simply swearing or speaking foolishly. Rather, it "is deliberately speaking untruth about God". Under the Mosaic Law, the penalty for blasphemers was stoning (cf. Lev. 24:10-16). [122] The Antichrist (aided by the False Prophet of Rev. 13) will demand that all people worship him and the Devil, and he will take his seat in the temple of God (2 Thes. 2). As he exalts himself, he will purposely and powerfully attempt to degrade and diminish the one true God. But whatever "success" he has will last those few short years.

A second evil activity of this man will be that of the persecution of God's people, Israel. The seven-year period of time will begin with his promise of protection for God's people Israel (cf. Dan. 9:27). At the midpoint of this period he will forsake his promised protection of Israel and launch the most horrendous persecution of them. The Lord Jesus (Matt. 24:9, 15) and many of the prophets (e.g. Jer. 30:4-7; Isa. 4:2-4; Zech. 13:8-9) foretold the coming of these terrible times.

> In the Holocaust under Hitler one third of the world Jewish population died. Under the fierce persecution of the Antichrist,

---

[122] Kenneth O. Gangel, *Daniel: Holman Old Testament Commentary* (Nashville: Holman, 2001), 216.

controlled and energized by Satan, two thirds of the Jewish population will die. This will be the largest and most intense persecution of the Jews ever known in Jewish history.[123]

This focused attack on Israel will be an emphasis later on in the visions of Daniel as it is seen in the end times and also prefigured by the activities of the wicked king Antiochus Epiphanes (cf. Dan. 8:24-27; 9:26-27; 11:30-32; 36; 12:7-10).

The third wicked activity of the future antichrist is to "make alterations in time and in law." In the context this expression most likely means that he intends "to change times of religious observations and religious traditions which characterize those who worship the true God."[124] Though we lack details on what will actually be done, it is not at all difficult to imagine what he might do as he sets himself up in the temple and demands worship of himself. The laws of God and the ceremonies and rituals found in the Word of God will surely be forbidden and replaced with those intending to honor Satan and the Antichrist.

> The Antichrist, speaking for the "father of lies," will seek to reverse this foundational law of the moral and spiritual universe… He will indeed be "the man of lawlessness" (2 Thess. 2:3) and will culminate the desire of fallen man throughout history to cast off every divine restraint that has been imposed upon the world for man's good (Ps. 2:1-3).[125]

We can speculate that he will have some success in his efforts. The text simply states that his intention is to change these laws that have been woven into the very fabric of life since creation. Though he will undoubtedly have some limited, external success, his attempts will prove futile in the end.

7:26-27 These verses emphasize the point that God's judgment will be executed on this man and his kingdom without any mercy. This judgment is

---

123 Arnold Fruchtenbaum, *The Footsteps of the Messiah* (Tustin: Ariel Ministries, 1977), 197.
124 Walvoord, 175.
125 Whitcomb, 104.

seen as complete and eternal and not subject to judicial review. The court of heaven with its complete records (the books of Dan. 7:10) has reached its final and authoritative verdict with the result that his kingdom will be thoroughly destroyed without any remnants left. The completeness of the judgment is attested to by the Apostle Paul (cf. 2 Thes. 2:8) and the Apostle John (cf. Rev. 17:14; 19-19-21), as well as by Daniel himself (cf. Dan. 2:35, 45).

With simplicity, but real clarity, the heavenly interpreter declares that the destruction of this evil empire will be followed by the establishing of the kingdom of God. There is here, as there was in the statue vision of chapter 2, a stated chronology of events. The sequence is the setting up of God's kingdom only *after the complete destruction and removal of the kingdoms of man*. Many conservative scholars, from all millennial positions, believe that the Apostle Paul's "man of sin" (2 Thes. 2) and the Apostle John's "beast" (Rev. 13) refer to the Antichrist who will appear at the end of the age. His appearance and subsequent destruction are future to us. Yet, many insist that God's kingdom was established at the first coming of Jesus Christ. They do this in spite of the chronology set forth by Daniel in chapters 2 and 7. Years ago Robert Culver made an appeal to some of these scholars.

> But now we call on our Amillennialist friends to look, and to look steadily for a moment, at the fact that the kingdom of Messiah which they contend was established at the beginning of the present age is in this chapter specifically predicted to appear after the appearance and the destruction of Antichrist, and *only* after the appearance and the destruction of Antichrist.[126]

And while we do not question the godliness of these scholars, we do resist their interpretations at this point. Not only is there a clear sequence presented but the kingdom that God sets up is one of power and glory and requires the absolute submission of *all* peoples on the earth. The language of

---
126 Culver, 131.

scripture relating to God's kingdom does not align itself well with what we see in the world in this present age.

The last words of the heavenly interpreter emphasize the place that God's people will have in the Messiah's kingdom. As noted earlier, the original purpose of God was that Adam and Eve would be the rulers of the earth. They lost that position to the Evil One and after millennia of anguish and struggle, this wonderful purpose of God will at last be realized. The nations, which now rage and war, will submit and live in peace as every knee will bow to Messiah. And the Son of Man (the Stone) will not only deliver His people but the Lord will give this ruling and kingdom to His people. Unlike the position of Post-millennialism, the people of God will not bring in the kingdom and, in a sense, give it to Him. He rules and delegates authority to rule to His people after His total victory over the enemy.

It is no wonder that Daniel was so overwhelmed by what he saw in this most graphic revelation. He saw God bringing to an end the authority of evil and reinstating the righteous rule of God.

QUESTIONS TO CONSIDER

1. In what ways does this chapter contribute to a biblical worldview; that is, how are we helped in seeing life/the world from God's perspective? Give several possibilities.

2. How might Daniel 7:13-14 affect the way we worship and approach the Father and the Son? What from this heavenly scene might assist in making our corporate worship qualitatively better?

3. How should the reality that evil and evil men will be brought to an end affect how we view the world we live in with its sin and evil?

4. In looking at the four beasts, what can be learned about sin and the way in which God deals with sin and sinners? What do we see of mercy and judgment?

5. There is an emphasis in this chapter on God's people ruling with the Son of Man. Will all believers have this opportunity or does it belong to just some? What would passages like 2 Timothy 2:11-12; Luke 19:15-26 and Matthew 19:27-30 contribute to the discussion?

6. What is the "kingdom of God"? Is it something in the present? In the future? Both? What does Daniel 2 and 7 tell us about the kingdom of God?

CHAPTER EIGHT

OBSERVING SOME HORNS

Preview: Two years after receiving his vision of the four beasts, Daniel had a second vision concerning two other beasts. Up to the giving of this second vision, very little had been revealed in the book of Daniel about the Second Kingdom (i.e. Medo-Persia) and the Third Kingdom (i.e. Greece). This vision tells of the rise of the Second Kingdom, which is seen as a ram with two horns, unequal in length. After a period of dominance, this kingdom would be destroyed by the Third Kingdom, which is pictured as a male goat with one very large horn between its eyes. Of the two beasts, the greater emphasis in the vision is on the goat. Its large horn is suddenly broken off and replaced with four horns. Out of one of the horns (i.e. its kingdom) arises a small horn which will have a great impact on the nation of Israel. This small horn becomes the focus of the vision and the interpretation because of its impact on Israel.

Daniel was around 65 years old when he had this vision of the Ram and the Goat. He apparently still had some sort of responsibility in the government of the kingdom (cf. Dan. 8:27) though we would assume that it was not a prominent one since some 12 years later at Belshazzar's infamous feast, the king seemed to be ignorant of the man Daniel. This vision begins to develop the bare outlines of chapters 2 and 7 as regards the kingdoms of Medo-Persia and Greece. It is the account of the conflict between these two empires.

With this vision the Aramaic section of Daniel (Dan. 2:4-7:28) is over and the final chapters (Dan. 8:1-12:13) are written in Hebrew. Generally, it is thought that the reason for the change back to Hebrew is that the focus of the final chapters is on history as it relates to Israel. In these final chapters, it is true that the Gentile nations remain important in the unveiling of this prophecy. But it is the oppression and deliverance of the covenant nation of Israel that is central to the prophecies.

THE SETTING OF DANIEL'S VISION (Dan. 8:1-2)

8:1 The reception of this vision by God's man, Daniel, was said to have been in the third year of Belshazzar. Remembering that 553 B.C. was the first year of the co-regency of Nabonidus and his son Belshazzar, this would set the Ram-Goat vision in the year 551 B.C. The fact of Belshazzar's co-regency with his father is well established based on the information found in the "Babylonian Chronicles" (see pages 96-98) with the result that the dating of this vision can be made with some confidence. As Daniel prepared to tell his readers of this second vision of his, he made reference to his first vision of the Four Beasts, which was received two years earlier. There is, however, a difference between the two visions. In chapter 7, Daniel apparently received information in a night dream/vision, while in chapter 8 he appears to have been fully awake as is seen by his emphasis on "looking" at the animals and events which he describes.

8:2 The question surrounding verse 2 has to do with where Daniel actually was when he received the vision. Was he in Babylon or in Susa (Shushan, KJV) in Persia? While some have argued that Daniel was in Persia, and not in Babylon, when he was given this vision, the majority of expositors believe that he remained in Babylon but was taken in vision to Susa. The transporting of an individual in vision to another location would, of course, be the experience of others, such as Ezekiel (cf. Ezek. 40:2).

> The probability is that Babylon did not control this city or area at this time, and this perhaps accounts for Daniel's astonishment

as he contemplated the vision to find that he was in this place rather at Babylon. The expression *Shushan the palace* reoccurs in historical sections dealing with the Persian Empire (Neh. 1:1; Esth. 1:2, 5; 2:3, 5). By *the palace* is probably meant the king's residence, which was more in the form of a castle or fortress than merely a luxurious building. Shushan the palace, nevertheless, was destined in the Persian Empire to become the capital rather than Babylon. This was unknown at the time that this vision was given to Daniel, although Susa had served as the capital of the Elamites in antiquity; and conservative scholars find a genuine prophetic prediction in this reference to Susa.[127]

Even more specifically, Daniel places himself near to the Ulai River which was a man-made canal near to the city of Susa. It should be observed that it is highly unlikely that a second century pseudo-Daniel would have knowledge of this kind of detail.

THE RAM AND THE GOAT AT WAR (Dan. 8:3-8)

8:3-4 The description and activity of the Ram is mentioned first. Daniel observed the two-horned Ram on the other side of the canal. It will be remembered that "horns" are used to represent kings and their kingdoms. The horns of an animal were seen as its strength and its glory and came to be used to communicate the concepts of power, authority and honor (e.g. Dan. 7:24; Ps. 89:17; 92:10). Apparently, the unusual nature of the horns on the Ram immediately caught Daniel's attention. The horns were unusual in that they were unequal in size and the larger ("higher") one came up last on the head of the Ram. This description of uneven horns corresponds nicely to the "lopsided bear" found in the "four beast vision" in chapter 7, which represents this same empire. It was observed in this present vision that the Ram was unstoppable in its conquests as it destroyed all nations ("other beasts") that it encountered. The conquests of the Ram were in all

---

127 John F. Walvoord, *Daniel: The Key to Prophetic Revelation* (Chicago, 1970), 180.

directions except for the east, which indeed was true of the military movements of Cyrus and those kings that followed him.

The identification of the Ram is not left to speculation as Gabriel was sent to Daniel to give the clear declaration that the Ram with the two horns represented the kings of Media and Persia (cf. Dan. 8:20). This unequivocal statement by Gabriel is another powerful proof that the second empire was a combination of the two empires of Media and Persia and that the second empire was not an independent Median empire, which would be followed by a separate Persian empire (see the earlier discussion, pages 55-59; 132-134). The two horns growing out of the Ram show that the second empire had two distinct parts to it.

> Thus we find here the one horn higher than the other. That is an indication of the greater power of the Persians over the Medes, for in the prophecies of Isaiah and Jeremiah, Cyrus is always presented as the conqueror of the world who would put an end to Babylon's power. When it says that the higher came up last, this agrees perfectly with history, for it was not Cyrus and the Persians who were the mightiest at first, but the Medes.[128]

As it would turn out in history, this conquering and dominance of the Ram would go on for about 200 years until finally defeated by the notable king from the west, Alexander the Great and the Macedonians.

8:5-7 The second animal in Daniel's vision was a male goat ("buck goat") that came swiftly from the west. This male goat not only moved with great speed, but it had a distinctive single horn in the middle of its head. Again, Gabriel saves us a great deal of discussion and speculation by giving the divine identification of this particular animal. He stated that the male goat represented the empire of Greece and that the large horn that protruded from between its eyes represented its first great king (cf. Dan. 8:21). There is general agreement among interpreters that this large horn represents Alexander

---

[128] Harry Bultema, *Commentary on Daniel* (Grand Rapids, Kregel, 1988), 240.

the Great and that the emphasis on the Goat's speed of movement refers to Alexander's amazingly quick conquest of the Persian Empire. It is worth noting that there is no way that Daniel by natural understanding and insight could have known about the rise to power of these peoples from the west who were so very insignificant in his day, much less the kind of rapid and devastating conquest that is pictured in the vision.

The conflict between the Goat and the previously identified Ram is discussed in the following two verses. There are two things that particularly stand out regarding the clash between these two world empires. First, there is a rapid and total defeat of the Medo-Persian Empire (the Ram) by the Greek/Macedonian Empire (the male Goat). And second, there is high level of anger and antagonism for the Ram in the heart of the Goat.

First, history tells us of the complete defeat of the Medo-Persian Empire by Alexander and that it was done with incredible speed. It will be remembered that this element of speed was also suggested in chapter 7 where the third empire was represented by the leopard with four wings. The four wings would be indicating that the leopard moved very swiftly. After consolidating his power and defeating rebellious elements within Greece, Alexander began his dismantling of the Persian Empire in 334 B.C. The first encounter with the Persians was at the Granicus River, which resulted in the utter defeat of the Persian army. In a matter of months all of Asia Minor was in Alexander's control. Darius III, the king of Persia, led an army of over 500,000 men against Alexander at the battle of Issus in 333 B.C. Alexander, though greatly outnumbered, slaughtered the massive Persian army, which resulted in the western half of the Persian Empire falling into his hands.[129] He then turned southward and city after city submitted to him with the exceptions of Tyre and Gaza. Both of these cities were eventually defeated, and Alexander controlled all of Syria, Palestine and Egypt. In 331 B.C. at Guagamela, near Nineveh, Alexander again met Darius III with his immense

---

129 A.T. Omstead, *History of the Persian Empire* (Chicago: Univ. of Chicago, 1963), 495-505.

Persian army and again decisively defeated him in battle. Also, at this time, Darius himself was assassinated by one of his own satraps. Alexander and his troops then proceeded east in their conquest and ended up destroying and burning the Persian capital of Persepolis and the neighboring city of Ecbatana. By 324 B.C. his conquests led him all the way to the borders of India where his battle-weary soldiers refused to go any further. In a matter of only ten years (which was amazing in those days), the second empire was replaced by the third.

The text of Daniel also reveals that there was a particular hatred that Alexander and the Macedonians had for the Persians. There are a number of reasons why the goat "rushed at him in his mighty wrath" (Dan. 8:6) and why he "was enraged at him" (Dan. 8:7). The Greeks deeply resented the Persians for their invasion of Greece in the days of the Persian king Xerxes and Alexander saw his role as avenging that invasion. "The king's ancestors had wantonly invaded Greece; as commander-in-chief of the Greeks he intended to take vengeance through the new crusade."[130] Retaliation against Xerxes' actions was the reason why Alexander plundered, vandalized, burned and massacred the inhabitants of Persepolis the Persian capital. And Alexander noted in more recent times that Darius III had sent money and other help to those opposed to Alexander and had played a part in the murder of his father Philip.[131] So even when Darius III eventually sought peace with Alexander, the Grecian king would have nothing to do with it. He had a deep and abiding hatred for the Persians, which would fuel his rapid conquest of their empire. The Goat indeed was "enraged" at the Ram.

8:8 Alexander ruled a vast empire, but for a very brief period of time. After his conquests halted at the border of India, Alexander returned back to Babylon where he intended to establish the capital of his empire. "While engaged in establishing his new organization, he died a victim of his profligate

---

130 Ibid. 505.
131 Ibid. 505-506.

eating and drinking coupled with an attack of malaria."[132] It is also noted by some historians that he had been wounded a number of times which likely played a part in his demise. Along the road of his conquests, Alexander had married a captive princess named Roxana. It was by her that his heir to the throne was supposed to have come, but that would never come to pass.

Instead, the empire of Alexander would end up being divided up among four of his generals. The process would take some twenty years before the final division of the Greek empire was firmly in place. There is general agreement that the four horns of this vision are fulfilled in the men given below.

> Great as his military conquests may have been, Alexander failed to create a unified empire. No sooner was he dead than his generals began to quarrel over the government of the empire. They are known as the *Diadochi* ("successors"). The four leading rulers were Antigonus of Babylon and North Syria (soon to be overtaken by Selecus I Nicator); Ptolemy I Soter of Egypt; Cassander of Macedonia; and Lysimachus of Thrace and Bithinia.[133]

There were more than four of Alexander's leaders who contended for positions of power, but it all ended up as Daniel predicted with four (not three or five) who divided up the empire. The text adds that their four empires would be toward the "four winds of heaven" (see the discussion of this phrase at Dan. 7:2). Of these four, however, only two would be of significance to the prophecies of Daniel because only these two would directly affect the people of Israel.

Gabriel's revelation made it clear that the four horns do indeed represent four kings and their kingdoms (cf. Dan. 8:22). He also noted that their combined power and authority would not at all match the power that Alexander the Great alone had after his conquests.

---

132 John F. Walvoord, *The Nations, Israel and the Church in Prophecy* (Grand Rapids: Zondervan, 1988), 77.
133 John C. Whitcomb, *Daniel* (Chicago: Moody, 1985), 110.

THE SMALL HORN (Dan. 8:9-14)

The part of Daniel's vision that is located in 8:9-14 is one of the more difficult sections found in this book as evidenced by the varieties of views found among the commentators. The identification of the "little horn", the "host" and the "stars" and the calculation of the "2300 evening and mornings" are central to the understanding of the vision.

8:9-10 From one of the four empires mentioned in 8:8 a small, or little, horn would emerge, which would play a very significant role related to the nation of Israel. This "little horn" becomes the focus of this prophecy. There has been some confusion at this point because a "little horn" was also the center of attention in chapter 7. Some have concluded that these two chapters are looking at the same individual.[134] But the consensus among scholars from various theological camps is that these two horns do not refer to the same person and kingdom.

A careful reading of the two chapters shows that these two "little horns" are not looking at the same individual. It will be remembered that the little horn in chapter 7 (the Antichrist) comes out of the fourth empire, but here in chapter 8 the little horn (who will be identified with Antiochus IV) emerges out of the third empire. The Antichrist/little horn of chapter 7 is intimately connected with ten other horns, which appear at the end of time while the little horn of chapter 8 has no such association with ten horns. The Antichrist/little horn of chapter 7 comes out of the body of the animal (the empire itself) while in chapter 8 the little horn does not come from the body of the animal itself but out of one of the four horns, which are seen as subdivisions of the empire. Furthermore, the Antichrist/little horn of chapter 7 rules a western confederacy of eleven nations and then quickly becomes ruler of the world (see pages 147-154) but again, no such scenario of ruling is seen regarding the little horn of chapter 8. And finally, when the Antichrist/little horn of chapter 7 is destroyed the kingdom of

---

134 Henry Morris, *The Defender's Study Bible*, (Iowa Falls: World Bible Publishers, 1995), 920.

Messiah immediately comes into existence, but no messianic kingdom arises after the appearance of the little horn of chapter 8.

One might wonder why the Lord would use such similar pictures. Why not use two entirely different symbolic pictures and avoid confusion? It is probable, that while they are not the same individual, there is an important connection that should be made by the interpreter. Obviously, the Lord could have used an entirely different symbol in chapter 8. He did not have to use animals with horns, but even if He did, He could have used something other than a horn, such as an ear or a tail or a wart. But He did not do that and that apparently is to encourage the interpreter to make a comparison between the little horn that emerges from the fourth empire and the little horn that arises out of the third empire. And there is important information that one obtains by doing so.

Identifying the little horn of chapter 8 must be done in the broad context of Daniel's prophecies, which are concerned about the nation of Israel during the time of gentile domination. Only two of the four divisions of Alexander's empire directly affected Israel, those of Ptolemy (Egypt) and Seleucus (Syria). It is from one of these two ruling dynasties that the little horn will likely come, and the interpreter should look there in making the identification. As one looks over the history after Alexander, the conquests and activities described in 8:9-14 can only really be applied to one king. Approximately 150 years after Alexander's death, out of the Seleucid (Syrian) kings, emerged the eighth king of that dynasty. This king was Antiochus IV who took the title Epiphanes ("manifest god") and ruled from 175-164 B.C. (Additional information about Antiochus and his activities are given in the prophecy found in Daniel 11 and will be dealt with at that time.) We would make the observation here that in many ways Antiochus IV is really not that significant an individual and is certainly not deserving of such scriptural attention (both in chapters 8 and 11). While admittedly nasty and depraved and an oppressor of Israel, he is rivaled or surpassed in history by many other haters of Israel. But he is spotlighted because he very likely is the most accurate picture of the future Antichrist. This can be supported by 8:17, which states that the vision has significance for the "time of the end." And the term "time of the end" is used elsewhere in Daniel for the time when the Antichrist will be on the world stage (cf. Dan. 9:26; 11:35, 40, 45; 12:4, 9). Again, this helps explain the usage of the same basic symbol of a "little horn" in both chapter 7 and 8 and why we should compare the two.

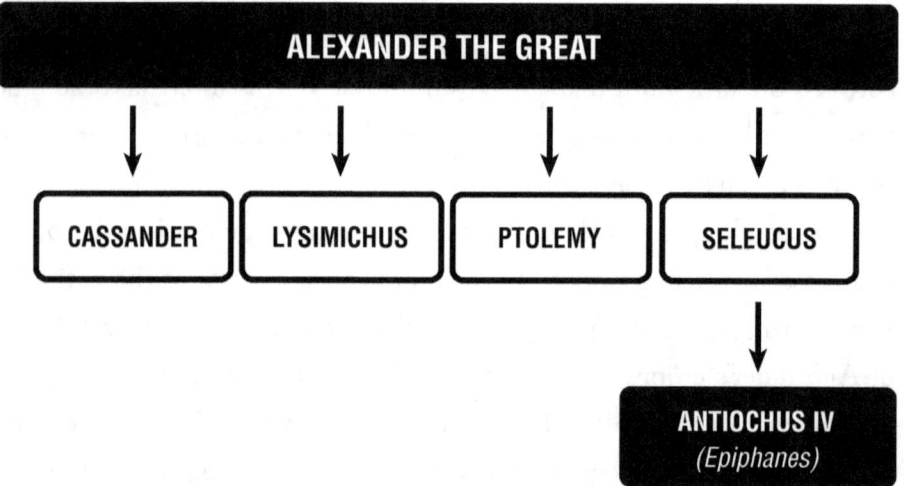

The military excursions of Antiochus IV met with much success. They included going south into Egypt and into the "pleasant" or "beautiful" land, as well as east into Armenia and Persia. The beautiful land is of particular interest and is certainly a reference to Israel "the land of milk and honey (cf. Ezek. 20:6, 15), the land considered most attractive by virtue of a divine perspective appreciated by Daniel."[135]

> The original for "pleasant land" actually means "beauty," with the word for "land" supplied from Daniel 11 (cf. Dan. 11:16, 41, 45:

---

[135] Tremper Longman III, *Daniel: The NIV Application Commentary* (Grand Rapids: Zondervan, 1999), 203.

Jer. 3:19; Ezek. 20:6, 15; Mal. 3:12). Actually, the meaning here may be Jerusalem in particular rather than the land in general.[136]

By conquering these lands, the "little horn" (Antiochus IV Epiphanes) did become "exceedingly great" for a little while. Some of his conquests are described in the book of 1 Maccabees. Though part of the Apocrypha, and not a part of the inspired Scriptures, the book of 1 Maccabees is generally considered to be fairly accurate historically.

> Now when the kingdom was established before Antiochus, he thought to reign over Egypt, that he might have the dominion of two realms. Wherefore he entered into Egypt with a great multitude, with chariots, and elephants, and horsemen, and a great navy, and made war against Ptolemee king of Egypt: but Ptolemee was afraid of him, and fled; and many were wounded to death. Thus they got the strong cities in the land of Egypt, and he took the spoils thereof. And after that Antiochus had smitten Egypt, he returned again in the hundred forty and third year, and went up against Israel and Jerusalem with a great multitude. And entered proudly into the sanctuary…And when he had taken all away, he went into his own land, having made a great massacre, and spoken very proudly.[137]

The temporary rise to greatness of Antiochus IV included victory over the "host" and the "stars." This success over the "host" and the "stars" must find fulfillment during the reign of Antiochus IV (and probably also in the career of the future Antichrist). But we must consider just what is meant by the terms "star" and "host"? The term "star" is used only once in 8:10 while the "host" is used four times in 8:10, 11, 12 and 13. Because of the fact that these terms are often used for angelic beings, it is thought that there is some kind of cosmic war that is in view or that damage was somehow inflicted on the armies of heaven. But as successfully evil as he was, it is quite clear that

---
136 Walvoord, *Daniel*, 185.
137 1 Maccabees 1:16-21. *The Apocrypha* (Oxford: Oxford University Press, n.d.), 151.

Antiochus IV could not and did not have actual victory over God Himself nor the angels of God. And yet, 8:11 is clear that some of the host were defeated by Antiochus. It would seem that the "stars" (Dan. 8:10) are most likely referring to the faithful Israelites who are closely associated to God by covenant and who suffered greatly under the reign of Antiochus IV. While stars often refer to angels, they are also used in relationship to people. It will be recalled, for example, that the stars in Joseph's dream (cf. Gen. 37:9-10) represented the sons of Jacob, who were the very foundation stones of the nation of Israel. And in the interpretation of the victories of Antiochus given by Gabriel in 8:24, the "holy people" is used of the same people and this is a reference to the people of Israel (cf. Dan. 7:25), which supports that idea that the stars symbolize the faithful people in Israel.

> That stars should signify God's holy people is not strange when one considers as a background the words that were spoken to Abraham concerning the numerical increase of the people of God, Gen. 15:5; 22:17.[138]

> ...probably the best explanation is that this prophecy relates to the persecution and destruction of the people of God with its defiance of the angelic hosts which are their protectors, including the power of God Himself.[139]

The faithful people of God are seen in Scripture as shining like stars (cf. Dan. 12:3 and Matt. 13:43). Since this vision is focused on the people of Israel, we can understand why commentators most often conclude that the faithful of Israel are being spoken of here. And the oppression of God's people Israel by Antiochus is well documented.

It is quite possible that the term "host" is actually used in apposition to "stars", that is, the two words are referring to the same group. If it is in apposition, then the text in 8:10 is saying "some of the host *even (that is)*

---

[138] H.C. Leupold, *Exposition of Daniel* (Minneapolis: Augsburg, 1949), 348.
[139] Walvoord, *Daniel*, 185.

some of the stars." This equating of the two seems plausible in view of the fact that "stars" are not mentioned again in the verses that follow. Only "host" is mentioned, which would make sense if they were essential the same entity, that is, faithful Israelites including faithful priests.

8:11-12 Antiochus IV deliberately chose his name when he declared himself as "Epiphanes" (the manifest god) and this is reflected in his arrogant defiance of the Lord God. He exalted himself and attempted to bring down Israel's God by attacking His people and polluting His sanctuary.

> Antiochus's coins picture his head surrounded with a star, and he entitles himself King Antiochus God Manifest (Βασιλευσ Αντιοξοσ Θεοσ Επιφανησ). Perhaps it is the case, then, that an attack on the Jerusalem temple, the people of Israel, and the priesthood is presupposed to be implicitly an attack on the God who is worshipped there and on his supernatural associates who identify themselves with Israel.[140]

The "Commander of the host" is often identified as the Jewish high priest. He did hold the most significant position in Israel both religiously and politically during these times. However, the real authority behind the high priest was the Lord God Himself. And in the coming interpretation given by Gabriel in 8:25 it would appear that it is probably God Himself that it in view as the "Commander" and identified as the "Prince of princes". But even if the high priest were in view here, he is serving at the pleasure and authority of the Lord and to oppose him is to oppose the Lord Himself. The stopping of all the sacrifices to God by Antiochus and the desecrating of the Jerusalem temple was an aggressive, defiant act of God Himself. 1 Maccabees gives a description of these events.

> And he entered proudly into the sanctuary, and took away the golden altar, and the candlestick of light, and all the vessels thereof, and the table of the shewbread, and the pouring vessels...He took

---
140 John Goldingay, *Daniel: Word Biblical Commentary* (Nashville: Thomas Nelson, 1989), 210.

> also the silver and the gold and the precious vessels…And forbid burnt offerings and sacrifice and drink offerings in the temple… and pollute the sanctuary and holy people…Now the fifteenth day of the month Casleu in the hundred forty and fifth year, they set up the abomination of desolation upon the altar and builded idol altars throughout the cities of Juda on every side…Now the five and twentieth day of the month they did sacrifice upon the idol altar which was upon the altar of God.[141]

At that time an old priest in Israel by the name of Mattathias cried out "behold, our sanctuary, even our beauty and our glory, is laid waste and the Gentiles have profaned it."[142] Antiochus Epiphanes had indeed done the unthinkable. And although he did not actually tear down the sanctuary of God, it was so desecrated by him that later on when it was reclaimed after the Maccabean revolt and cleansed by the Maccabees, they did in fact tear the desecrated altar down and rebuild it.

The prediction was that Israel would suffer significantly under Antiochus, much as they will in the days of Antichrist (cf. Dan. 9:26-27; Rev. 13:6-7). Daniel 8:12 states that because of "transgression" this host will be given over to Antiochus along with the sacrifices in the Jerusalem temple. God was going to allow these terrible events to take place because of the "transgression." In other words, the reason given for the successes of Antiochus IV over God's people has to do with sin. Is it the sin of Israel or of Antiochus that is in view here? It is unclear and has been interpreted both ways. But it would appear that both might be in view since it is true of both. First, these matters took place in order for Antiochus to be able to sin greatly against God and His people. This sinner was allowed to prosper no doubt because he was to prefigure the future Antichrist. This point would be validated by 8:13 where the transgression of Antiochus is apparently in view. But it is also very likely that Israel's sin is also in view. It is interesting

---

141 1 Maccabees 1:21-23, 45,-46, 54, 59.
142 1 Maccabees 2:12

to observe that 1 Maccabees 1:11 declares that "in those days went there out of Israel wicked men who persuaded many" to become co-conspirators with Antiochus IV in opposing the truth and ways of the Lord. And it records in 1:52 that "many of the people" forsook the law of God and aligned themselves with Antiochus and that they ripped apart and burned the "books of the law" (1 Maccabees 1:56). The sins of both appear to be in view here as it will be in the coming time of tribulation when the willful sins of the Antichrist and the stubborn sinning of Israel are both present.

8:13-14 With the success of Antiochus over the faithful in Israel as well as his damaging of the sanctuary and the Word of God, the concern was now over the duration of his victories. Daniel heard two angels discussing the matter (cf. Dan. 4:13 and 10:5), one of whom seemed quite concerned about how long this terrible condition would persist. He is informed that it will last for 2300 "evenings and mornings." It is clear that the successes of Antiochus would be temporary in nature, which of course was good news. But the perplexing question has to do with the exact amount of time that is being presented here.

There are two basic positions held concerning the meaning of the phrase "2300 evenings and mornings", not counting the day to year view of Seventh-Day Adventism.[143] One view is that it means 1150 actual days. This is based on the reference to the evening and morning sacrifices that took place in the Jerusalem temple.

> "Change…the words "two thousand and three hundred days" to "two thousand and three hundred *evening-mornings.*" The "evening-mornings" were of course the morning and evening burnt-offerings prescribed in Leviticus. This would be only 1,150 days, somewhat over three years.[144]

---

[143] The father of Seventh-Day Adventism, William Miller, believed that the 2300 "days" were actually 2300 years. This year-day theory was used to calculate the end of the world and the coming of Christ. He proposed that Christ would return in 1843/44. But since Christ did not come to earth in that year, the view was altered to the idea that a heavenly sanctuary was in view in Daniel 8. This theory left Daniel 8 without any real fulfillment as it simply does not fit the text. The year-day theory is simply not a viable option for the interpreter.

[144] Robert Culver, *The Histories and Prophecies of Daniel* (Winona Lake: BMH Books, 1980), 128.

> This phrase probably does not simply mean one day, as it does in Genesis 1, but instead is to be understood as referring to the two sacrifices offered daily in the temple. One day implies two sacrifices; therefore, 2300 evening and morning sacrifices equal 1150 days or about 38 1/3 lunar months of 30 days each, which equals 3 years plus 70 days.[145]

The other view is that the phrase "2300 evenings and mornings" is simply stating that the time frame of the desecration by Antiochus would be 2300 days.

> Based upon the very strong precedent of Genesis 1, where each of the creation days bears a similar formula ("there was evening and there was morning"), we must understand the 2,300 evenings and mornings to mean 2,300 literal days.[146]

> A Hebrew reader could not possibly understand the period of 2,300 evening-mornings of 2300 half days or 1150 whole days, because evening and morning at the creation constituted not the half but the whole day. Still less, in the designation of time, 'til 2300 evening-mornings', could evening-mornings be understood of the evening and morning sacrifices, and the words be regarded as meaning that till 1150 evening sacrifices and 1150 morning sacrifices are discontinued. We must therefore take the words as they are, i.e., understand them as 2300 whole days.[147]

There are, obviously, real differences in understanding the "2300 evening and mornings". It is possible to fit both views into the history of the days of Antiochus. Does the time period of 2300 begin with the actual desecration of the temple in 167 B.C. or does it begin earlier around 171 B.C. with the removal of the high priest Onias III? Most all agree that the period ends with the taking back of the temple and its rededication in the days of the

---

145 W. Sibley Towner, *Daniel* (Louisville: John Knox, 1984), 122.
146 Whitcomb, 113.
147 C.F. Keil, *Biblical Commentary on the Book of Daniel* (Grand Rapids: Eerdmans, n.d.), 304.

Maccabees (in December of 164 B.C.). But it is the starting point that is debated. While there is room for opinion here, it is probably best to take the 2,300 evenings and mornings in their normal and usual sense of 2,300 literal days. This is then a period of between six and seven years. This would then mean that the period of time began in 171/170 B.C. and ended in December of 164 B.C. Again, the book of 1 Maccabees gives some helpful information (cf. 1 Macc. 1:10-21; 4:52-59).

> We can see from this portion of the remarkably accurate historical document of 1 Maccabees that the beginning of the 2,300 days of tramping of "the host" (8:13), as well as the holy place, could very easily have occurred in the fall of 170 B.C. It was when the apostate Jews "abandoned the holy covenant" and received official authorization from Antiochus "to observe the ordinances of the Gentiles" that this six year and four month period of horror began.[148]

It has also been noted that the legitimate high priest, Onias III, was put to death and false priests were established around the time of 171/170 B.C. Such an action would certainly deprive the sanctuary and the sacrifices of their legitimacy and would seem to qualify as being "thrown down" and flinging "truth to the ground" (Dan. 8:11-12).

THE FUTURE REVEALED (Dan. 8:15-27)

The second half of chapter 8 records the interpretation of Daniel's vision by Gabriel. A number of the specifics of Gabriel's interpretation have already been mentioned in our discussion of 8:1-14. This interpretive section of chapter 8 has been approached in several ways by Bible expositors. First, there are scholars who believe that this chapter is simply history written after the fact but put in a prophetic format.[149] Naturally this approach, which sees

---
148 Whitcomb, 114.
149 Towner, 115-127.

Daniel as a second century work, is rejected by conservative scholars. Secondly, there is the view that chapter 8 was completely fulfilled by Antiochus IV and, as a result, there is no future fulfillment to be anticipated.[150] This perspective is generally rejected by most Premillennialists. The third view is that chapter 8 was fulfilled historically in the person and activities of Antiochus IV, but that this king who lived in the second century B.C. pictures the future Antichrist. There is, therefore, information of importance about the coming Antichrist that can be gleaned from these verses. This section will be approached from the viewpoint of this third position.

8:15-16 Unlike many believers today, Daniel passionately wanted to understand the meaning of prophetic statements. His desire to know prophetic truth would be honored. Daniel saw an individual near the Ulai River who is said to be like a man. This apparently is a reference to the angel Gabriel (whose name means "man/hero of God") who will give the requested interpretation of the vision. Gabriel is ordered to give the interpretation and we would surmise that this is the voice of God giving the order, since Gabriel is a messenger angel who "stands in the presence of God" and to whom God gives His messages to be delivered to men on the earth (cf. Luke 1:19 and Rev. 8:2). This is the first time that the angel Gabriel is mentioned by name in the Bible though he will appear again on the earth bringing crucial messages from God (cf. Dan. 9:21; Luke 1:19, 26).

8:17-19 Daniel naturally was overwhelmed by the presence of this glorious and powerful angelic being and fell to the ground. Daniel was merely a weak and fragile human being ("son of man") and this experience simply was too much for him. But Gabriel strengthened and encouraged Daniel in order that Daniel would comprehend the prophetic message.

Gabriel immediately indicated that the ramifications of this vision were far reaching, even to the end of time: "the vision pertains to the time of the end" (Dan. 8:17); "at the final period of the indignation, for it pertains to the

---

150 Longman, 205.

appointed time of the end" (Dan. 8:19). While this is not a denial of fulfillment in the days of the second and third empires, as is evident in 8:20-22, it takes a perspective beyond that time frame. Daniel is not merely interested in the rise and fall of gentile powers, but rather in their rise and fall as it leads to the final days and the establishment of the future Messianic kingdom; the kingdom of the "Stone" (chapter 2) and the "Son of Man" (chapter 7).

Most Premillennial writers see some kind of application or fulfillment of this prophecy in the days of the future Antichrist.

> But what did Gabriel mean when he said that "the vision pertains to the time of the end"? This expression cannot properly be applied to the career of Antiochus IV Epiphanes. Not only did he die a hundred years before his kingdom came to an end, but also his kingdom was followed by another world empire, namely, Rome. "The time of the end" is actually a technical expression that refers to the events that will accompany the second coming of Christ to destroy the kingdoms of this world and to establish His own everlasting kingdom (see the contextual use of this expression in Dan. 11:35 and 11:40).[151]

> "This chapter constantly points to the time of the end (see vv. 19, 23, 26). "The time of the end" is a standing expression in Daniel for the time of the Antichrist (see Dan. 9:26; 11:35, 40, 45; 12:4, 6, 9). It is the time of the last year-week of Daniel and particularly the second half of it.[152]

> It may be concluded that many premillennial expositors find a dual fulfillment in Daniel 8…most of them find the futuristic elements emphasized, especially in the interpretation of the vision.[153]

So, while the days of Antiochus IV were terrible times for the nation of Israel, even worse times lie ahead for God's people Israel. The atrocities

---
151 Whitcomb, 115.
152 Bultema, 246.
153 Walvoord, 196.

of Antiochus IV will be far surpassed by those of Antichrist, which he will execute during the last 3 ½ years of gentile rule on the earth.

8:20-22 These verses were absolutely critical in the earlier discussion of Daniel 8:3-9 as they clearly identified the nations and persons involved in the rise and fall of the Medo-Persian and Grecian empires. The verses state unequivocally that Medo-Persian is one, not two empires, and these verses give the road map to understanding who the significant "little horn" would be.

8:23 Based on our belief that the following three verses (Dan. 8:23-25) refer to both the historical figure Antiochus IV Epiphanes as well as the prophetic figure Antichrist, there will be an attempt to generally apply what is said in the text to both individuals. It is recognized that some statements may appear to be more applicable to one of the individuals than the other, but both will find some point of application.

This verse (Dan. 8:23) states that a king will come to power in the latter part of the kingdom and his rising to rule will coincide with the ending of some sort of rebellion. Further, this king will be particularly noted for being a master of manipulation and for being ruthlessly bold ("stern faced").

Antiochus Epiphanes. Antiochus did arise in the latter times of the Seleucid dynasty. He appeared as the eighth ruler in that line some 160 years after the emergence of the "conspicuous horn", Alexander the Great. But what about the idea of his appearing at the end of the age in the time of indignation? One author is speaking about the words "end", "time", "closing part of wrath" and "distant days" says that they are everyday words in Hebrew just as they are in English. He then makes the following statement: "None inherently refers to the absolute End, and only their contexts tell us whether the expressions in the various combinations refer to the end of a particular period of time of to the End of Time."[154]

---

154 Goldingay, 215.

This same author then makes the following observation.

> The "end" must still be the punctiliar moment of the termination of the Antiochene persecution and the vindication of the sanctuary, but this more absolute expression hints that v. 17 sees this as *the* End; at least it implies that the end of the Antiochene oppression (v.19) is also the end of the era, the closing scene of the history of Israel and the nations (Dan. 2:28), and the moment of final judgment.[155]

This author does not believe that the final, absolute end is in view in Daniel 8, but nevertheless his observations are helpful. There is a sense in which Antiochus' reign would conclude Syrian oppression would usher in a time when Israel would have a greater independence. But *the End* would come to pass only when the pre-figured Antichrist came out on the world stage. So, both a near and a far view of "the end" can be found in chapter 8. And while the final "wrath" (Dan. 8:19) will only take place during the tribulation (the days of Antichrist), it is also true that Israel experienced "wrath" in the time of Antiochus. 1 Maccabees 1:64 declared that "there was very great wrath upon Israel." Zechariah 1:12 uses the term "wrath" in relationship to the exile of Israel, thus indicating that "wrath" can have application other than the very end of the times.

The verse under discussion (Dan. 8:23) further indicated that the king will rise to power when the "transgressors have run their course." As observed earlier, there were many wicked people in Israel who were in league with Antiochus. And while they are probably included in this rise in rebellion and transgression, it is most likely that the rebellion of the Gentiles is primarily in view (see Dan. 8:11-12). It is a rebellion against the true God that is being discussed which was spearheaded by Antiochus, but which included both gentiles and Israelites. Antiochus' time spiritually was a far cry from the days of Cyrus, Ezra, Nehemiah and those who returned

---

155 Goldingay, 216.

back to the land from the Babylonian exile when God was honored and respected by the Persian king as well as the people of Israel. There was in the days of Antiochus a bold rebellion against the true God.

The verse (Dan. 8:23) further declares that the king would be ruthlessly bold and artfully clever. Antiochus was clearly both. He was a master political manipulator who took the kingdom away from his nephew and he was a tyrant who used his power for selfish and evil purposes. His intrusion into and desecration of the sanctuary of God is the kind of activity that is being alluded to in these descriptive statements of him.

Antichrist. The Scriptures are abundantly clear that at the end of the age, immediately prior to the Second Coming of Jesus Christ to establish the final, forever kingdom of God, the Antichrist will rise to power (cf. Dan. 7:23-27; 9:26-27; 2 Thes. 2:3-10; Rev. 13:3-8; 17:12-17). His coming will be in the end of days when the great eschatological wrath of God will be poured out on mankind. He is the ultimate human rebel and transgressor against the true God.

Antichrist too will be known for his ruthless boldness and his political skills, which will compel kings and nations to do his bidding. This is certainly what is indicated in 2 Thessalonians 2 and Revelation 13 and 17. Men and nations will not be able to resist his oratory, his political genius as well as his military skills. Like Antiochus, he too will enter into the sanctuary of God and desecrate it with the "abomination of desolation" (cf. Matt. 24:15). He too will present himself as the "manifest god."

8:24 This verse focuses on the destructiveness of the king who will wreak havoc on the people of God ("the holy people") as well as on gentiles ("mighty men"). His power source is said to be received from outside of himself.

Antiochus Epiphanes. As was noted earlier, 1 Maccabees 1 chronicles the military activities of Antiochus as he killed many in Egypt and then in Israel. It is not stated, but it could be that the verse is indicating that the real source of his authority was the "god of this world", Satan. Antiochus' deep and abiding hatred for Israel, Israel's God and Israel's worship seems to reflect a satanic connection. Satan has employed willing men through the ages to do his bidding and it would not be surprising if Satan was directly involved in those dark and terrible days of Antiochus' reign.

Antichrist. According to the scriptures given above, the reign of Antichrist will be characterized by death and destruction. Multitudes of gentiles and Israelites will die because of his rule. He too will have a deep and abiding hatred for God and God's people Israel. And his satanic connection is quite clear. Revelation 13 declares that the Antichrist receives his power, throne and authority directly from the Devil.

8:25 This verse informs us that the king will be characterized by deceit, pride and brutality. It also says that the king will not come to his end because of some human effort or activity, which points to direct divine involvement.

Antiochus Epiphanes. His deception is clearly stated in Daniel 11:21-24, 27 and 32, where he will lie, practice deception and use "smooth" words in his dealing with both gentile nations and the people of Israel. 1 Maccabees 1:29-30 records the fact that he came "peacefully" to Jerusalem persuading the people that his intentions were good. It was then that he fell upon the city and destroyed many people in it. And in 2 Maccabees 4:7ff., his deceptive dealings regarding the priesthood are recorded. As noted earlier (Dan. 8:11) his pride was seen in his arrogant defiance of the true God. The verse further states that he would come to his end by divine intervention. After a failed military campaign in the east he angrily headed for Jerusalem to do harm to the Jews, but it was at this time that the Lord struck Antiochus with a horrible and fatal disease.

The Lord Almighty, the God of Israel, smote him with an incurable and invisible plague; for as soon as he had spoken these (proud) words, a pain of the bowels that was remediless came upon him, and sore torments of the inner parts…but it came to pass that he fell down from his chariot, carried violently so that having a sore fall, all the members of his body were much pained…(he was) now carried in an horselitter, shewing forth unto all the manifest power of God. So that the worms rose up out of the body of this wicked man and whiles he lived in sorrow and pain, his flesh fell away, and the filthiness of his smell was loathsome to all his army … Thus, the murderer and blasphemer having suffered most grievously … died he a miserable death in a strange country in the mountains.[156]

Antichrist. Antichrist's pride is prophesied in Daniel 7, 2 Thessalonians 2 and Revelation 13. His arrogance and boastful words against the true God are emphasized in those passages. He will seat himself in the holy place of the Jerusalem temple and make a claim of deity and will welcome the worship of the whole world (2 Thes. 2:4; Rev. 13:4). Using satanically energized miracles he will pawn himself off to the world as the Messiah (Matt. 24:24; 2 Thes. 2:8-10; Rev. 13). Is this not the ultimate "opposing the Prince of princes"? He will deceitfully deal with Israel, making and then breaking a covenant with them (Dan. 9:26-27). And his end will not come because of anything related to man but from the returning Lord Jesus Christ. The Lord Jesus will take him alive and cast him into the lake of fire where he and his sidekick, the False Prophet, will become the first residents of the lake of fire (Rev. 19:20).

8:26-27 Gabriel then informed Daniel that this vision was absolutely accurate. The terrible 2,300 days were indeed going to come upon his people Israel. The atrocities of that time would pale in comparison to the final days when Antichrist would appear on the world scene and do even great harm to Israel. Daniel is further informed that the fulfillment of the vision will not come for many days. He is then instructed to "seal up" the vision, probably not allowing its contents to be seen by the ruling authorities of the coming Persian Empire who probably would not respond well to the prophesied destruction of their kingdom.

---

156 2 Maccabees 9:5, 7, 8, 9, 28.

The vision left Daniel weak and confused. He was overwhelmed by the magnitude of trouble coming on his people Israel. His nation faced some prolonged days of suffering and humiliation. And on top of that, the coming evil was so great that even the Lord Himself was affected by it as His sanctuary would be desecrated and His worship stopped. Although he understood some of the vision, there was so much that someone living in the sixth century B.C. simply could not put together and this clearly bothered him. Perhaps Peter had Daniel in mind when he wrote that the prophets of old desired to know prophetic truths but just could not fathom their meaning though they gave themselves diligently to try and understand (cf. 1 Pet. 1:10-11).

But in spite of the affects of the vision on him, Daniel faithfully returned to his duties. It would be another twelve years before the Ram would appear as the world empire spoken of in this vision.

QUESTIONS TO CONSIDER

1. Why does God allow such wicked people, like Antiochus, to have significant success and prosperity in their lives? Why doesn't God judge them quickly for their aggressive evil? Would not an immediate judgment cause people to have a greater fear and respect of God?

2. While it is true that all of us are sinful, it is nevertheless evident that there are levels of wickedness in the world. Why does God allow those who are sold out to sin to have victories and domination over the righteous?

3. In your opinion is Daniel 8 dealing mainly with the Antichrist to come or Antiochus from past history?

4. What does this eighth chapter reveal about the ways and the character of God?

5. What value does the information gleaned from this chapter have to do with the way in which we as believers live our lives today.

6. In what ways would this chapter in Daniel reinforce our high view of the inspiration and authority of the Scriptures?

CHAPTER NINE

COUTING THE YEARS

Preview: This prophecy of the "seventy weeks" is set in the first year of the Persian Empire. In reading the prophet Jeremiah, Daniel became very aware that the time of Israel's seventy-year captivity period was shortly to end, and yet there seemed to be no movement towards that happening. An impassioned Daniel prayed and confessed to the Lord with the result that the angel Gabriel was sent with critical information about Israel's future. There would be "70 weeks" of God's special dealings with Israel, and then, the Messianic Kingdom would come.

This key prophetic portion found in 9:24-27 is one of the most significant Bible prophecies found in all of the Old Testament. These four verses contain an amazing wealth of information. The chronological structure provided by this prophecy would become the basis for understanding numerous other prophecies as well as giving a clear framework for the last days of man upon this earth.

THE SETTING OF THE PRAYER AND THE PROPHECY (Dan. 9:1-2)

9:1 The previous two prophecies given to Daniel (in chapters 7 and 8) were given during the reign of the Babylonian king Belshazzar. The giving of this prophecy of the "Seventy Weeks" took place some thirteen years after the Ram-Goat vision of chapter 8. Daniel would now be in his early eighties; the infamous feast of Belshazzar is now history and the Medo-Persian Empire has arrived on the world stage.

This chapter is dated in the first year of Darius, the son of Ahasuerus, of Median descent. (See page 109 for a previous discussion of Darius the Mede). Darius' first full year of ruling would have been from the spring of 538 B.C. to the spring of 537 B.C. and so the giving of this prophecy occurs somewhere during that year. This is same time frame for the incident of the lion's den (chapter 6), but we do not know if the night spent by Daniel in the lion's den took place before or after this vision was given. This opening verse states that Darius was *made king* over the Chaldean empire. This statement suggests that Darius was appointed and, therefore, is to be seen as a different individual from Cyrus the Great. John Whitcomb, who supports the distinction between the two individuals, sees this as a significant statement.

> It is important to note that Darius "was made king" (*homlak*, the passive form of the Hebrew verb is used here), and thus Darius cannot be another name for Cyrus as some evangelical scholars have claimed. Instead, he was a subordinate of Cyrus the Great.[157]

9:2 It happened that in this first year of Darius that Daniel had given particular attention to the prophecies of Jeremiah related to the captivity of Israel in Babylon. Jeremiah had been very specific that the Babylonian captivity would last for seventy years.

> And this whole land shall be a desolation and a horror, and these nations shall serve the king of Babylon seventy years. Then it will be when the seventy years are completed I will punish the king of Babylon and that nation, declares the Lord… (Jer. 25:11-12)
>
> For thus says the Lord, 'When seventy years have been completed for Babylon, I will visit you and fulfill My good word to you, to bring you back to this place. For I know the plans that

---
[157] John C. Whitcomb, *Daniel* (Chicago: Moody, 1985), 120.

I have for you,' declares the Lord, 'plans for welfare and not for calamity to give you a future and a hope. (Jer. 29:10-11)

The scriptural reason for the length of the captivity, according to 2 Chronicles 36:21, was that Israel had violated the law concerning the Sabbath year land rest seventy times. During the Sabbath year (every seventh year) and the Year of Jubilee (every fifty years) Israel had been commanded by Moses to let the land lie dormant. It was not to be worked but was to be unused. This was good agricultural policy but primarily was an issue of faith in the Lord that He would provide for them. During the years from the conquering of the land under Joshua (c. 1390 B.C.) to the beginning of the captivity in 605 B.C., there had been about 130 years when the land was to have remained idle and unworked. Out of those 130 years (114 Sabbath years and 16 years of Jubilee) they had violated that law of God more than half the time. Israel probably assumed that God had not taken notice of their Sabbath year violations, confusing His patience with indifference. But as is seen, God was actually keeping very good records. Since Israel would not voluntarily let the land "rest", then the Lord would give the land its rest by removing Israel from it.

The meticulous records kept by God in this matter should not go unnoticed. God is not carelessly indifferent to the obedience or disobedience of people regarding His laws and standards. People very often assume that God overlooks or really does not care about the details of life or about how they live. But God does care about violations of His moral order and about adherence to His precepts. As noted earlier (in Dan. 7:10), precise records are kept in preparation for the judgment and evaluation of both believers[158] and unbelievers alike. In many places and in many ways the Scriptures warn us and encourage us to live our lives with a consciousness of our ultimate

---

158 The subject of the believer's evaluation is an issue that pervades the New Testament scriptures and is, therefore, most vital for believers to be alert to. This matter of the believer's appearance at Christ's judgment seat is dealt with in some detail in my book *The Believers Payday* (Chattanooga: AMG Publishers, 2002).

accountability to our Creator-Savior God. The believer in Jesus Christ too faces a time of evaluation, which we commonly refer to as the "judgment seat of Christ" (2 Cor. 5:10). But now, we return back to Daniel and his prayer and the prophecy given to him.

The Babylonian captivity officially began in 605 B.C. and, therefore, some 67 or 68 years had elapsed when this chapter opens. This would mean that in about two more years the captivity should be over. But apparently Daniel could not discern any evidence that God was at work to do anything to fulfill the words of Jeremiah. And it may be that the nation of Israel did not appear to be spiritually ready for God to work on their behalf. And furthermore, there was likely some confusion in Daniel's mind about the coming restoration to the land and the establishing of the Messianic kingdom. At any rate, Daniel became highly motivated to seek the Lord on these matters and his great and impassioned prayer is the cause for Gabriel being sent by God to Daniel with the truth of the "Seventy Weeks" (cf. Dan. 9:23).

THE PRAYER OF DANIEL (9:3-19)

9:3 Daniel says that he "gave attention" to seek the Lord. This simply means that he set everything else aside to pursue the Lord on this matter concerning the end of Israel's captivity. Other legitimate activities were put on hold in order that he might concentrate on an issue of great importance to himself and to his people. It was not by lobbying government officials or by setting up focus groups that the matter must be dealt with, but rather by coming humbly with faith to the sovereign Lord God of Israel. He alone could resolve the questions and concerns in Daniel's heart. Daniel prayer would contain things that were general truths and realities as well as specific matters of supplication to God. Daniel did everything he could to be effective and focused in his praying. The external elements of fasting, sackcloth and ashes would not impress God, nor would they contain some sort of mystical key to enter the door into God's presence. But Daniel knew that these externals would help him focus on his praying. He would not be diverted into other things (such as preparing and eating food) and he would be helped in his own attitude as he approached God by reminding himself (sackcloth and ashes) that he must remain contrite and humbly as he approached his God. These are good lessons for all who would pray as Daniel did.

9:4 Effective praying is built upon the knowledge of who God is and what He has said to be true. Daniel's understanding of the character of God and the commitments of God is clearly seen in his prayer. God's character is immediately recognized as Daniel speaks to Him as the "great and awesome God" (cf. Neh. 1:5). However, Israel has not treated the Lord with honor and respect. Daniel's approach to the Lord is based on the fact that God had made a covenant commitment to Israel and that He is a God characterized by faithfulness and a love that is loyal. In other words, God had made a commitment to Israel and it is expected that He will fulfill that commitment because of who He is. And, of course, if this covenant is unconditional (and it is) then it must be completely fulfilled by the Lord. Daniel, like many of the prophets of God, knew the great self-revelation of God that was given to Moses on Mount Sinai. While sin must be dealt with, God patiently deals with sinners with the intention of bringing men to the place where He can forgive them and restore them. The account of Moses and God on Mount Sinai is instructive.

> Then the Lord passed by in front of him and proclaimed, "The Lord, the Lord God, compassionate and gracious, slow to anger and abounding in lovingkindness and truth; who keeps lovingkindness for thousands, who forgives iniquity, transgression and sin; yet He will by no means leave the guilty unpunished, visiting the iniquity of fathers on the children and on the grandchildren to the third and fourth generations. (Exo. 34:6-7)

Therefore, Daniel is not approaching an arbitrary, vindictive God but rather One who is loyal to His covenant commitments, and thus to the people of the covenant. He is One who is characterized by compassion, grace, truth and love.

9:5 Daniel now addresses the matter of Israel's sinfulness and confesses that sin to the Lord. It should be said here that Daniel fully and completely identified himself with his people Israel. It is not "they have sinned", but rather "we have sinned." Although there is no record of sinful behavior in Daniel, he was obviously a sinner, along with the rest of the human race, and acknowledges that fact (cf. Dan. 9:20). He understood, as we today generally do not, the meaning of "community". He really saw himself as truly guilty because he was part of the covenant community called Israel who stood guilty before God. Their sins were his sins. And, therefore, more than thirty times in this prayer he speaks in the first-person plural, "we", "us" and "our". This is not flowery rhetoric but firm conviction. What made Daniel great in God's eyes was not his sinless perfection, but like King David, he was very sensitive to his sinning, as well as the sins of his "community", and repented of it.

Daniel used a number of words in order to reveal the depth and breadth of their sinning. One word would simply not communicate the depth and breadth of Israel's depravity. He declared that Israel has "sinned" (Heb. **chata**), which carries with it the point of missing the mark. "The idea is not merely a passive one of missing, but also an active one of hitting. It is used of moral evil, idolatry, and ceremonial sins."[159] Israel has "committed iniquity" (Heb. **awon**), which emphasizes their sinning as morally crooked and ethically perverted.[160] Israel has also "acted wickedly" (Heb. **rasha**), which speaks of their doing that which is the opposite of the righteous standard of God. The word carries with it the idea of criminality. Israel's behavior was criminal because it broke the law of God. Israel also descended into a willful, stubborn rebellion (Heb. **marad**) against the clear instructions of God (cf. Ezek. 2:3; 17:15). Thus, they veered off course departing purposefully from the commandments and the

---

[159] Charles Ryrie, *Basic Theology* (Colorado Springs: Chariot Victor, 1997), 209.
[160] George Zemek, *A Biblical Theology of the Doctrines of Sovereign Grace* (Little Rock: G. Zemek, 2002), 61.

ordinances of God (Heb. **sur**).[161] It is one of their "moral detours which beg for divine judgment...looks upon sin as apostasy."[162] To all this Daniel will add in verse 7 that Israel's has acted unfaithfully to the Lord. This word (Heb. **maal**) adds yet another dimension to the sinfulness of Daniel's people Israel. It is, in some ways, the worst of Israel's sins because it is a word that can only be committed by those in a covenant type of relationship. For example, it is a word that is used of a woman's infidelity in the marriage relationship (cf. Num. 5:12, 27).

> In almost all the biblical references *ma'al* is used to designate the breaking or violation of religious law as a conscious act of treachery. The victim against whom the breach is perpetrated is God...It is the cause of Judah's exile (Ezek. 39:23; Dan. 9:7) ... This word does not describe the sins of unbelievers but of believers, covenant peoples, those who 'break faith'...[163]

The inclusion of this word by Daniel raises the culpability of Israel to the highest level. They were a people in covenant relationship with God, but they purposely broke their word and went against the covenant commitment. Not even an unbeliever can sin this badly!

9:6 In his prayer, Daniel revealed that their sin was compounded by the fact that God graciously, patiently worked to bring them back onto the path of righteousness by sending warnings through His prophets. They sinned against repeated warnings. The Lord sent prophet after prophet who told Israel the truth about their spiritual condition. Jeremiah (Dan. 7:25-26) made this point about the role of God's prophets years before Daniel's prayer, and the writer of Chronicles (2 Chron. 36:15-16) looked back on the captivity of Israel with the same perspective.

---

161 *Theological Workbook of the Old Testament*, R. Harris, G. Archer, B. Waltke, eds. (Chicago: Moody, 1980), II. 635.
162 Zemek, 50.
163 *Theological Workbook*, I. 519-520.

> Since the day that your fathers came out of the land of Egypt until this day, I have sent you all My servants the prophets, daily rising early and sending them. Yet they did not listen to Me or incline their ear, but stiffened their neck; they did evil more than their fathers.
>
> And the Lord, the God of their fathers, sent word to them again and again by His messengers, because He had compassion on His people and on His dwelling place; but they continually mocked the messengers of God, despised His words and scoffed at His prophets, until the wrath of the Lord arose against His people, until there was no remedy.

And as these texts make clear, the rejection of the prophets' messages was nearly universal in the nation of Israel. Daniel explained that just about all in Israel resisted the call of the prophets to return to the Lord, including the kings and other leaders.

9:7-12 Daniel continued to emphasize the culpability of all Israel by contrasting them with the Lord. The Lord is righteous and keeps His covenant commitments, but Israel is treacherous, violating their covenant commitments (cf. Dan. 9:5). The Lord is righteous in His dealings, not just because of His character, but because He clearly spelled out these issues to Israel from the very beginning. There is absolutely no injustice in the way that the Lord dealt with Israel in allowing their defeat and captivity at the hands of the Babylonians. Later, in the prayer of confession, Daniel would mention the "law of Moses" (Dan. 9:11, 13) where many of these specific warnings were to be found. There were many places where the results of obedience and the consequences for disobedience were spelled out. The penalties for lawbreaking was given in such clear detail that no one could claim ignorance. These two scriptures will suffice to illustrate that God was completely just in the way that He dealt with Israel. He finally enacted the penalty ("curse") that had been set forth years earlier after He had exhorted Israel again and again through the prophets.

> But if they do not obey Me and do not carry out all these commandments, if, instead, you reject My statutes, and if you soul abhors My ordinances so as not to carry out all My commandments, and so break My covenant, I, in turn will do this to you… I will lay waste your cities as well, and will make your sanctuaries desolate; and I will not smell your soothing aromas, and I will make the land desolate so that you enemies who settle in it shall be appalled over it. You, however, I will scatter among the nations and will draw out a sword after you, as your land become desolate and your cities become waste. (Lev. 26:14-16, 31-33)
>
> But it shall come about, if you will not obey the Lord your God, to observe all His commandments and His statues which I charge you today, that all these curses shall come upon you and overtake you…Moreover the Lord will scatter you among all peoples, from one end of the earth to the other end of the earth; and there you shall serve other gods, wood and stone, which you or your fathers have not known. And among those nations you shall find no rest… (Deut. 28:15, 64, 65)

Daniel was certainly knowledgeable of these warnings and they are reflected in his prayer. And to him, the stated penalties for law violation only accentuated the wonderful character of God who patiently endured for centuries and who stood ready to forgive at any time (Dan. 9:9). And yet, he understood the absolute righteousness of the Lord in His disciplines of the nation. Daniel prayed in line with the revealed will of God. Certainly, the most effective type of praying is that which accurately reflects the Word of God, and perhaps it is our ignorance of the Word of God that accounts for many of our unanswered prayers. We must pray according to the will of God, which is revealed in the Word of God.

9:13-14 Again the justice of God in His dealings with Israel is stated, but this time there appears to be a hint of a way out of their dilemma. Daniel notes that Israel had not "sought the favor of the Lord" nor had they given "attention to Thy truth." If Israel would seek the Lord and obey the truth, then things would be different. Daniel certainly knew the other parts of the passages quoted above as well as statements made in 1 Kings 8 by King Solomon (see Dan. 6:10). There was hope given by the Lord in the warning passages found in the Mosaic Law.

> If they confess their iniquity and the iniquity of their forefathers, in their unfaithfulness which they committed against Me, and also in the acting with hostility against Me--- I also was acting with hostility against them, to bring them into the land of their enemies---or if their uncircumcised heart becomes humbled so that they then make amends for their iniquity, then I will remember also My covenant with Jacob, and I will remember My covenant with Isaac, and My covenant with Abraham as well, and I will remember the land…I will not reject them, nor will I so abhor them as to destroy them, breaking My covenant with them; for I am the Lord their God. (Lev. 26:40-42, 44)

> So it shall become when all of these have come upon you, the blessing the curse which I have set before you, and you call them to mind in all nations where the Lord your God has banished you, and you return to the Lord your God and obey Him with all your heart and soul according to all that I command you today, you and your sons, then the Lord your God will restore you from captivity, and have compassion on you, and will gather you again from the peoples where the Lord your God, and from there He will bring you back. (Deut. 30:1-3)

Based on the promises of God that He would restore Israel following their judgment, and their repentance, and based on His word that the captivity would last just 70 years, Daniel now prays to the Lord to act on His word and to restore the people of Israel back to the land of Israel.

9:15-16 These verses transition from the confession to the request. Daniel thinks back to the Exodus out of Egypt where the delivering power of God was manifested. God's mighty deliverance of Israel out of Egypt had made a deep impression on all, both Israel and the gentile nations. A deliverance of Israel out of Babylon would also bring great glory to God and allow the nations of the earth to be impressed with the greatness of Israel's God. The departures and returns of Israel testify to the power of the Lord.

> The three dispersions of Israel from the land and their re-gatherings are among the more important demonstrations of power in relation to Israel. God had allowed them to go into Egypt and delivered them in the Exodus. He had punished them by the captivity, but now Daniel is pleading with Him to restore His people to their land and to their city. The future final regathering of Israel in relation to the millennial kingdom will be the final act fulfilling Amos 9:11-15, when Israel will be regathered never to be dispersed again. In both the dispersions and the re-gatherings, God's righteousness, power, and mercies are evident.[164]

After acknowledging one more time the depth of Israel's sinning, Daniel began to implore the Lord to deliver and restore His people and their land. Although it is true that Israel was to have been a light to the gentiles but had instead become a "reproach" among the nations, Daniel believed that God could still act in righteousness and deliver His people. They had experienced the righteous anger of the Lord and the plea is that God will now turn away from His righteous anger and restore Israel. It is always the righteousness of God and not the righteousness of Israel that would cause such a deliverance to come to pass.

> He makes all the righteousness of God the solid foundation of this plea. The righteousness of God often appears in the Old Testament as the principle and the source of the deliverance of God…The expression "all Thy righteousness" indicates that there is not only an avenging righteousness that demands punishment, but also a rewarding righteousness. Thus the word "righteousness" often appears in the sense of mercy, faithfulness, favor, grace (1 Sam. 12:6; Ps. 23:3; 32:2; 143:1; Mic. 6:5).[165]

---

164 John Walvoord, *Daniel: The Key to Prophetic Revelation* (Chicago: Moody, 1971), 211.
165 Harry Bultema, *Commentary on Daniel* (Grand Rapids: Kregel, 1988), 272.

The direction of Daniel's prayer at this point (Dan. 9:16) is of great importance to the interpretation of the coming "Seventy weeks" prophecy. The focus of Daniel's prayer is on the two subjects of **the people of Israel** and **the land of Israel**. In various ways in verses 16-20, Daniel speaks of these two subjects. His praying is about the restoration of *Israel the people* and *Israel the land*. Daniel is not praying about the fate of the gentiles or about the unknown Church of Jesus Christ. And when Gabriel comes to answer his prayer, the angelic messenger is equally as clear. He came to tell Daniel about his people and his holy city (Dan. 9:24). To force any other subjects into this section is to ignore the context of the prayer and the response to the prayer and is reading things into the text that are not found there.

> There are those who wish to interpret the answer of the prayer... as having really small reference to the Jewish people, their land and temple, supposing it to refer to the New Testament church. Contrariwise the prayer is especially clear. Every word of it relates to "thy city Jerusalem, thy holy mountain (Zion)...Jerusalem and thy people".[166]

> It is of great importance that we recognize what Daniel prayed for---and what he did *not* pray for. He did *not* pray for the spiritual well-being of the church, the Body of Christ. He did *not* pray for the prosperity of the saints of all ages. He *did* pray for "Thy city Jerusalem, Thy holy mountain...This distinction is highly important because God's answer is just as specific as Daniel's prayer. The answer sent by God through Gabriel centers *exclusively* on Jerusalem and Israel, and thus bypasses the entire church age.[167]

Failure to make this distinction leads only to obscurity in interpretation and a departure from real exegesis of the text of Daniel.

9:17-19 It is impossible for a person not to see the two subjects of Daniel's request if they will only just read the text. The land of Israel, with

---

166 Robert Culver, *The Histories and Prophecies of Daniel* (Winona Lake: BMH Books, 1980), 144.
167 Whitcomb, 126.

its focal point of the temple mount in Jerusalem, is seen in a variety of terms: "Thy city Jerusalem", "Thy holy mountain", "Jerusalem" (vs. 16); "Thy desolate sanctuary" (vs. 17); "the city which is called by Thy name" (vs. 18); "Thy city" (vs. 19); and "the holy mountain of my God" (vs. 20). The people of Israel are mentioned as well in this section: "Thy people" (vs. 16); "Thy people" (vs. 19); "my people Israel" (vs. 20); and the several times where "our" and "we" are found. It is, therefore, no surprise when Gabriel arrives and states that his message has to do with "your people and your holy city" (vs. 24). As obvious as this seems to be, it is often overlooked or ignored by interpreters.

A second matter of importance is that Daniel's appeal is motivated by His desire for the Lord to be honored. Twice he declares that God's reputation is at stake in this matter (Dan. 9:17, 19). It is more than Israel getting liberated from captivity. God has promised to restore Israel after 70 years. He has given His word and if He does not do it then God is going to look bad and He will be evil spoken of among people. The Lord no doubt delighted in the prayer of His servant Daniel who was so concerned about His reputation.

As we read this prayer, we cannot help but notice the urgency of it and the depth of his passion for the things of God. There is no vain repetition here and no meaningless "fillers". There is no flippant, irreverent approach to the Lord and no mind wandering into thoughts of the day's activities. Here is praying of the kind that moves the hand of God. And it did.

Most everyone is impressed by Daniel's wonderful prayer. And his prayer does align itself well with the pattern for effective praying that Jesus set forth (cf. Luke 11:1-4). The disciples had observed that Jesus' praying was of a different quality than theirs and so asked the Lord to teach them to pray in that effective way. The Lord Jesus gave them the important elements that should be part of our prayers. Prayer first must be based upon a relationship with God that is real ("our Father"). It must focus on the worship and adoration of the Lord and reflect a clear desire for God's will to come to be experienced. The confession of sin, recognition of personal weakness and the recognition of personal need and dependence as request is made must also be present. These are the ingredients of effective praying and Daniel's prayer includes them all.

THE COMING OF GABRIEL (Dan. 9:20-23)

9:20-21 Very often it seems as though the Lord delays in answering prayer (cf. Luke 11:5-13; 18:1), but that was not the case with Daniel's prayer. In fact, while Daniel was still in the process of praying to the Lord and confessing sin, the angel Gabriel was sent to Daniel with a message from God. A previous appearance of Gabriel is mentioned, which probably is referring to his instructing of Daniel over a decade earlier in the Ram-Goat vision (Dan. 8:16). He arrived in Daniel's presence around the time of the evening offering (about 3 pm). There was, of course, no Jerusalem temple and no sacrifices since all had been destroyed and done away with decades earlier by the Babylonian armies. However, as discussed earlier (cf. pages 117-119), Daniel had apparently ordered his prayer life according to the daily times of worship that he had experienced as a boy growing up in Jerusalem. When the angel arrived, he found that the impassioned praying of Daniel had left him emotionally and spiritually drained. But Gabriel's words would bring understanding and encouragement to Daniel.

9:22-23 Daniel was informed of three wonderful truths by Gabriel. First, he was going to give Daniel an understanding of the future of Israel and Jerusalem. There were a number of issues that related to Israel's future that Daniel was unsure of and he needed help in understanding. The second truth communicated to Daniel was that he was greatly loved or desired by God. God looked at him and considered him a very precious follower. What an amazing and encouraging statement! What believer would not want that kind of commendation from the Lord God! The devotion, loyalty and faithfulness of Daniel throughout his life were not unnoticed by the Lord. He could not help but cherish those words given by the angel Gabriel and similar words given later on by other heavenly beings (cf. Dan. 10:11, 19).

And the third encouraging truth was that his prayer had moved the hand of God. Notice that Gabriel tied the giving of the information about the "Seventy weeks" directly to the prayer of Daniel. When Gabriel stated that "at the beginning of your supplications the command was issued", it was more than a chronological statement. It was a cause and effect statement. It is fair to assume that if Daniel had not prayed as he did that God would not have given to him the information about the "Seventy weeks". This is a great example of the truth that prayer does make a difference (cf. Isa. 37:21).

In addition to the above truths, the "Seventy weeks" prophecy would give a prediction about the Messiah's coming into this world. It is certainly appropriate that it was Gabriel who delivered this truth to Daniel since several centuries later he would be sent to the Virgin Mary to announce to her the birth of the Messiah.

THE PROPHECY OF THE SEVENTY WEEKS (Dan. 9:24-27)

Few would debate the critical value of this passage to Bible prophecy. One author declares that in these verses "we have the indispensable chronological key to all New Testament prophecy."[168] Another echoes this sentiment.

> We could call this the heart of Daniel's prophecy as well as the backbone of all predictions. It is the unanimous opinion of all students of prophecy that whoever does not understand these four verses cannot possibly obtain a clear concept of unfulfilled predictions.[169]

Dispensational writer John Walvoord wrote that "in the concluding four verses of Daniel 9, one of the most important prophecies is contained."[170] Even amillennarian Philip Mauro says that this portion "is one of the most marvelous and most transcendently important in the Word of God."[171]

---

168 Alva McClain, *Daniel's Prophecy of the 70 Weeks* (Grand Rapids: Zondervan, 1969), 10.
169 Bulterma, 279.
170 Walvoord, 216.
171 Philip Mauro, *The Seventy Weeks and the Great Tribulation* (Ashburn, VA: Hess, n.d.), 13.

But at this point such agreement evaporates and there occurs widely divergent interpretations of the prophecy. Liberal interpreters do not, of course, see this as prophecy but as history written by the pseudo-Daniel who badly confused Jeremiah's seventy years with Gabriel's seventy sevens. The belief is that the numbers of this prophecy (history) cannot be matched to actual events, but the prophecy (history) is nevertheless somehow fulfilled in the days of Antiochus IV.[172]

Conservative amillennial writers vary in their approach. Some see the "Seventy weeks" as an indefinite period of time[173], while others see the first sixty-nine weeks as a literal period of time (of years) leading up to coming of Christ but believe that the last week is an indefinite period of time.[174] The perspectives and problems of the amillennial views of the "Seventy weeks" has been discussed elsewhere.[175] The amillennialist, who insists that Israel has been set aside and replaced by the Church is forced to allegorize, which always leads to subjectivity and vagueness. As is the case, whenever allegorical interpreting occurs there is, with this scriptural passage, a significant subjectivity that enters the picture. The amillennial view has problems in one place or another in lining up the events of this prophecy with known history. In commenting specifically on Daniel 9:27, Randall Price observes that "the amillennial interpretation has difficulty reconciling this event with historical events. For this reason, Young (traditional school) advises against an emphasis on dates, while Leupold (symbolic school) abandons any historic fulfillment to the Seventieth Week."[176] But a literal/normal reading of Daniel 9:24-27 does not lead into interpretive obscurity but to an opening up of astounding truths about the comings of the Messiah.

---

172 Daniel L. Smith-Christopher, *Daniel: The New Interpreter's Bible* (Nashville: Abingdon: 1996), 128.
173 Edward J. Young, *The Prophecy of Daniel* (Grand Rapids: Eerdmans, 1949), 220.
174 Mauro, 20, 79ff.
175 Walvoord, 217-219. Randall Price, *Daniel's Seventy Weeks, Amillennial Interpretation*, "Dictionary of Premillennial Theology", ed. M. Couch (Grand Rapids: Kregel, 1996), 75-76.
176 Price, 76.

9:24 This verse reveals both the critical chronological framework of the prophecy as well as God's six stated purposes for this period of time. Gabriel's words to Daniel began with **"Seventy weeks have been decreed for your people and your holy city."**

The very first matter for the interpreter is to determine the angel's meaning of "seventy weeks." The term "week" is somewhat unfortunate since we usually think of a week as being 7 days. However, the Hebrew word in the text (*shavuim*) simply has reference to a unit of seven. So seventy units of seven (or 490) have been determined for Israel the people and Israel the land. The context in which the word is found determines the meaning. It is like the English word "dozen" which is a unit of measurement indicating twelve of something. If I were to say, "I have a dozen", the listener would only know that I had twelve of something but would not know exactly what I possessed. But if our conversation was about blue shirts, then the listener would know that I had twelve blue shirts. So *the context* of Daniel will determine the exact meaning of "seventy sevens". And for the following reasons, the evidence is that it is seventy sevens of years (490 years) that is being spoken of by Gabriel.

First, it is nearly universally acknowledged that the verse could not be speaking of a period of 490 days. In this prophecy the city of Jerusalem must be rebuilt, destroyed and rebuilt again. This could hardly be accomplished in a little over a year much less have all the other details of the prophecy come to pass.

Second, in the context of the prophecy, Daniel had been thinking in terms of years as he contemplated Jeremiah's seventy *years* of captivity (Dan. 9:1-2). He knew that in just about two years the Babylonian captivity should be over. His thoughts, therefore, are not about days but about years.

Third, the length of Israel's captivity was based on their violation of God's law regarding the Sabbath year (cf. pages 182-183). It is no accident that Israel's violations in years would be matched in years by their ultimate restoration.

> Since according to 2 Chronicles 36:21 the Jews had been removed from off the land in order that it might rest for *seventy years*, it should be evident that the Sabbatic years had been violated for 490 years, or exactly seventy "sevens" of years. How appropriate, therefore, that now at the end of the judgment for these violations the angel should be sent to reveal the start of a *new era* of God's dealings with the Jew which would extend for the same number of years covered by his violations of the Sabbatic year, namely, a cycle of 490 years, or "Seventy Sevens" of years (9:24).[177]

Fourth, Daniel's use of "sevens" is found just one other time in his book and that is in the next chapter (Dan. 10:2-3). There, Daniel relates the fact that he had been fasting for three units of seven, but, in this case, carefully adds the fact that it was units of days. It is clear that Daniel adds "days" to the phrase because "he did not want his readers to think of the unit of seven the same way it was used in chapter nine."[178] If the "weeks" in chapter nine were to be understood as being days, then there would have been no need for that added word of clarification in chapter ten. Chapter nine is speaking about years.

Fifth, the final "week" (the Seventieth) aligns well with other scriptures if it is seen to be a period of seven years. The final "week" begins with the signing of a covenant, which is broken at the half way point. It is at that time that the great time of tribulation comes on Israel.

> ...this would mean that the covenant will be broken at the three and one-half year point and the last three and one-half years will be a time of trouble and desolation. This fits well with the trouble described by the temporal note "time, times, and half a time" in Daniel 7:25 and 12:7 as well as in Revelation 12:14.[179]

---

177 McClain, 19-20.
178 Harold Hoehner, *Chronological Aspects of the Life of Christ* (Grand Rapids: Zondervan, 1978), 118.
179 Ibid., 119.

In fact, the Apostle John, in Revelation 11:2-3, 12:6 and 13:4, uses additional chronological terms to speak of a period of three and one-half years, which ends human history. These terms all refer to the second half of Daniel's "Seventy weeks."

So, the evidence is strong and compelling that we are looking at a designated period of 490 years during which God will deal with His people Israel to bring them back to the place where He wants them to be. And if part of this prophecy is to be understood in terms of years we would believe that, apart from evidence to the contrary, all of it is to be understood that way. Those scholars who have interpreted some of the years as literal years and other parts as indefinite are engaged in a somewhat arbitrary and inconsistent approach to the text.

Further, Gabriel stated that this 490-year period has been "decreed". God had ordered the events of the future and these 490 years are an integral part of what God has ordained will certainly come to pass.

> The Hebrew word translated "decreed" literally means "to cut off" or "to determine"…Now the prophet was told that a total of 490 years was to be "cut out" of the Times of the Gentiles. This 490 year period had been "determined" or "decreed" for the accomplishment of the final restoration of Israel and the establishment of Messiah's kingdom.[180]

Again, it is very important interpretively to emphasize that the 490-year period does not concern the Church of Jesus Christ nor does it concern the gentile nations. The Church, the Body of Christ, is made up of Jews and gentiles who are equal, and this concept would have been completely foreign to Daniel's thinking. Furthermore, the Church has no relationship with the land of Israel and the temple in the city of Jerusalem. To be consistent in the handling of this text, the subject would have to be the people of Israel and the land of Israel. And this must be true for all 70 of the "weeks". It was

---
180 Arnold Fruchtenbaum, *Messianic Christology* (Tustin: Ariel Ministries, 1998), 95.

true of the first 69 and will be true of the future 70th. Again, this would tell us that the Church of Jesus Christ is not the focus of the 70th week and the Church most likely has no part in the events of the 70th and final week.

The main emphasis of this verse (Dan. 9:24) is on the six goals of God. There are six very specific purposes for the 490-year period. These are the things God is committed to accomplish. And because of this, there is no question that the Almighty God will completely do what He said He will do. Generally speaking, when the 490 years have run their course, God will have brought Israel back into a right relationship with Himself and because of that will have established the long-awaited kingdom of the Messiah. Specifically, the goals focus on the work of Christ and the application and results of that work as it particularly relates to Israel.

TO FINISH THE TRANSGRESSION

The first divine goal of the 490 years will be to bring to completion the transgression (Heb. *pesha*) of Israel. This word "transgression" focuses on the deliberate rebellion and apostasy of Israel and it is declared that this will be brought to an end. The definite article is used so that it is not just Israel's rebellion generally in view, but *the* rebellion of the nation. Throughout history, the nation of Israel has distinguished itself for its disobedience, unbelief and rebellious spirit. But what must be in view here is Israel's rebellion greatest act of rebellion as it was manifested in their rejection of the Lord Jesus as their Messiah. This is *the* rebellious act of Israel that will be brought to completion within the Seventy Weeks.

In order for the Messiah to return and for His kingdom to be established, Israel must turn in faith to Him. This was Peter's point when he told Israel that they must turn back to the Lord as a prerequisite for Messiah return.

> Repent therefore and return that your sins may be wiped away, in order that times of refreshing may come from the presence of

the Lord; and that He may send Jesus, the Christ appointed for you, whom heaven must receive *until* the period of restoration of all things about which God spoke by the mouth of His holy prophets from ancient times. (Acts 3:19-21)

Jesus Himself declared that the one thing that must be true before He would return is the change in Israel related to their view of Him.

> O Jerusalem, Jerusalem, who kills the prophets and stones those who are sent to her! How often I wanted to gather your children together, the way a hen gathers her chicks under her wings and you were unwilling. Behold, your house is being left to you desolate! For I say to you from now on you shall not see Me *until* you say, 'Blessed is He who comes in the name of the Lord. (Matt. 23:37-39)

National Israel's rejection of their Messiah will be all over and Israel will be restored, which is a great desire of Daniel's heart. This dramatic change is integral to God's overall plans for this earth.

TO MAKE AN END OF SIN

In this goal of God, the idea appears to be that sin generally will be brought into judgment and forgiveness granted. Israel, whose national life had been so characterized by its waywardness, will live apart from sin because their sins have been judged and they have been forgiven. There is a final culmination of Israel's sinful condition.

> The Hebrew word translated "to make an end" literally means "to seal up" or "to shut up in prison." It means "to be securely kept, locked up, not allowed to roam at random." The Hebrew word translated as "sin" literally means "to miss the mark." It refers to sins of daily life, rather than to any specific sin. Even these sins are to be put to an end and taken away. This, too, is quite in keeping with predictions by the Prophets who proclaim that in

the Messianic Kingdom, sinning would cease from Israel (Isaiah 27:9; Ezekiel 36:25-27; 37:23; Jeremiah 31:31-34).[181]

So, the vain, purposeless life lived by Israel as they walked far from God will covered up, and therefore, removed out of the sight of God. There will be a new spirit in Israel, a new attitude towards sin and righteousness. This reality will be in place as the Seventy Weeks concludes.

TO MAKE ATONEMENT FOR INIQUITY

The third purpose of the Seventy Weeks is to deal with the sin issue by making atonement for it. This is undoubtedly looking at the cross of Jesus Christ, since it is the only thing that takes care of sin. It is the cross alone that makes it possible for anyone to be reconciled to God whether gentile or Israelite (cf. 2 Cor. 5:17-21). Chronologically, it is after the completing of the Body of Christ, in the times of the gentiles, that national Israel will turn in faith to the Lord Jesus, their Messiah (cf. Rom. 11:24-28). One of the God's great goals for the Seventy Weeks is to save Israel, based on the cross work of Jesus Christ, and to bring them into the New Covenant. Jesus cannot and will not return until Israel's spiritual salvation is a reality. The great purpose of Daniel's Seventieth week is to bring Israel to the point that they will repent and to embrace the salvation that is provided by their Messiah, Jesus. The total and complete payment for sin was in the past at the cross, but it will be in the future that the provision of the cross will be applied to national Israel (cf. Zech. 12:10; 13:1; Isa. 59:20-21; Ezek. 36:25-27; Jer. 31:31-34). It is interesting to observe what the Book of Revelation has to say about salvation during the period of the Tribulation. When Israel begins turning in massive numbers to the Lord during the Tribulation, they will become what God always intended them to be: a light to the gentiles. Their "light" will bring untold millions of gentiles to a saving faith in Jesus Messiah (Rev. 7:9-14).

---

181 Ibid.

TO BRING IN EVERLASTING RIGHTEOUSNESS

The first three goals deal with the negative issue of sin and how sin, particularly Israel's sin, will be dealt with and removed. The next three goals relate to the establishment of Messiah's kingdom, which was spoken of in Daniel 2 and 7. It is significant to observe that all six of these divine purposes are related to the earth.

According to the Old Testament prophets, one of the marvelous characteristics of the Messiah's kingdom is that of righteousness (cf. Isa. 11:2-5; Jer. 23:3-6). Righteousness, not sin, will prevail in the realm of mankind and the nations of the earth. This will be a time unlike any other. There has never been in Israel, or anywhere else on earth since the fall, the domination of righteousness. While the believer is certainly to be considered "righteous" today because of justification, this goal of God finds it ultimate fulfillment in the Messiah's kingdom when Daniel's people and Daniel's land will be righteous and will live righteously. The nation that has lived in rebellion will then live in righteousness (cf. Isa.1:26; Jer. 33:14-16).

> Concerning righteousness (*sedeq*), also a legal term, one must of course acknowledge that the believing Christian today has the very righteousness of God and that, by its nature, that righteousness must be everlasting (cf. 2 Cor. 5:21). In this sense, the work of Christ on the cross made this fourth goal possible for the individual. But the nation of Israel and the city of Jerusalem are in view in Daniel 9. If "everlasting righteousness" based on the atoning work of Christ is to be brought in for Israel as a nation, it must be brought in while Israel is still constituted as a nation, i.e., before the eternal state begins. The only possible point in time when this could occur and remain within the time parameters offered (i.e., within the 490 decreed years) would be at the end of the Great Tribulation and at the inception of an earthly kingdom.[182]

---

182 Kenneth L. Barker, "Evidence from Daniel" in *The Case for Premillennialism*, ed. Campbell and Townsend (Chicago: Moody, 1992), 143.

The point can also be made that this fourth goal included the idea that it is actually an age of righteousness that will instituted and not simply that righteousness will become the order of the day. "This could more literally be translated 'to bring in an age of righteousness' since the Hebrew word *olam* is better translated as 'age' rather than as 'everlasting'."[183] A time of righteousness is clearly in view in this passage.

One of the very real problems for those who see Christ's kingdom being established at His first coming is the absence of righteousness in this world. The entrance of "everlasting righteousness" into this world at Christ's first coming has certainly not affected the nations of the world that remain under the domination of the "god of this world", Satan. The level of righteousness in the world after the cross seems no different than it was prior to the cross. Even if one were to argue that this "everlasting righteousness" applies just to believers today, it becomes problematic to prove that the church today is dominated by righteousness in its actions, attitudes and motives. The best one might do is to say that "everlasting righteousness" is looking at the positional truth of believers today, which really does not fit well with the emphases and context of Daniel 9. It is quite a stretch to attempt to prove that we see everlasting righteousness in the world today!

TO SEAL UP VISION AND PROPHECY

The term "seal up" "indicates a complete fulfillment of all prophecy"[184] coupled with the idea that there will be no additional prophetic information given. With the Lord Jesus present in all His glory, the forever kingdom of God established, and the earth reclaimed from the usurper, Satan, prophecy is seen as completely fulfilled. Those who live at that time will be recognize that all has been fulfilled. There will be no need for people to have prophetic visions or for God, who will then dwell among believers, to give revelation.

---

183 Fruchtenbaum, 96.
184 Walvoord, 283.

The presence of the Shekinah (glory indicating the very presence of God) in Jerusalem (Ezek. 43:1-8) removes the need for prophets or the prophetic gift.

TO ANOINT THE MOST HOLY

While some have suggested that this refers to the anointing of the Lord Jesus, others have observed that the "expression is never used of a person."[185] Another has declared that "it has nothing whatever to do with Him, but it is the anointing of the Holy of Holies in another temple, which will stand in the midst of Jerusalem."[186]

In only one passage in the entire Old Testament (1 Chron. 23:13) can these Hebrew words be used of any other than the temple or some one of its parts. It would be exceedingly strange for Gabriel to depart from the usually meaning here in a passage so closely tied in thought to the rebuilding of Solomon's temple.[187]

And so, it seems best to understand this anointing as the setting apart of the millennial temple for the ministry to which it was ordained.

The sixth goal is "to anoint the most holy" (lit., "to anoint a holy of holies," *welimsoah qodes qodasim*)...the most frequent use of *qodes qodasim* is in reverence to the Holy of Holies, first in the Tabernacle, later in Temple (cf. Exo. 26:33-34; 2 Kgs 7:50) ... If the anointing of a holy of holies in Daniel 9:24 refers to a temple, its provenance must be earthly, inasmuch as there is no temple in the New Jerusalem (cf. Rev. 21:22). The only possible point in time for the anointing of an earthly temple must be late in the Great Tribulation or early in a millennial kingdom...[188]

The "anointing" refers to the consecration of the chamber that housed the Ark of the Covenant, whose presence sanctified the Temple by virtue of the Shekinah (the divine presence).[189]

---

185 Bultema, 284.
186 A. C. Gaebelein, *Daniel* (Grand Rapids: Kregel, 1968), 133.
187 Robert Culver, *Daniel and the Latter Days* (Chicago: Moody, 1977) 158.
188 Barker, 145.
189 Randall Price, *The Coming Last Days Temple* (Eugene: Harvest House, 1999), 249.

The final fulfillment of God's six goals for the Seventy Weeks is based on the work of the Lord Jesus on the cross. Once the full and complete redemptive price for sin was paid, it then became possible for God to act to restore Israel and to fulfill His covenant commitments to the descendants of Abraham. The fulfillment of the covenant promises, according to the Apostle Paul (cf. Rom. 11:12, 15) brings the greatest blessing possible to the gentiles as well. And so it will be in the future kingdom of God.

9:25 Gabriel then gave to Daniel the starting point of the 490 years of God's special dealings with Israel. Normally, it would be assumed that the period of 490 years would begin with Gabriel's arrival and the giving of this prophecy to Daniel in the year 538 BC. But such is not the case. The 490 years would not commence with Gabriel's giving of the Seventy Weeks prophecy but when a command was issued to restore and rebuild the city of Jerusalem. The words of Gabriel require that a complete, not partial, rebuilding of the city is in view.

> First, the words "to restore and rebuild" suggest that the city was raised to its former state. It is not a partial rebuilding but a complete restoration. Second, the words "plaza and moat" give weight to the position for a complete restoration of the city…it is best to take the first word *plaza* as referring to the interior of the city and the second word *trench* as referring to a moat going around the outside of the city. Part of Jerusalem's natural defenses consisted of a great cutting in the rock along the northern wall…these two items present a graphic picture of the complete restoration. Third, it should be noted that the rebuilding of Jerusalem would be done in times of distress and oppression.[190]

But what command is being referred to by Gabriel? Commentators have observed that there are four possibilities. First, there is a decree given by Cyrus concerning the rebuilding of the temple (Ezra 1:1-4); second,

---

190 Hoehner, 119-121.

the scriptures record the decree of Darius reaffirming the decree of Cyrus (Ezra 6:6-12); third, there is the decree of Artaxerxes that was given to Ezra permitting him to proceed with temple service (Ezra 7:11-26); and finally, the decree of Artaxerxes allowing Nehemiah to rebuild the wall of Jerusalem (Neh. 2:1-8). It should be noted here that the second and third views do not have many adherents. The second view can be dismissed quickly because it is not a new decree but only confirms the original decree of Cyrus, which did not include any statement about rebuilding the city. There would be no real basis for starting the Seventy Weeks with such a duplicate decree. The third view is not widely held because its focus is on allowing Ezra to enhance the ongoing temple worship, and because there is no explicit degree to allow the city to be rebuilt. Ezra's own response of thanksgiving does not include the city but just the temple (cf. Ezra 7:27). While it is true that Artaxerxes' statement had a possible loophole in that it gave Ezra some latitude in using any excess funds, that is a far cry from a *decree* to restore Jerusalem.

The first decree mentioned; that is, the decree given by Cyrus (Ezra 1:1-4), does not mention the rebuilding of the city, but only references the "house of God which is in Jerusalem." However, those who believe that Gabriel is indeed referring to Cyrus' decree for the starting point of the Seventy Weeks point out that if Isaiah is brought alongside (Isa. 44:28; 45:13), then rebuilding the city is included.[191] They note that it is unlikely that Cyrus would allow the rebuilding of the temple and prohibit some sort of fortification of the city at the same time. This idea, however, is countered by others who do not believe that Cyrus' decree really fits well the requirements of Daniel 9:25.

> It is true that God had promised long years earlier that Cyrus would declare of Jerusalem, "She will be build" (Isa. 44:28). But the context of that prophecy indicates that his purpose in having the city rebuilt and repopulated was that the Temple might

---
191 Fruchtenbaum, 140-141.

> function again. It was certainly *not* refortified, as the prophecy requires ("with plaza and moat").[192]
>
> Cyrus' edict refers to the rebuilding of the temple and not the city. Although it is granted that there were inhabitants and a city was built in Cyrus' time as predicted by Isaiah, certainly it was not a city that could defend itself as described in Daniel 9:25…a distinction should be made between the rebuilding of a city and the restoration of a city to its former state…The commencement of the rebuilding began with Cyrus' decree was the city's complete restoration was not at that time.[193]

It seems best to take the decree mentioned in Daniel 9:25 as the one given by Artaxerxes in Nehemiah 2. This decree is the first one specifically allowing the actual restoring and refortifying of Jerusalem, which seems to be what the statement of Gabriel required. The decree of Artaxerxes called for the rebuilding of Jerusalem's walls and for the resources of the empire to be used in that rebuilding (cf. Neh. 2:3, 5, 8). And, as the scriptures record the history of this rebuilding, it was done in times of distress and difficulty, fulfilling the requirement in Daniel 9:25. This decree was issued in the twentieth year of Artaxerxes' reign, which would place it in the spring of 444 B.C.[194]

From the issuing of the decree of Artaxerxes to the time of "Messiah the Prince" there would be a total of 483 years (69 of the weeks). This would seem to put the time involved a little beyond the ministry of Christ on earth. However, if the late Sir Robert Anderson's lead is followed, then the chronological computation is easily made. He believed that the years were to be measured, not as the 365+ day solar years, but as the 360-day "prophetic years.[195] Also following Anderson's lead, Harold Hoehner shows that the 360-day year is used in the prophetic literature of the Bible.[196] And when

---

192 Whitcomb, 131.
193 Hoehner, 122-123.
194 Ibid.127-128.
195 McClain, 25.
196 Hoehner, 134-138.

we recall that the Apostle John, in the Book of Revelation, apparently used 360-day years in his calculations (cf. Rev. 11:2-3; 12:6, 14; 13:5), it is likely that he was walking in step with Daniel. With a 360-day year, the end of the sixty-ninth week, after which the Messiah will be cut off, is the year 33 A.D.

In Daniel 9:25 two distinct periods of time are mentioned; namely a period of 7 weeks and another period of 62 weeks. In fact, the prophecy of the Seventy Weeks has three distinct subdivisions to it; that of 7, 62 and 1. The 7 weeks (49 years) and the 62 weeks (434 years) are consecutive with no breaks in the flow of history indicated. The only reason given for distinguishing these two groups of years is that the rebuilding of Jerusalem is assigned to the initial 7 weeks (49 years). The rebuilding of the walls by Nehemiah in some 52 days is not what is in view here. It is the rebuilding and restoring of the entire city of Jerusalem to the functioning entity that it once was before being destroyed by the Babylonians. After Nehemiah's initial efforts the city was still so desolate that people were conscripted to live inside the city walls. When we analyze Daniel 9:26 and 27, we will set forth the point that there was a programmed gap between weeks 69 and 70. Between those two weeks, two highly significant events would occur; namely the death of the Messiah and the destruction of the city of Jerusalem. With that in mind, the seventy weeks can be charted in the following way.

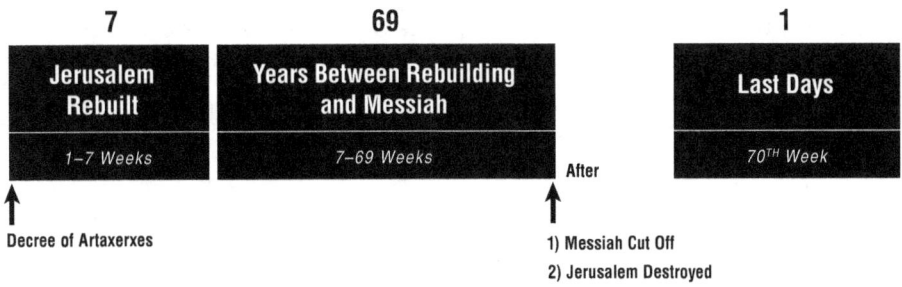

The consensus among conservative scholars is that "Messiah the Prince" is Jesus Christ. Some of the more liberal scholars have attempted to find reference here to Alexander the Great, Onias III and a number of others, but these attempts are quite arbitrary and end up in the wilderness of obscurity. But Gabriel is as clear as he can be on this. After 483 years, the Messiah will appear, and He will be killed. It is obvious that those who have a bias against predictive prophecy must find someone else to attach this title to, and those who do not want Jesus of Nazareth to be identified as the Messiah of Israel must scramble for another solution. But to those who take the text in its plain and obvious sense they see the wonderful forecast of the coming of Jesus.

9:26 Gabriel informed Daniel that after the second subdivision of 62 weeks, two very significant events would occur. A natural reading of these verses points to the existence of a gap in time that would occur between the 69th and the 70th weeks. Daniel 9:25 revealed that Messiah the prince would appear towards the end of the time frame of the 69 weeks. Daniel 9:26 states that *after* the 69th week two important events would occur and then 9:27 speaks of the 70th week and the events of that 7 years, including its commencement.

There are two main theories among evangelical interpreters about the relationship of the 70th week to the first 69 weeks. One view is that the weeks are unbroken, one following immediately after the other. In other words, there is absolute continuity of the Seventy Weeks. According to this view, the 70th week followed the 69th without any interruption and is, therefore, already history. The second view is that there is a period of time between weeks 69 and 70, in which the two events of the death of the Messiah and the destruction of Jerusalem takes place. Some of those holding to the first view see the death of Christ (April, 33 A.D.) being referred to in 9:27 where the temple sacrifices cease half way through the 70th week. However, there are major problems with this view. First, the death of Christ did not cause the animals sacrifices in the Jerusalem temple to cease. They continued on for almost four decades. Second, the view is forced to identify the "he" in 9:27 as Christ, which, as we will see, is highly questionable. Third, there is no way for this view to explain the 70 A.D. destruction of Jerusalem, which would be 38 years beyond the end of the 70th week. And fourth, there is no ability in this view to match the events described in 9:27 with anything found in history.

The second view sees a required period of some time length between the 69th and 70th weeks. During this time interval the historical fulfillment of the two stated events (the killing of the Messiah and the destruction of Jerusalem) would take place. These events need to occur between the 69th and 70th weeks and not during the 70th week.

> If this was intended to occur *in* the seventieth week, the text would have read here "during" or "in the midst of" (cf. Daniel's use of *hetzi*, "in the middle of," v. 27). This language implies that these events *precede* the seventieth week but do not *immediately* follow the sixty-ninth. Therefore, a temporal interval separates the two.[197]

In support of the second view there is, first and foremost, the evidence of the normal reading of the text, which would indicate the need for a time interval to accommodate the two events mentioned above.

> That the opening of the seventieth week is subsequent to the events of verse 26 is manifest by the text itself. The seventieth week is not picked up for mention till verse 27 is reached. When that point is reached it is introduced by a *waw consecutive*, indicating that the contents of verse 27 are subsequent and consequential in relation to verse 26. All attempts to place the events of verse 26 (the cutting off of Christ and the destruction of Jerusalem) in either the period of the sixty-two weeks (Keil and Leupold) or in the seventieth week (Young and a host of writers in the past) stumble and fall on the simple language of the text itself.[198]

In addition to the plain reading of the text, there is the matter of the purposes of God for this period of time that is found in Dan. 9:24. It will

---
[197] Randall Price, "Prophetic Postponement in Daniel 9 and Other texts", *Issues in Dispensationalism*, ed. Willis and Master (Chicago: Moody, 1994), 152.
[198] Culver, *Daniel and the Latter Days*, 149-150.

be remembered that there are six distinct goals of God that will be accomplished during the 490 years and that these goals relate to the people of Israel and the land of Israel. These six goals have not been fulfilled historically in relationship to Israel. For example, where do we observe the finishing of Israel's apostasy or an end to their sinning or the bringing in of everlasting righteousness or the anointing of the Holy place in the temple? If the 70 weeks are continuous, then it would be required that all of the six goals be fulfilled by around A.D. 40. This would place the end of the Seventy Weeks in the early days of the church in the Book of Acts. The death of Christ, of course, did occur prior to Acts with the accomplishing of the "atoning for sin." But the Book of Acts does not record the fulfilling of most of these six purposes of God, but actually the opposite in several cases.

But the history of those years contains nothing that in any reasonable way corresponds with what Daniel saw at the end of the Seventy Weeks. Where in the history of Acts, for example, can you find any finishing of Jewish transgression or an ending of Jewish sins? On the contrary, the transgression of the chosen nation increases by leaps and bounds until the crisis comes in the twenty-eighth chapter, where the Apostle Paul turns definitely to the Gentiles. Or where in the period of the Acts can we find any "sealing up of vision and prophecy"? On the contrary, it is during this very period and beyond that we find the greatest loosing of "vision and prophecy" in all the history of revelation.[199]

Some have objected to the entire idea of "gaps" in the biblical record and, therefore, rule out such a phenomenon in Daniel 9. But there are many places where a single text of scripture includes events that are separated by great amounts of time. For example, all Christians believe that "for unto us a Child is born" (Isa. 9:6a) took place in Bethlehem centuries ago. But the statements given by Isaiah (Isa. 9:3-5, 6b-7) concerning the future kingdom and the ruling of this Son have yet to be fulfilled. Jesus simply did not sit

---
199 McClain, 36.

"on the throne of David" where He ruled "over his kingdom"; a kingdom characterized by "justice and righteousness." The same holds true with Isaiah 61:1-2, Zechariah 9:9-10 and a great many other passages. This reality of such prophetic postponements has been discussed thoroughly by others.[200] There are numerous places, particularly in the "major" prophets where near judgment and future judgment are blended together in a single passage.

The text of Daniel 9:26 declares that *after* the groupings of 7 weeks and 62 weeks (i.e. 69 weeks or 483 years) have past the "Messiah will be cut off." In the Old Testament this is the standard expression for capital punishment. And it is the consensus among evangelical writers that this is a reference to the Lord Jesus and to His death on the cross.

The Hebrew word translated "cut off" is the common word used in the Mosaic Law and simply means "to be killed." The implication of the term is that the Messiah would not only be killed, but also that He would die a penal death by execution.[201]

There is less of a consensus on the next expression, "and have nothing", which literally says "nothing for him." But this does seem to be communicating the truth that Jesus "came to His own and His own received Him not" (John 1:11) and that He was "despised and forsaken of men" (Isa. 53:3). At His first coming, Jesus was rejected and died for the benefit of others. It was for us that He suffered in order to redeem us from our sins. But as far as receiving that which rightly belonged to Him, such as the kingdom and great honor, He did not receive those things. As one author notes, "nothing that rightly belonged to Him as Messiah the Prince was given to Him at that time."[202] So these phrases give the revelation that the Messiah would be executed but at that time did not benefit personally from it. Of course, believers understand that

---

[200] Price, "Prophetic Postponement", 133-165.
[201] Fruchtenbaum, 97.
[202] Walvoord, 230.

Messiah Jesus will, in the future, receive all the glory and honor due to Him, and that every knee will indeed bow before Him, acknowledging Him as the great King.

The sad news is then given that both the city and the temple would again face destruction. This destruction would come at the hands of "the people." From history the identification of "the people" is clear and certain. It was the Romans who came in A.D. 70 and fulfilled this prophecy. These people are clearly evil and are not, as some have supposed, connected with the Messiah. Daniel is also informed about "the prince who is to come." This prince will not be the one who destroys the city (in A.D. 70), but will come from those people (the Romans) who do destroy it. This second prince is a reference to the Antichrist who does come from the Roman Empire (the fourth empire of Daniel 2 and 7) and is to be distinguished from the first one, Messiah the Prince. This second prince in the prophecy is the subject of 9:27. And once again, in the progress of revelation, much more about this individual is given.

The verse (Dan. 9:26) concludes with the ominous warning about what awaits Jerusalem and the people of Israel. The destruction of the city of Jerusalem is likened to a "flood", which is a term that designates an overwhelming catastrophe or desolation. As a flood can obliterate a town that is in its path, so Jerusalem will be completely overwhelmed and destroyed. This is just what happened in A.D. 70 (though not what will take place during the time of tribulation, the Seventieth Week). Gabriel also seems to be communicating the idea that "from the time of the destruction of the city of Jerusalem, trouble, war and desolation will be the normal experience of the people of Israel."[203] Trouble and war would be the usual experience of God's people and land until, of course, Messiah comes and establishes His great kingdom.

9:27 The final verse in this prophecy of the Seventy Weeks reveals the monumental events of the Seventieth week. These final seven years prior to the

---

203 Ibid. 231.

Second Coming of Jesus Christ are absolutely crucial in fulfilling the purposes of God. Some of the key events of those years are mentioned in this verse but await further revelation in scripture for additional details and emphases.

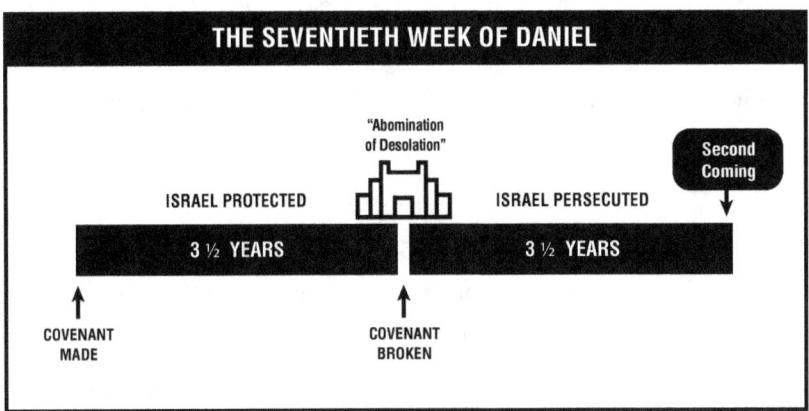

The first problem that must be settled in this verse is the identification of the "he" who makes the covenant. The identification of this individual is the key to unlocking the rest of the verse. Is this chief player in the drama of the Seventieth Week referring to Jesus the Messiah or to the man commonly known as the Antichrist? The ordinary rules of grammar establish the "he" as the Antichrist because its nearest antecedent is "the prince that shall come" from verse 26. Furthermore, there a number of other points that establish the Antichrist as the subject of verse 27.

First, this individual enters into a seven-year covenant with "the many". In His ministry on earth, the Lord Jesus never entered into a seven-year covenantal agreement with anyone and, of course, never broke the covenant after 3 ½ years. "The many", in the context of Daniel 9, can only refer to Israel, Daniel's people and the Bible student searches the gospels in vain to try a find such a covenant. To try and have this covenant refer to the New Covenant, as some have done, simply does not fit Daniel 9:27. The New Covenant was not a seven-year covenant, it did not involve animal sacrifices and it was not broken after 3 ½ years. In fact, the Book of Hebrews, in describing the "new" covenant, also calls it the "eternal" covenant. This covenant has no end and will not be superseded by another covenant.

Second, the description of what this person does fits the Antichrist but does not fit the Lord Jesus. Jesus Christ did not oppress and destroy Israel, and He did not cause the temple sacrifices to stop. The temple sacrifices in the days of Christ did not cease with the death of Christ but were terminated by action of the Roman army. But, on the other hand, Antichrist is seen doing very terrible things to Israel in a number of passages. The 3 ½ years of Daniel 9:27 corresponds to the "times, time and half a time" of Daniel 7:25 where the Antichrist ("little horn") does harm to God's people and sets aside the laws of God. The Apostle John adds that he is given authority for 42 months (3 ½ years) and overcomes the saints and blasphemes God and His tabernacle (Rev. 13:5-7).

Third, identifying the "he" as Christ then puts the events of the Seventieth Week in the past. As we have seen, this is impossible since it would require all six of God's goals to be fully fulfilled by A.D. 40 and this simply is not true. But we must add here that Jesus Himself placed the event of the "abomination of desolation" (mentioned in Dan. 9:27) in the future in connection with His return to the earth (cf. Matt. 24:15). If the "abomination of desolation" was future in Jesus' day, it cannot, therefore, refer to a past event that took place in the early 30s A.D. Rather, this event takes place at the mid-point of the Seventieth Week and is connected with the future evil work of the Antichrist (cf. Rev. 13 and 2 Thes. 2). It cannot, therefore, be a past event.

This key personage, who occupies center stage in the Seventieth Week, is the Antichrist. If the interpreter will follow the clear details of these verses there can be no other conclusion than that all of the Seventieth Week is yet future and that there is simply no historical fulfillment of these details during and immediately after the life of Christ. The Roman Prince will emerge out of the fourth empire (Rome) and will deceitfully enter into a covenant with "many", which is probably a reference to unbelievers in Israel since there is no reason for believers to enter into a pact with the evil Antichrist. At the beginning of the Tribulation (the 70th week), Israel is in unbelief and quite capable of entering into an agreement with this foreigner from a western nation. This signing of the covenant is the event that actually starts the Seventieth and final week of Daniel. It should be noted that the Rapture of the church is not the event that commences the last seven years. Theoretically they could occur on the same day, but it is also possible, and perhaps likely, that they will be separated by weeks or maybe a few months.

The covenant made between the Roman Prince (Antichrist) and the people of Israel requires that Israel will be at least partially restored to the land. And this covenant that is made will undoubtedly include Israel's ability to rebuild a temple on the sacred mount in Jerusalem and to once again carry out the full and complete Levitical sacrificial system. The political genius and military power of the Antichrist is suggested by this reality of an actual functioning Jewish temple in Jerusalem. There is no word on the exact time for the rebuilding project to begin, but it most likely will not be until after the covenant is in force. The text does not say how long Israel will be sacrificing in the temple when the covenant is broken by the Antichrist. So Israel might have been sacrificing for a few months or perhaps for the greater part of the 3 ½ year period. But there does come a point in time when the Roman Prince breaks the covenant.

At the mid-point of the Seventieth week the Antichrist breaks the covenant he has made with Israel and the one who was the protector of Israel now becomes the persecutor of Israel. According to the Lord Jesus, this is when Israel's time of "great tribulation" will begin (cf. Matt. 24:15-26). There are monumental events that take place at the middle of the Seventieth week, including the removal of Satan from the heavenly places (Rev. 12), the destruction of the great world religion (Rev. 17) and the assassination and return to life of the Antichrist himself (Rev. 13). These events all flow together resulting in a great one world religion, the worship of Satan and the Antichrist (cf. Rev. 13:3, 8). The return to life after receiving the "fatal wound" (cf. Rev. 13:3, 12, 14) is directly linked to the worship of the Antichrist and to the erecting of the life possessing image of Antichrist. Also, Satan. who has always desired to be like God, will understand at the mid-point of the Seventieth week that his time is severely limited (cf. Rev. 12:9, 12). This confinement to the earth will apparently motivate him as never before to receive worship. These events will be instrumental in the abolishing of all religions (including Israel's) and establishing the worship of the Antichrist. This enforced worship will center in the newly rebuilt temple in Jerusalem where Antichrist will present himself as deity (cf. 2 Thes. 2:3b, 4, 9). Therefore, at the mid-point of the Seventieth week Israel will be forced to stop their Levitical worship and it will be replaced with a forced worship of the Antichrist. This will be inaugurated by the evil act of setting up of the "abomination of desolation" (Dan. 12:11 with Dan. 9:27).

The phrase "on the wing of abominations will come one who makes desolate" is a difficult one, but other scriptures help in understanding its meaning and significance (cf. Matt. 24:25 and Dan. 11:31; 12:11 as well as the non-canonical book of 1 Macc. 1:54, 59). What is clear in this expression is that the temple will be terribly defiled by the Antichrist. Randall Price demonstrates that the scriptures taught that the defilement of the temple could be in differing degrees because some acts were simple acts of negligence while others were intentional.[204] This event will clearly fit into the category of the intentional.

The mention of "wing" has spawned numerous ideas. It clearly has some connection with the temple. Some have suggested that it is a reference to the pinnacle of the temple (the highest point of the temple), which would

---

204 Price, *Last Days Temple*, 482.

represent the entirety of the temple being defiled.[205] Another possibility is that the "wing" is a reference to the winged cherubim of the Ark of the Covenant located in the Holy of holies.[206] This might find support from Paul's statement in 2 Thessalonians 2, where the Antichrist will present himself as deity and sit in the very Holy of holies. Can anything be any more evil and defiling than that? In any case, what is seen in Daniel 9:27 is the highest level of desecration where idols permanently reside in the Jerusalem temple. The temple is completely defiled by this evil man and his willful act of setting up an idol in the sanctuary. This will be the greatest demonstration of temple defilement ever, which is rivaled only by the works of Antiochus Epiphanes during the intertestamental period. The term "abomination" is "used of any detestable thing (Hos. 9:10; Nah. 3:6; Zech. 9:7), but predominately in connection with idolatrous practices."[207] So what is being foretold by Gabriel will be the amazing defilement, by means of idolatry, of a rebuilt Jerusalem time in the end of times.

    The verse ends by making clear that the Lord has "decreed" that the one who did such damage to the temple of God and the people of God will suffer a like fate. His rebellion will not go on forever but will be terminated. God will deal harshly with this Roman Prince ("the desolating one"). This statement will be fulfilled at the Second Coming of the true Christ when the Antichrist, along with his co-conspirator the False Prophet, will be taken alive and cast into the eternal Lake of Fire (cf. Rev. 19:19-21; 20:10). And before all of creation the righteousness and justice of God will be manifested. And God will be true to His word that "Seventy sevens" will fulfill six great purposes by the time they have come to an end.

---

205 Walvoord, 235.
206 Price, *Last Days Temple*, 487-488.
207 bid.

QUESTIONS TO CONSIDER

1. Daniel's prayer reflects the basic elements that Jesus said were essential for effective praying. What were those elements and which of them seems to be absent from the prayers of Christian? Which of the elements are more or less likely to be found in your prayers?

2. Daniel fasted and put on sackcloth when he prayed. Should these kinds of externals have a place in our individual praying or in our corporate praying?

3. Daniel's prayer was filled with confession. What place is confession of sin to have in our prayers? How specific must we be? Should confession of sin be part of corporate praying? Use scriptures to back up your conclusions.

4. What were the subjects of Daniel's prayer and why is knowing them important in interpreting the prophecy?

5. Explain in an understandable way the six purposes of God for the Seventy Weeks. Which ones do you think are fulfilled or partially fulfilled? Are there any that await future fulfillment.

6. Summarize, either verbally or in writing, the contents of the Seventy Weeks prophecy. Imagine that you are summarizing the truths in this prophecy to a new believer in Christ.

CHAPTER TEN

MINISTERING TO DANIEL

Preview: Two years after the seventy weeks prophecy, Daniel received a vision of the end times which would give information about the history of Israel during the seventy weeks. This vision, which continues through Chapter 12, would be the last vision that Daniel received. This tenth chapter is actually the introduction to this final prophetic vision, which gives amazingly intricate details as well as a broad sweep of coming events. This chapter highlights the role that the angelic realm plays in the events that take place on earth. And in the middle of the angelic conflict stands the faithful man of God, Daniel.

This introduction to Daniel's final vision unveils the significant involvement that both men and angels have in bringing to pass the purposes of God. It is unfortunate that the final vision of Daniel has been divided into three different chapters since that lends to some confusion. It would have been better to have one lengthy final chapter to the book of Daniel.

The tenth chapter contains some of the clearest revelations concerning angelic activity that are found anywhere in Scripture. The key to understanding this vision is to be found in 10:14 where Daniel is informed that the vision is intended to give him an understanding about what would happen to "your people in the latter days, for the vision pertains to the days yet future." Even though there will be much information given, in chapter 11 especially, about gentile nations, the focus remains on the people of Daniel and their land.

THE SETTING OF DANIEL'S VISION (Dan. 10:1-3)

10:1 The events of this chapter took place in the third year of Cyrus' reign, which would be 536 B.C. This would make Daniel around 85 years old at the time that this vision was given. He had recently witnessed the wonderful event of the return of some 50,000 Israelites back to their land as a result of God's faithfulness and Cyrus' decree (cf. Ezra 1:1-4). These Israelite who had been led back to the land by Zerubbabel had begun to lay the foundation for the Jerusalem temple (cf. Ezra 3-5; Hag. 1). So, 536 B.C. was an eventful year for this aging servant of God. It is worth noting that Daniel had not joined the thousands who had returned back to his beloved land of Israel. We cannot imagine that he lacked a desire to return. It has been suggested that it was because he was too old a man that he did not return. But the Scriptures are quite clear that many older men, who had seen the Jerusalem temple before its destruction, were part of the 50,000 who returned with Zerubbabel (cf. Ezra 3:12). We must assume that Daniel had not been given permission by the Lord to do so since the Lord's will for Daniel apparently was to remain in exile because he had many things yet to do for the Lord in the Medo-Persian Empire. This may be reading more into the account than we should, but it would be entirely consistent with his manner of living for Daniel to subjugate his own desires to the desires of his Lord. Not a bad example for us.

Daniel came to a more complete understanding of coming events as a result of this vision. It became clearer to him that in fulfilling God's purposes there was to be a long time of destructive warfare ahead. Daniel is here identified by his Babylonian name, Belteshazzar, which is the first time since chapter 5 that he has been so identified. We cannot be sure as to why this name is suddenly mentioned again. However, we can speculate that it may be a simple reminder that Daniel remains in exile and has not had the joy of going home to Israel.

10:2-3 The reader is informed that Daniel spent three entire weeks in mourning and fervent praying (cf. Dan. 10:12) prior to the receiving of this vision. During these three "weeks of days" (in contrast to the "weeks" found in Dan. 9:24-27. See page 197) he did not eat rich and fancy foods, but limited himself to "bread and water". These twenty-one days were not a period of strict fasting, but rather a time that he placed significant restrictions upon himself as he set aside the normal activities of life. The normal comforts of life were temporarily set aside as he diligently sought the Lord. It is instructive to observe here that all through his life he faced times of "mourning", which come to all of God's faithful servants in this world where we are strangers and aliens. And it is good to remember that the Lord Jesus said that the blessed ones were those who "mourn", and not blessed are the lighthearted seekers of pleasure, profit and comfort. But what caused Daniel to spend three weeks like this? We cannot know for sure, since the text does not state a specific reason. However, we can speculate that it may have had something to do with the negative events that were taking place in his beloved land about this time. The clearing of the rubble from the temple mount in Jerusalem and the laying of the foundation for the temple received significant opposition from the non-Jews living in the land (cf. Ezra 4:1-5). This kind of intense resistance to their work for God may have caught Daniel and others by surprise, and thus perhaps this time of mourning and prayer by Daniel.

THE GLORIOUS PERSON AND DANIEL (Dan. 10:4-9)

10:4-6 The period of mourning and partial fasting ended on the twenty-fourth day of the first month of the year, which would have placed the entire week of the Passover celebration in the midst of these three weeks (Passover was from the 14th to the 21st of the first month). When the three-week period ended he was on the banks of the Tigris River and there he met a glorious being, who is described in terms of brilliant light, beautiful stones and shining metals. No reason is given for Daniel being by this great river, so he may have been there on government business or enjoying a post-Passover holiday. But this detail is probably mentioned so that the reader understood that Daniel had not returned back to Israel with the 50,000 but remained in the land of his captivity.

The main issue in these verses is the identification of this glorious personage who appeared to Daniel. The opinion is basically divided between those who believe that this is an angel of God and those who see it as an appearance of God Himself (or an appearance of Christ). While he was human-like in general appearance, he clearly was not a man. The author struggled with his words to try and describe the absolute splendor of this person. While one can build a case for this personage being an angel, it is better to see this as an appearance of the Lord Himself. There are several reasons for this. First, the previous times when angels appeared in this book, they are not described at all in this way. Angels are simply not described in such majestic terms. But, on the other hand, the description of God the Father (the Ancient of Days) in 7:9-10 and other places (such as Ezek. 1) has a real resemblance to the language of these verses. Second, the description given here has significant similarities to the glorified Christ in Revelation 1:14-16, from the splendor of glowing metals to the roar of the voice. It seems to be an attempt to describe the glories of deity. And third, Daniel's response to the presence of this person and to his words is not the reaction one would expect when facing a fellow creature, but it does seem appropriate if that individual was the Lord Himself.

10:7-9 Daniel was in the company of others that day on the banks of the Tigris River, but he alone saw the powerful, glorious person and was overwhelmed by the experience. The others with Daniel did not see the vision but they were aware that something momentous was going on. Fear gripped their hearts and they fled the scene leaving Daniel by himself. A similar situation would occur centuries later on the road to Damascus when Saul of Tarsus would see the glorious risen Lord Jesus. He alone saw Him, but those with Saul heard something and were aware of the light, but were speechless and did not see the vision (cf. Acts 9:3-8; 22:9; 26:12-14). On another occasion the Father spoke to Jesus, but those around Jesus did not understood the words, thinking that it thundered or that an angel had spoken (cf. John 12:28-30). These events seem to suggest that unbelievers may well be aware of divine interventions into human experience while at the same time not really understanding the reality of what is transpiring. Such might be the case among unbelievers when the church is suddenly and powerfully raptured out of the world.

The vision had a profound effect on Daniel, causing him to fall to the ground in great weakness. Daniel was left alone when his companions fled, which was good since the vision was for Daniel. Men who constantly wish for such visions should take careful note of the reaction of such spiritual giants as Daniel and John (cf. Rev. 1:17) to these times when heaven opens to them. The sight of this divine Person and the roar of His words sapped him of all strength and he lay helpless on the ground.

THE MINISTRY OF AN ANGEL TO DANIEL (10:10-14)

10:10 The text does not tell us how long Daniel lay incapacitated on the ground. But while lying there, Daniel received the first of three angelic "touches" (cf. Dan. 10:16 and 18). This first touch enabled Daniel to rise up so that he was resting on his hands and knees although shaking badly from this experience. He can now hear the words of the angel and is no longer in the coma that he had been in a short while before.

If in fact the being that appeared to Daniel previously (in Dan. 10:4-9) was the Lord Himself (a theophany), then this must be a different individual.[208] But this change in persons is objected to by some commentators.

---

208 John F. Walvoord, *Daniel: The Key to Prophetic Revelation* (Chicago: Moody, 1971), 245.

There is, however, justification for it. First, it should be noted that Daniel was touched by "a hand" and not "His hand" (the being of verse 5-6). Logically we would have expected the text to say "His hand" if the same person was in view. Second, the being said to Daniel, "I have now been sent to you" (Dan. 10:11). This is rather an odd thing to say if he had already been with Daniel before he fainted and fell to the ground. One must postulate that he departed from Daniel when he fainted and returned to him again and touched him and lifted him up. But the matter of much greater significance is the issue of 10:13 where the person now speaking with Daniel states that he was hindered in coming to Daniel for a period of 21 days. If this is still the Lord speaking to Daniel, then this would be stating that the Lord (Dan. 10:4-9) was kept from coming to Daniel by some being who is called the "prince of Persia." But certainly, this could not be referring to the Lord being thwarted by another being for three weeks. Who can resist Him for three weeks or three seconds? Yet this one who spoke with Daniel needed the help of the great angel Michael to make his way to Daniel. This strongly points to the being of 10:10-14 being an angel who had been sent by the Lord (Dan. 10:11) while the Lord is the one seen in 10:4-9.

10:11 As Daniel rested on his hands and knees, the angel encouraged Daniel with the words that he was a "man of high esteem." When Gabriel came two years earlier to Daniel with the information of the Seventy Weeks (Dan. 9:23), he had declared the same encouraging truth to Daniel. Daniel had honored God and the Lord in turn had a special relationship with Daniel (cf. 1 Sam. 2:30b). The frightened, exhausted Daniel needed this reminder. The angel, who is not identified by name, encouraged Daniel to stand up and to listen carefully to the message. When God speaks to man, they must not be drowsy or distracted but rather must give focused attention to what is being declared, which is a good reminder to us when we sit under the teaching of God's Word. Otherwise, Satan is given free-reign to snatch away the good seed of the Word before it can produce good fruit in the life of an individual. The angel had specifically come to Daniel with this message and Daniel needed to understand this word from God. A weakened Daniel stood but still was shaking from the overwhelming experience.

10:12-13 The messenger angel then gave to Daniel some amazing information. He told Daniel that he had actually been dispatched from God with information immediately after Daniel began his humble, fervent praying. But it had taken the angel twenty-one days to reach Daniel! It may well be that Daniel became burdened during those twenty-one days with the thought that God was not listening to him. And is this not the sense that many of us have when our prayers are not quickly answered? But delay in the answering of prayer is quite common as the Lord Jesus noted (cf. Luke 11:1-13; 18:1-8). Daniel's praying contained those necessary elements of humility and persistence. But why was the answer delayed in coming to him? It was not because the angel was unusually slow or had gotten distracted. The angel's explanation for the three-week delay pulls back the curtain on the spirit world for a brief moment. It reveals that our praying may well have an impact on another dimension of reality; namely the angelic world. "And it throws a flood of light on many a dark problem and many apparently unanswered prayers or prayers which have not been answered for a long time."[209] That which goes on in this world is not simply visible human activity, but includes powerful, invisible angelic forces. The worlds of angels and men intersect time and time again as the biblical record indicates so that believers have even unknowingly entertained angels (cf. Heb. 13:2).

The angel explained to Daniel that his mission to reach Daniel with God's answer had been thwarted for three weeks by the "prince of Persia". The most obvious question at this point has to do with the identification of this "prince of Persia." While some have dismissed this simply as fictional apocalyptic imagery or as a figurative way of depicting a prevailing bad attitude in the Persian court, the majority of commentators do not do so.

---

209 Harry Bultema, *Commentary on Daniel* (Grand Rapids: Kregel, 1988), 302.

Rather they see the "prince" as a reference to a human figure (such as the Persian kings Cyrus or Cambyses) or as an angelic being (either good or evil). However, most do see the "prince" as an angelic being since a normal reading of the text, and the immediate context, seems to point that direction. And, the evidence is in favor of the "prince" being identified as an evil angel. The fact is that he stands in opposition to angelic beings that work for God. This resisting of the purposes of God would only be true of those fallen, rebellious angels. Furthermore, a human being is ruled out because a human cannot stand against the angels of God. And the fact that Michael, one of the most powerful angels, was needed to free the angel from the harmful activity of the evil angel, shows this to be conflict in the angelic realm and not the realm of mankind. So, warfare in the spiritual realm is most obviously the issue in the giving of this revelation to Daniel.

The fact that this evil being is referred to as the "*prince* of Persia" suggests that he is a particularly powerful angel. The reality that "one of the chief princes", Michael, was needed to help out points to this evil angel being of high rank. The Scriptures reveal that within the angelic realm there are differences in power, authority and ability. It should not be surprising to us, therefore, that one angel (even an evil one) could have power over another angel (even a holy one). This "prince of Persia" is evidently assigned by Satan to work on behalf of Satan's purposes in that particular kingdom. The presence of evil angels of differing ranks and authorities in the army of Satan is documented in the Bible. This idea is included in the Apostle Paul's discussion in Ephesians 6:10-18 concerning the warfare of the believer in this world. Paul's teaching supports and illuminates this section of Daniel.

> Put on the full armor of God, that you may be able to stand firm against the schemes of the devil. For our struggle is not against flesh and blood, but against the rulers, against the powers, *against the world forces of this darkness*, against the spiritual powers of wickedness in the heavenly places. (Eph. 6:11-12)

Of particular interest to this discussion in Daniel 10 is the group the Apostle refers to as "the world forces of this darkness." These Satanic agents are aligned against God and His people with the primary purpose of sabotaging God's plans for this world by using the nations of this world particularly against the nation of Israel. There is one word used by the Apostle for those identified as "world forces".

> It can be used for one who is the ruler of the whole world, or for one whose authority is in the world, in the sense in which the devil is so described in John 12:31, 14:30 and 2 Corinthians 4:4. The world is frequently spoken of thus in the New Testament as in the power of the evil one (1 John. 5:19), and in consequence in *darkness* (cf. Luke. 22:53; Rom. 13:12; Col. 1:13). Those who, under the devil himself, hold such power in the world, and in consequence keep people in *darkness,* are those against whom Christians have to do battle.[210]

God has apparently given specific assignments to the holy angels in order that His purposes might be fulfilled in the world. These exalted beings do not simply sit around the heavenly realm idly passing time but have been actively involved in bringing God's revelations to mankind (e.g. Rev. 1:1; 10:1-9), protecting individual believers (e.g. Heb. 1:14) and performing innumerable assignments (e.g. Ps. 103:20-22). And, there are some that apparently are assigned jurisdiction over individual nations in the world. Moses spoke of God's dividing up of the nations of man with a parallel assigning of angels ("sons of God") in Deuteronomy 32:8, "When the Most High gave the nations their inheritance, when He separated the sons of man, He set the boundaries of the peoples according to the number of the sons of God."[211]

---

[210] Francis Foulkes, *Ephesians: Tyndale New Testament Commentaries*, Rev. Ed. (Grand Rapids: Eerdmans, 2000), 180.

[211] While there is some dispute in the manuscript evidence, modern scholars are in general agreement that "sons of God" is to be preferred over "sons of Israel."

It is quite clear that the chief angel Michael has been assigned to the nation of Israel and will rise up to give them support in the coming days of tribulation, according to Daniel 12:1. God's apparent strategy and deployment of His angelic forces seems to have brought a corresponding response from Satan, as is evidenced by the assignment of his followers to both Persia and Greece in Daniel 10:13 and 20.

But why would there be an attempt by the "prince of Persia" to keep the holy angel from delivering this revelation to Daniel? The information that would be given to Daniel was probably far more extensive than the concerns he had which caused him to go to prayer. Those concerns were about the trouble that Israel was experiencing at that time back in the land in connection with the rebuilding of the temple.

> Since the vision extended to the overthrow of the Satanic world system at the Second Advent, it aroused intense demonic opposition through one of Satan's powerful spirit agents…The attempt was being made to thwart the purpose of God for His earthly people; they knew full well that the divine plan invoked challenge to their sway in the world system. In this instance this was true in a pre-eminent sense; for Daniel was about to be given a momentous vision, looking forward to the Second Advent and the establishment of the Messianic earthly kingdom over Israel, which would ultimately spell the doom of Satan's rule through human governments.[212]

Daniel would learn that it was not simply evil men that harassed and harmed Israel, but that there were diabolical spirit beings that were actively involved also. And the truth revealed here ought to open our spiritual eyes to the fact that beyond human politics and wars there is fierce and intense warfare within the unseen angelic ranks. There are forces that promote God's agenda in this world and those that resist it. And those human leaders who

---

212 Merrill F. Unger, *Biblical Demonology* (Wheaton: Scripture Press, 1963), 194-195.

abandon God's truth and God's agenda become pawns in the wicked hands of these powerful spirits. Did we not witness this in the cruel, godless leaders that led the world into the atrocities of World War II? And while we focus on the depth of evil found in those leaders, we must remember that behind them were the wicked, fallen angelic beings who have aligned themselves with Satan. "Wicked rulers and dictators…renouncing Christianity and abandoning themselves to pride, ambition, conquest and rebellion against God, offer the ideal medium for the untrammeled operation of these evil ruling spirits."[213]

The purposes of the Lord God on this earth revolve around the nation of Israel and the satanic forces remain committed to thwarting these purposes of God. While the battle rages on, the outcome of it all is certain. When the Messiah comes, according to Daniel 2 and 7, the nations of the world, which are under Satan's control, will be completely and permanently eliminated.

10:14 After explaining reason for the three-week delay in his arrival, the angel informed Daniel that the revelation he is about to receive has to do with his people Israel and that it has to do with the "latter days." This phrase was discussed earlier (in connection with Dan. 2:28) and it was concluded that while it is sometimes a general term, it has definite eschatological significance in Daniel. The perspective is from the time of the prophet to the consummation of all things in what is known as the kingdom of the Messiah. In other words, it extends to the time of the second coming of Christ and does not terminate at the time of the Maccabees or some other time other than the establishment of the messianic reign on the earth. And as it will be seen, this final vision of Daniel (in chapters 10-12) proceeds through to the end of man's rule with the Antichrist, which is then immediately followed by the Messiah's rule.

---

213 Ibid. 196.

THE FURTHER MINISTRY TO DANIEL (Dan. 10:15-18)

10:15 The angel's words implied there was to be a considerable amount of time for Israel to experience before the end would come. This had a negative effect on Daniel who once again was overcome with weakness. Daniel either bowed down under the weight of the revelation or again assumed his previous position on his hands and knees. In either case, he needed help in this time of great burdens.

10:16-18 At this moment, Daniel received strengthening from one who is identified as "one who resembled a human being." Who is this person? Some have seen this as the angel who had been speaking to Daniel while others see him as a reappearance of the divine being in 10:5-6. Angels can minister physically and emotionally to a person as is seen in the Garden of Gethsemane where angelic beings ministered to the Lord Jesus (cf. Luke 22:43) or where they ministered to Jesus after His temptation (cf. Mark 1:13; Matt. 4:11). However, the identification of this one as like a human being calls to mind the "son of man" in Daniel 7. But perhaps the solution is to found in the possibility that multiple persons were present with Daniel. On more than one occasion the Lord God and His angels did appear together to men in the Old Testament record.

> When He visited Abraham, He was not alone but was accompanied by two other persons who, like Himself, were called men. In Ezekiel 9 we come across the same thing. There He marches up to Jerusalem with a company of six men. In the night visions of Zechariah, we find this representation again and again...Hence, it appears to us that we are dealing here with the Son of God surrounded by a group of angels who carry out His commands. And we do not consider it absurd that every time we must picture different heavenly spirits...[214]

---

214 Bultema, 307.

Therefore, the apparent multiple persons in Daniel 10 are really not at all different from other heavenly appearances in the Old Testament. And it is perhaps helpful to view the account in this manner.

Daniel was too weak to stand up or even to talk. The heavenly being touched Daniel with the result that he was enabled to speak again (vs. 16) and to receive the needed strength to hear and respond to the soon to be revealed vision (vs. 18).

THE PROPHECY INTRODUCED (Dan. 10:19-21)

10:19 For the third time Daniel was encouraged by the word that he is highly esteemed by God (cf. Dan. 9:23 and 10:11). He was in great need of these words because the appearance of these glorious beings and the monumental nature of the revelation had brought a great deal of fear to him as well as having the effect of completely sapping him of emotional and spiritual energy. The kindly words did bring strength to Daniel and he then became ready to receive the word from God.

10:20-21 Daniel was again asked if he understood why the angel had come. This was not needless repetition as some have suggested. Rather it was a necessary question in light of Daniel's depleted strength and capacities.

The angel again pulls the curtain back into the angelic realm of activity and warfare when he informed Daniel that he must now go and continue the battle against the "prince of Persia." This continuing battle will eventually bring about victory over the prince of Persia, but warfare will not cease at that point. After the demise of the Persian Empire, the empire of Greece would come onto the world stage. And it too would have a powerful, evil spirit being trying to use that nation against Israel. When the "prince of Greece" arrived on the scene, then battle with that evil angel would commence.

> The mention of both Persia and Greece also directs our attention to the second and third major empires which are involved in the prophecies of Daniel 11:1-35. From this we can learn that, be-

hind the many details of prophecy relating to the history of this period, there is unseen struggle between angelic forces that the will of God may be accomplished.[215]

The angel then informed Daniel that he would give him information that was found in the "writing of truth." This is probably not a reference to the Scriptures but is more likely "a figurative expression for the decrees of God"[216] as it is sometimes used this way in the Old Testament (e.g. Deut. 32:34; Ps. 56:8; 139:16; Mal. 3:16). God has His sovereign purposes, some of which He has chosen to reveal to man, but many of which He has not. Daniel would be given some truth from the treasures of God's wisdom.

Daniel was informed by the angel that the angel must now head for the court of Persia where only Michael the prince of Israel was doing battle for God. Michael is here referred to as "your prince", which undoubtedly brought comfort to Daniel. Michael has been given the special assignment of giving protection to the nation of Israel. It is clear that Michael has his hands full when it comes to spiritual warfare because Satan and his forces have a deep and abiding hatred for Israel. But Satan will not have free reign when it comes to the nation of Israel. Satan will be opposed by Michael until Satan and his followers are removed from heaven by Michael and his angels (cf. Rev. 12). This great battle will take place half way through Daniel's Seventieth Week. After being confined to the earth, Satan will persecute Israel as never before, but will not succeed in destroying God's people. Then Michael and the holy angels will have the satisfaction of seeing Satan and all his evil agents cast into the abyss and eventually into the lake of fire (cf. Rev. 20:1-3, 10).

---

215 Walvoord, 250.
216 Robert Culver, *The Histories and Prophecies of Daniel* (Winona Lake: BMH Books, 19800, 170.

QUESTIONS TO CONSIDER

1. What are some lessons that this chapter might teach believer's today about prayer and the answers to prayer?

2. What perspectives does this chapter give to us about the activities of political leaders and their nations? How much emphasis should we make related to angelic activity in all of this? Would the USA have a powerful demon and a holy assigned to it? If so, how might this affect how we view the increasing political struggles that exist in this nation?

3. How might this chapter help we who are in the church in our understanding of spiritual warfare? Compare this chapter with the Apostle Paul's discussion in Ephesians 6:10-18.

4. What do you believe about the activities of angels and demons in the world today? Is there greater or lesser activity today than compared to the days when Jesus was on the earth? Will there be greater or lesser activity in the end times (support your view with scripture)?

5. What place does "holy wars" have, if any, in fulfilling God's purposes on the earth? What about Joshua and the conquering of Canaan? What about World War II and the establishing of a homeland for Israel? What about the Crusades of Medieval times?

6. What are some of the specific areas given in the New Testament where Christians are "at war'?

CHAPTER ELEVEN

PREPARING FOR THE END

Preview: The circumstances surrounding the reception of the final vision were given in the previous chapter. There, many details concerning Daniel's interaction with those bringing the revelation from God were related. This present chapter contains most of the content of that message, covering the time from the Persian rulers to the very end of times and the reign of the Antichrist. This chapter gives the prophetic history of the first sixty-nine weeks (Dan. 11:3-35), which is followed immediately by the prophetic history of the seventieth week (Dan. 11:36-45). The dozens and dozens of prophecies found in this chapter set it apart as one of the most amazing prophetic chapters in the Bible.

The detailed prophecies in this chapter number over one hundred and are so clear that they can be matched up with the persons and events that eventually did appear on the stage of history. Their identity is so clear that liberal theologians and conservative theologians generally agree on what the text is saying. However, it is this fact that has made Daniel 11 a flash point of controversy between scholars. For some, it is impossible for this kind of detail to be given ahead of time and, therefore, it had to be history written in the literary form of prophecy[217], a sort of "quasi-prophecy".[218] But for others, the appearance of detailed prophecies given

---

217 W. Sibley Towner, *Daniel* (Louisville: John Knox Press, 1984), 152.
218 John E. Goldingay, *Daniel: Word Biblical Commentary* (Nashville: Thomas Nelson, 1989), 282-283.

well ahead of time by the Divine Author is not a problem. In the study of the Scriptures, the interpreter must never relegate the Holy Spirit to some minor role of negligible influence on the human author. It is true that no man (even with demonic help) can predict the future in detail. But men moved along by the Spirit of God can record the most amazing details from the exact birthplace of the Messiah to the number of months that the Antichrist will rule the world. Dr. John Walvoord's evaluation of this issue in Daniel 11 is accurate and to the point.

> Daniel 11:1-35 is either the most precise and accurate prophecy of the future, fully demonstrating its divine inspiration, or as Porphyry (the third century A.D. heathen philosopher) claimed, it is a dishonest attempt to present history as if prophesied centuries earlier. Modern critics of Daniel have not gone much beyond the basic premise of Porphyry, namely, that such detailed prophecy is impossible, and, therefore, absurd and incredible.[219]

THE PROPHECIES OF PERSIA (Dan. 11:1-2)

11:1 There is nearly universal agreement that those people who divided the scriptures into chapter divisions did not do it right at this point in Daniel. This verse should have ended chapter 10 rather than beginning chapter 11. This first verse is a continuation of the explanation given to Daniel by his angelic visitor. This unnamed angel had been explaining that he was the only one who had come to the aid of the great angel Michael in the battle against the "prince of Persia", the powerful demonic being assigned to Persia. He then made it clear that this help had been given in the first year of King Darius. Some have understood the "him" in 11:1b to be a reference to Darius, and this is possible. However, in light of the present context, as well as other details given earlier in this book, it is better to understand "him" as a reference to the angel Michael who has been the subject of the discussion.

---

[219] John F. Walvoord, *Daniel: The Key to Prophetic Revelation* (Chicago: Moody, 1971), 253.

Both the incident of the lion's den and the giving of the Seventy Weeks prophecy took place during the first year of Darius; the date spoken of here by the angel. Those were monumental days for Daniel and his people Israel. The people of Israel had been allowed to return back to their land, which was a wonderful moment for them and for Daniel. But, at this time, there was also an attempt to turn Darius against Daniel and Israel with the writing of a decree. This resulted in Daniel ending up in the lion's den. Apparently the "prince of Persia" was instrumental in the composing of that human decree (another doctrine of demons) which caused Daniel to spend a night in the den of lions. But Daniel was delivered out of that situation by an angel. And around that same time, Daniel was deeply distressed, perhaps by the opposition that Israel was experiencing back in the land, as described in Ezra 4. This was apparently the work of the "prince of Persia". As a result of all this, Daniel received from the angel Gabriel information concerning the Seventy Weeks.

We cannot help but believe that the angel's statement here to Daniel (Dan. 11:1) must have opened his eyes to realities he had never understood before about those days several years earlier (chapter 6 and 9). Behind those events on the human plane there was significant and powerful angelic activity as well. The battle rages on today between the forces of God and the evil agents of Satan, and we are not wrong to assume that behind the events on the human stage there is equal or greater activity taking place in the realm of angelic beings.

11:2 There would be great interest on the part of Daniel as to the course of events in the second empire, that of Medo-Persia. Daniel, who was told that he would get nothing but truthful facts from the angel (Dan. 10:31 "the writing of truth"), was given a brief summary of the next few Medo-Persian rulers. He was informed that after the present reign was over, three more kings would rule and then a fourth one who would be greater in power and wealth than the others who preceded him. It would be this king that would initiate warfare against the Greeks and ultimately set the stage for the transition to the third world empire discussed in the book of Daniel; that is, the kingdom of Greece. (See discussion about the transition from the second to third empire on pages 158-162).

When Daniel was receiving this revelatory information, the king on the throne was Cyrus/Darius (See discussion on page 109). Following the death of Cyrus, the Persian throne was occupied by Cambyses, Pseudo-Smerdis, and Darius I (Hystaspes). After these kings, it was Xerxes who ruled the empire. Xerxes (the Ahasuerus of the book of Esther) was the one who spearheaded the attack on the Grecian city-states. There is often confusion in identifying these kings in 11:2 because Pseudo-Smerdis is not acknowledged as a ruler of Persia since his reign lasted but seven months. However, when he is rightly included in the list, then the verse becomes clear and the valid identification of Xerxes is established. It was Xerxes who led this prophesied attack against Greece.

> In his great campaign against Greece from 481 to 479 B.C., with an army of probably 200,000 men and a navy of many hundreds of ships gathered from all over his vast empire, Xerxes desperately sought to avenge the humiliating defeat suffered by his father, Darius I, at the battle of Marathon (490 B.C.). But his army was defeated north of Athens at Plataea (479 B.C.), just after his navy was smashed at Salamis, to the west of Athens.[220]

This verse does not state the outcome of the Persian king's attack on Greece, but the fact that the next verses speak of the rising of mighty Grecian king would suggest that things did not go well for the Persians. Historically, in Xerxes one can see the height of Persian power and wealth and at the same time see the beginning of its demise as an empire. It is perhaps for this reason that the revelation does not find it necessary to give out any information about the next eight kings of Persia.

---

220 John C. Whitcomb, *Daniel* (Chicago: Moody, 1980), 146.

Before going any further, it might be helpful to pause and identify in a general way the focus of the upcoming prophecies. It is important to remember that what is being given to Daniel, though having significant detail, is nevertheless only a summation of things to come. The revelation does not include every single individual who ruled, nor does it include every event of significance. Like with many of the biblical genealogies, there is selectivity involved here, and the intent is to give a picture of the ebb and flow of events up to the key figure of Antiochus IV, who in turn prefigures the future Antichrist.

VERSES	DATE	PERSONS WHO WOULD RULE
2	539-465 B.C.	Cyrus (Darius); Cambyses; Pseudo-Smerdis; Darius I; Xerxes
3-4	334-323 B.C.	Alexander the Great
5-20	323-175 B.C.	Kings of the North (Seleucid dynasty) and Kings of the South (Ptolemaic dynasty)
21-35	175-164 B.C.	Antiochus IV (Epiphanes)
36-45	???	Antichrist (The "little horn")

THE PROPHECIES OF GREECE (Dan. 11:3-4)

11:3 The declaration of this verse could find innumerable applications in history if it were not for the explanation of the verse that follows. We might assume that the subject of this verse was some Persian ruler who would follow Xerxes. But that assumption would, of course, be incorrect. The king here described would be especially powerful and independent. But it is the next verse that makes clear who is here being referred to.

11:4 Three basic facts are set forth in this verse, which describe Alexander the Great and his empire. First, it would be while rising to the heights of power that he would die. This points to the fact of history that Alexander did indeed die a premature death. Second, it is noted that when he died his empire would be divided up into four parts among those who were not his own descendants. This was fulfilled when four of Alexander's generals took over the Grecian empire at the death of Alexander. Third, these four rulers would not possess, either as individual rulers or collectively, the power that Alexander once possessed. When Alexander died the glory and might of the Grecian empire was never the same.

Many of these same facts were given in the Ram-Goat vision found in Daniel 8 where the transition from the second to the third kingdom was discussed. However, that chapter did not reveal that behind Alexander the Great and those that would follow him was the "prince of Greece" (Dan. 10:20). In this present revelation, Daniel was informed of the presence of demonic forces at work in the world. Behind the mighty king Alexander stood a mightier being, the prince of Greece. This truth would have given Daniel an even clearer perspective on these events.

THE PROPHECIES OF EGYPT AND SYRIA (Dan. 11:5-20)

The biblical account is only interested in those generals of Alexander who would have an impact on the nation of Israel. Two of the four played no direct role in relationship to Israel (namely Lysimichus and Cassander). As a result, the prophetic focus is on the kings of the south (General Ptolemy and his descendants) and the kings of the north (General Seleucus and his descendants). Naturally these directions of "south" and "north" are in reference to the land of Israel. The people of Israel would become deeply involved with both of these kingdoms. Israel would first fall under the domination of the "south" and then it would be the "north" that would hold sway over them. Israel often became a battleground as these two nations fought each other. These verses (Dan. 11:5-20) record the cooperation and conflict that existed between these two powers for a period of about 150 years. This century and a half will be dealt with briefly in the comments to follow. There are a number of sources that that can be used in constructing the summary that is given below.[221]

The kings that are referred to in these verses are given below. The many details are quite amazing, but the significant moment in time was the year 198 B.C. when the rulers of the south (Egypt) lost control of Israel to the north (Syria). The rise to power of Syria over Israel in that year prepared the way for the terrible persecution of Israel by the Syrian king, Antiochus IV (Epiphanes). In a sense, this is where the chapter was heading. His reign receives a significant amount of attention, as it did in Daniel 8, since he pictures the future Antichrist.

KINGS OF THE SOUTH (EGYPT)	KINGS OF THE NORTH (SYRIA)
Ptolemy I (Soter) 323-285	Seleucus I (Nicator) 312-281
Ptolemy II (Philadelphus 285-247	Antiochus I (Soter) 281-261
Ptolemy III (Euergetes) 247-221	Antiochus Theos 261-246
Ptolemy IV (Philopater) 221-203	Seleucus Callinicus 246-226
Ptolemy V (Ephiphanes) 203-182)	Seleucus III 226-223
	Antiochus III (Great) 223-187
	Seleucus IV (Philopater) 186-175
	Antiochus IV (Epiphanes) 175-164

11:5 The king of the south refers here to Ptolemy I (Soter) who founded the powerful dynasty in Egypt. However, it would turn out that Seleucus I

---
221 Arno C. Gaebelein, *Daniel* (Grand Rapids: Kregel, 1968), 166-178; Walvoord, 258-264; Harry Bultema, *Commentary on Daniel* (Grand Rapids: Kregel, 1988), 316-325.

would eventually gain greater power. Initially Seleucus I did not rule the area of Syria, but rather it was ruled by Antigonus of Babylon. Seleucus I joined forces with Ptolemy I and eventually defeated Antigonus thus establishing his dynasty in Syria and Palestine. However, Ptolemy I broke with Seleucus I and took Palestine, making it part of the Egyptian empire. This, of course, did not make for good relations between the two empires.

11:6 After a number of years had passed, perhaps in an attempt to ease tensions between the two empires, the daughter (Berenice) of Ptolemy Philadelphus was married to the Syrian king, Antiochus Theos. In order to be able to do this, Antiochus Theos divorced his wife (his half-sister Laodice). The idea was that any children born to Berenice and Antiochus Theos would be heirs to the Syrian throne and thus cement the ties between these two dynasties. However, these political and marital maneuverings did not accomplish anything of lasting good. When Ptolemy Philadelphus died, Antiochus Theos decided to bring back his former wife, Laodice. And she came back with a vengeance. She eventually poisoned her husband Antiochus Theos, as well as Berenice and the son of Berenice and Antiochus Theos thus fulfilling the word that they would all lose their power. Apparently, a number of those who accompanied Berenice from Egypt ("those who brought her in") died as well. So much for bonding the nations together through marriage. Seleucus Callinicus, son of Laodice, became the ruler of the dynasty of the north.

11:7-9 These next verses focus on the exploits of Ptolemy III (Euergetes), the brother of the recently poisoned Berenice. With vengeance in his heart he headed north and conquered the northern king, Seleucus Callinicus, taking Syrian strongholds and a significant amount of wealth. A counter attack later on by Seleucus Callinicus was a disastrous effort, except that some of the strongholds were recovered.

11:10 The two sons of Seleucus Callinicus (Seleucus III and Antiochus III) eventually had the kind of military success that had eluded their father. When Seleucus III died in a battle in Asia Minor, the throne of the north was taken over by Antiochus III (the Great) who became one of the most powerful and successful of the kings of the north. In three military campaigns against the Ptolemies of Egypt, he took city after city in Israel from Ptolemy Philopater who was not noted for being much of a warrior. Antiochus the Great brought the kingdom of the north to the very borders of the kingdom of the south.

11:11-12 Apparently the constant victories of Antiochus III and the possibility of Egypt itself falling to the Syrians aroused the lethargic, seemingly inept Philopater. In 217 B.C. a major battle took place at the border of Egypt and Israel/Syria involving some 70,000 soldiers in each army and dozens of battle elephants. And amazingly, although the forces of Antiochus III were slightly larger, and the momentum of war was his, the Syrians were soundly defeated by the once docile Philopater with Antiochus barely escaping with his life. History tells us that at that point Antiochus III wanted peace. Peace was granted by Philopater, who should have followed up on his victory and crushed the Syrians. But apparently Philopater preferred not to fight, instead desiring a life of ease and sensuality. For a short period of time there was peace between the two nations. But long term this great victory would do no good for Ptolemy Philopater.

11:13-16 As time went by Antiochus III (the Great) recovered from his terrible defeat in 217 B.C. at the hands of Ptolemy Philopater. In the years that followed he had some military successes in the eastern part of his empire. But in 203 B.C. Ptolemy Philopater and his queen died suddenly and mysteriously. The throne of Egypt then became occupied by their son Ptolemy V (Epiphanes) who was only a boy of about six years of age. With the sudden demise of his enemy, Antiochus III saw this as an opportunity to invade Egypt. He amassed a great army and headed for Egypt with his new ally Phillip of Macedon. The Egyptian situation was weakened as well by the fact that there were many rebels in Egypt as well as many Jews who were weary of Ptolemaic rule and sided with the northern invaders (Dan. 11:14).

As a result, no one could stop Antiochus III and he did what he pleased (Dan. 11:16). Antiochus III took Palestine ("the Beautiful land", Dan. 11:16) from Egypt and Israel was now firmly in the hands of the kings of the north, which would soon lead to the terrible persecution of Israel prophesied in Daniel 8. This perhaps is the meaning of "to fulfill the vision" in 11:14.

11:17 Antiochus III then determined to gain control over Egypt by marrying his daughter, Cleopatra, to the young Ptolemy V. This attempt to control the nation of Egypt through marriage did not produce the intended results because Cleopatra's loyalty was more often to her husband than it was to her father. It should be noted that at this time Antiochus III was observing with some uneasiness the rising power of Rome, who had taken an interest in the young king of Egypt. Some believe that this marriage was a ploy to keep Rome from turning against him by joining together the Syrian and Egyptian dynasties.

11:18-19 Antiochus III was not content with the gains and successes that he had achieved but was determined to invade Greece and add to his holdings. He had some limited successes, but this turned out to be an ill-conceived venture as it alerted the new power to the west, Rome. Antiochus was warned by Rome to leave Greece alone, but he did not listen. Instead of reaping the benefits of another victory, Antiochus III was soundly defeated twice by the Roman general, Cornelius Scipio. These Roman victories would open the door to Roman conquests later on. As a result of Roman intervention, Antiochus III then retreated to his own territory where he decided to rob the temple of Jupiter in order to address his problem of depleted funds. This act caused a rebellion, which in turn brought about the death of Antiochus III.

11:20 This verse looks at Seleucus IV, the son of Antiochus III, who was quite unpopular with his people because of the heavy tax burden that he placed on them. He was forced by Rome to pay huge sums of tribute money annually. In order to assist in the accomplishment of this task, he sent his tax collector, Heliodorus, to Jerusalem where he plundered treasure from the temple. As it turned out, Selecucus IV's reign was short ("few days"), apparently being brought to a sudden end by a dose of poison administered by the same Heliodorus. All of these events were leading up to the next king who would sit on the throne of the north, Antiochus IV (Epiphanes). This is where the storyline has been heading.

THE PROPHECIES OF ANTIOCHUS IV (Dan. 11:21-35)

The next king of the north was Antiochus IV, who only reigned about 10 years and normally would not be considered all that significant historically.

> The importance of Antiochus IV Epiphanes (175-164B.C.) in prophetic Scripture is very great. Though he was a relatively unimportant monarch in the ancient Near East, he gained eternal notoriety through his devastating attack upon the people of God and their religion. Thus he prefigured the final Antichrist.[222]

Earlier in Daniel 8, Antiochus IV was mentioned under the designation of the "small horn" (see page 162). His desecration of the Jerusalem temple and his deep hatred for the Jews who followed the Lord God set him apart among the many kings mentioned in this chapter of Daniel. In the text of Daniel 11, the story of the kings of the north and the south ends with him because he is, in a sense, the climax of the story related to the kings of the third empire. He is, however, not the end of this story, because he prefigures the wicked man of the end times, the Antichrist.

11:21 Upon the death of Seleucus IV, Antiochus IV was not the obvious successor to his throne. Others were in line ahead of Antiochus IV, especially Seleucus IV's son Demetrius. Demetrius left Syria, however, and was sent to Rome as a hostage to take the place of the exiled Antiochus.[223] So after a period of time filled with intrigue and maneuverings, when the dust settled, Antiochus IV Epiphanes sat on the throne. He saw himself as a glorious,

---
222 Whitcomb, 150.
223 Goldingay, 299.

god-like person, but the scriptures reflecting God's perspective refers to him as a "despicable person". While his rise to power has some uncertainty about it, the following seems to be a plausible reconstruction of events preceding his rise to power in Syria.

> When Antiochus IV was allowed to leave Rome, he was replaced by Demetrius, his nephew, who would have been his father's successor. Antiochus received the news of his brother's death while in Athens. He also heard that Heliodorus, perhaps behind the death of Seleucus, was plotting to seize power. Antiochus rushed home to come to the aid of another nephew, who was also named Antiochus. On the way back, he received the support of Eumenes, the king of Pergamum, who wanted to support he native dynasty over a pretender like Heliodorus. Antiochus, with this help, reached Antioch and ruled for the next five years as coregent with young Antiochus. In 170 B.C., the latter died and Antiochus IV ruled alone.[224]

With the most legitimate heir to the throne, Demetrius, held in Rome by the Romans and the scheming Heliodorus disappearing from the scene after his failed attempt at the throne, Antiochus IV and his young nephew Antiochus shared the power. However, this arrangement did not last for too long as the young Antiochus was later murdered. The murderer himself was then put to death by Antiochus IV. Rumors persisted that Antiochus IV was actually behind the assassination of his young coregent. In any case, a great deal of intrigue with his total lack of honor brought Antiochus IV to the throne as this prophesy in Daniel indicated.

11:22-24 These verses apparently are speaking in general terms concerning the military activities of Antiochus IV, and they note that he would initially enjoy several successes with his forces "overflowing" his opponents.

---

[224] Tremper Longerman III, *Daniel: The NIV Application Commentary* (Grand Rapids: Zondervan, 1999), 278.

Of some significance also is the reference to the "prince of the covenant" (Dan. 11:22) who would be destroyed. While there are a number of interpretations given for this phrase, it is best to see this as a reference to the murder of Onias III, the high priest. "The high priest bore the title 'prince of the covenant' because he was the de facto head of the theocracy at that time."[225] Antiochus IV did not want Onias III in office because he had a clear bent towards the Ptolemies of Egypt. Instead Antiochus IV favored Jason, the brother of Onias III, who favored the Syrians and the adoption of Greek culture and ways into Israel. Furthermore, Jason promised a significantly higher annual tribute. Antiochus, of course, viewed the office of the high priest as a political office and one which he had the right to appoint whomever he wished. Naturally this perspective was not shared by the pious in Israel. Onias III was removed as high priest and Jason was elevated to that position, which resulted in a much greater support of Antiochus in Israel.

The next verse (Dan. 11:23) is fairly vague probably because it is a general summary of the life and times of this evil king. His life and rule was characterized by manipulation, deception, intrigue and evil schemes with the result that the statement that he would "practice deception" does not help in pinpointing any particular event. "These verses speak of his duplicity and serpentine character. He was a true child of hell whose greatest cunning and vehemence."[226] He is not someone we would want to live next door to.

Antiochus' pattern was to achieve his ends in any way possible even if that meant attacking others in times of peace. Part of his pattern was to plunder wealthy areas, such as Israel, and then distribute that wealth to other cities and individuals for the clear purpose of buying their favor and support. This "Robin Hood" approach apparently gained him the loyalty of many.

11:25-30 The general subject of these verses is the military activities of Antiochus IV as they related to Egypt and to Israel. But it is more than a

---

225 Walvoord, 265
226 Harry Bultema, *Daniel* (Grand Rapids: Kregel, 1988), 327.

record of wars and military maneuvers. These recorded events unveil, in the book of Daniel, the emerging of the fourth great empire of Daniel, that of Rome. The third empire of Greece was clearly fading and in its place was arising this powerful empire from the west. Rome. This fourth empire of Rome would soon dominate the world. These verses also record that key past and future event known as "the abomination of desolation."

11:25-26 Once again the text focuses on the Ptolemies of Egypt and an invasion of Egypt by Antiochus IV. The king of the south at the time was Ptolemy VI Philometer, the son of Cleopatra. Historians believe that it was probably the Egyptians who were readying themselves to attack Antiochus IV and the Syrians, which subsequently brought about this preemptive attack from Antiochus IV. Antiochus was successful in this battle partly because of disunity and conspiracy at the highest levels in Egypt. This victory by Antiochus brought further confusion to Egypt with many of the mercenary troops defecting from Ptolemy. One result was that some in Egypt established a rival throne with the younger brother of Ptolemy VI Philometer (who was called Ptolemy VII Physkon) as ruler. It is likely that Antiochus left Egypt anticipating that the Ptolemies of Egypt would soon destroy themselves and become an easy prey for him.

11:27 But since warfare was not decisive or conclusive there were various treaties and agreements put on the table. This was done, not out of a desire for peace, but for the purpose of gaining advantage over the other side. This sitting down together usually was an indication of friendship and peace in the middle-east. But these men were liars and deceivers and violated all such codes of conduct. Their deceptions, however, were not at all successful.

11:28 In spite of his inability to decisively and completely conquer Egypt, Antiochus IV nevertheless went home with many of the spoils of war. As he headed back to Syria he revealed his contempt and hatred for the people of Israel (the people of the covenant). He paused long enough in Israel to plunder the temple, to destroy much and to kill many people.

1 Maccabees 1:20-25 records some of the actions of Antiochus in those terrible days.

> "And after that Antiochus had smitten Egypt, he returned again in the hundred forty and third year, and went up against Israel and Jerusalem with a great multitude, and entered proudly into the sanctuary, and took away the golden altar, and the candlestick of light, and all the vessels thereof, and the table of the shewbread, and the pouring vessels, and the vials, and the censers of gold, and the veil, and the crowns, and the golden ornaments that were before the temple, all which he pulled off. He took also the silver and the gold, and the precious vessels; also he took the hidden treasures which he found. And when he had taken all away, he went into his own land, having made a great massacre and spoken very proudly. Therefore there was great mourning in Israel, in every place where they were."

11:29-30 Several years later, Antiochus again launched a military campaign against the Ptolomies of Egypt. This time, however, the outcome was much different, and he tasted defeat and humiliation. The two Ptolemy brothers had decided to end their rivalry and now ruled together over a united Egypt. And as important as this was, it was the intervention of Rome that put an end to Antiochus' attempts to bring Egypt under his control.

The reference to "ships of Kittim" is a reference to Rome and is so translated in the Septuagint. The name "Kittim" (or Chittim) is found in Genesis 10:4 as one of the descendants of Japheth, who would end up living on the islands of the Mediterranean. And historically it was indeed Rome that put the brakes on Antiochus' attempts at conquering Egypt. Rome simply did not want either side to conquer the other and thus establish a single powerful empire in that part of the world. So they intervened in the situation and sent Caius Popilius Lenas to Egypt with soldiers with the demand that Antiochus stop his aggressions against Egypt and return home to Syria. Not to do so would be to face Rome. Antiochus had spent time in

Rome and had developed an appreciation for Rome's power and authority and did not want to come into direct conflict with this emerging power. But he did not want to give up his dreams of conquest either. The Roman envoy Caius Popilius Lenas, a former friend of Antiochus, forced him to make an immediate decision when he took a bamboo stick and drew a circle in the dirt around Antiochus.

> In a famous scene outside the city of Alexandria, the Roman envoy demanded that Antiochus, before he stirred from a circle drawn around him on the ground, promise to evacuate Egypt. With dreams of grandeur suddenly dissipated, Antiochus turned back in bitterness.[227]

Humiliated and angry, Antiochus left Egypt and entered Israel where the rumor was alive that he had been killed. A minor rebellion was under way because of this rumor and Antiochus moved with speed and wrath to kill and enslave tens of thousands of Jews. As never before, he believed that he must tighten his grip on Israel in order to ensure that the Ptolemies of Egypt did not succeed against him. He would now demand that those divisive elements (that is, the righteous ones) in Israel must be done away with, and so, with new motivation he vented his deep anger against Israel; or more precisely against those in Israel who faithfully served the Lord. He found in Israel many who had no loyalty to the Lord or to His commands and statutes. With these Antiochus aligned himself and brought terrible destruction and desecration to the things of God.

11:31 Antiochus aggressively removed Judaism and promoted Hellenism. Some of the darkest days in all of Israel's history would now descend on the covenant people.

> A systematic attempt was made to Hellenize the country by force. An edict demanded the fusion of all the nationalities of

---

227 Charles F. Pfeiffer, *Between the Testaments* (Grand Rapids: Baker, 1965), 81.

the Seleucid Empire into one people. Greek deities were to be worshipped by all. An elderly Athenian philosopher was sent to Jerusalem to supervise the enforcement of the order. He identified the God of Israel with Jupiter, and ordered a bearded image of the pagan deity, perhaps in the likeness of Antiochus, set up upon the Temple altar…Greek soldiers and their paramours performed licentious heathen rites in the very Temple courts. Swine were sacrificed on the altar. The drunken orgy associated with the worship of Bacchus was made compulsory. Conversely, Jews were forbidden, under penalty of death, to practice circumcision, Sabbath observance, or the observance of the feasts of the Jewish year. Copies of the Hebrew Scriptures were ordered destroyed. These laws promulgating Hellenism and proscribing Judaism were enforced with the utmost cruelty.[228]

Much of this is detailed in 1 Maccabees 1:37-64, where the desecrations of the sanctuary, atrocities committed against the godly in Israel and ruthlessness of the Syrians is recorded. (See also the previous study of Dan. 8:23-26).

While all of this actually took place in history, it must be noted that these events picture the future desecration of the temple and the future persecution of the nation of Israel during Daniel's Seventieth Week. The Antichrist will do a very similar thing in the Jerusalem temple at the halfway point of that final week, as predicted by the Lord Jesus in Matthew 24:15. The idol that Antichrist will set up in that rebuilt temple will have incredible demonic powers (Rev. 13:12-15) and will undoubtedly play a part in the 3 ½ years of intense persecution of Israel. And it is likely that, like Antiochus, Antichrist will present himself as deity to the people of the earth (cf. Rev. 13:4 and 2 Thes. 2:4). So, Antiochus IV is a type of the future Antichrist, a man yet to appear on the stage of history.

11:32-35 These verses give some of the events that came out of the days of Antiochus' brutal dealings with Israel and the response of some Jews to

---

[228] Ibid.

him. Within Israel there were two very distinct groups of people; those who embraced the lies, deceptions and benefits of Antiochus and those who boldly resisted him with a deep conviction that they must be faithful to the Lord. These would not passively accept the Hellenization efforts of Antiochus but would aggressively resist and challenge them. In view here is undoubtedly the Maccabean revolt that eventually would throw off the Syrian domination of Israel and bring about the cleansing of the Jerusalem temple in December 165. These righteous ones initially were few in number to begin with (as the "little help" of Dan. 11:34 suggests) but grew in number as these few faithfully instructed and encouraged the people (Dan. 11:33). Their efforts brought down the full wrath of Antiochus and many died as a result. This also caused some in Israel to defect from fighting Antiochus (Dan. 11:34). This painful process had the effect of purifying the nation of Israel, as the faithful and the faithless were revealed. And actually, according to this verse (Dan. 11:35) this purification process will go on *"until the end time"*. This verse also transitions us into the end times, as Daniel leaves his prophesying about Antiochus and the third kingdom of Greece and looks ahead to the very end of times and the arrival of Antichrist and the final phase of the fourth empire. God's dealings with His covenant people Israel did not come to an end with the days of Antiochus IV. He has made covenant commitments to Israel, which He has not fulfilled and, therefore, which He must fulfill in the future.

> God makes no mistakes with His people. Nothing is left to chance, 'because it is still to come at the appointed time.' And thus the Lord of all history and destiny lifts Daniel's eyes to see the coming centuries (omitting the age of the church entirely) down to the seventieth week, which is introduced next in terms of the Antichrist and his global domination.[229]

It is estimated that there are a little over 125 distinct prophecies found in Daniel 11:1-35, all of which have been fulfilled. This is absolutely amazing.

---
[229] Whitcomb, 152.

It is so amazing that those with a bias against predictive prophecy demand that it be read as history. But the God who can give this kind of detail about events that are now past to us is fully capable of giving us details about events that have not yet taken place. We can have total confidence in such an awesome God. And we are wise to listen attentively to what He says about events yet to come.

At this point in Daniel's prophecy (Dan. 11:35-36) the interpreter is faced with a significant decision that must be made. When the text reads that "the king will do as he pleases", is this a continuing discussion of Antiochus IV or is it referencing someone else? There are two primary views about this king; one is that the text is speaking of Antiochus IV[230] and the other view is that it is looking at the future Antichrist.[231]

Those who believe that this is a continuing account of Antiochus IV point to the lack of any clear statement in these verses, which would indicate that Daniel is moving on to a new and different subject. And, it is reasoned, that the lack of a clear transitional statement would indicate that the subject has not changed. It is also noted that Daniel 11:36 speaks of "the" king, which would suggest that the text is simply continuing the discussion of the king that has been the subject all along. While these points must not be dismissed as having no merit, they can be addressed. Regarding the definite article ("the" king) it can be observed that the definite article is often used to indicate the significance or extraordinary nature of something and that seems to be the way it is used here. Regarding the lack of a clear transitional statement, which would indicate that a new subject was being revealed, it should be noted that there are such indications in the broader context of Daniel 11 and 12, so that the passage really is not devoid of any indicators of subject change. The major problem of the Antiochus view is that these verses do not fit very well with what is known about the rule of

---

230 Goldingay, 304.
231 Walvoord, 270.

Antiochus IV, and even, in several places, contradict what we know of his reign. Those who believe that 11:36 and following refers to Antiochus IV candidly admit that the points made in these verses often do not fit the rule of Antiochus IV. One writer states that "here we are dealing with speculative material, most of which did not come to pass as here predicted."[232] For example, it is pretty obvious that the reference in this section to the taking of Egypt and to the place of his death simply do not match with the career and death of Antiochus IV. This causes another proponent of the Antiochus view to state that "we know we are at the point at which the seer actually begins to look into the future because, historically speaking at least, he gets it all muddled."[233]

The inability to match the statements of these verses with the rule of Antiochus IV stands in stark contrast to the precise nature of the prophecies up to 11:35, where liberal (seeing it as history) and conservative (seeing it as prophecies) commentators are in agreement on what is being said. James Boice's observation is certainly correct about the section of 11:36-45.

> If the section were referring to past events, there is no reason it should not be as clear in talking about them as the earlier portions of the chapter have been in talking about the history of the ancient Near East from the time of Cyrus to Antiochus Epiphanes. If it were dealing with past, commentators would agree.[234]

It seems far better to understand 11:36-45 as referring to the significant end time figure known at the Antichrist. In fact, we would expect that Antichrist would somewhere appear here because Antiochus IV is really not that important an individual, being emphasized in scripture because he prefigures the Antichrist. And for Daniel to simply end the section focused on this king who lived in the mid-100s B.C. does not align well with Daniel's

---

[232] Daniel L. Smith-Christopher, *The Book of Daniel: The New Interpreters Bible* (Nashville: Abingdon, 1996), 147.
[233] Towner, 165.
[234] James M. Boice, *Daniel* (Grand Rapids: Baker, 1989), 114.

emphasis on the great end time personality "the little horn" (Dan. 7) nor on his emphasis of man's days ending with the establishing of Messiah's kingdom. But beyond our expectation that Antichrist ought to appear somewhere in the passage, there are a number of good reasons why we can legitimately see a change of subject here at 11:36. First, in reading through this section it becomes apparent that the "willful king" (as he is commonly referred to) of 11:36 is neither the king of the north nor the king of the south. Up to this point in Daniel 11. the discussion has been on the activities of the king of the north and the king of the south. But 11:40 indicates that the "willful king" is a third king who is in conflict with both the north and the south. He does not arise from the northern dynasty or the southern dynasty, and since Antiochus IV is clearly a king of the north, this "willful king" is not Antiochus. This fact has been recognized by scholars over the years, though some have identified him with rulers other than the Antichrist.

An important line of evidence in identifying this person as the Antichrist is the chronological references in this final vision of Daniel. Of great significance in this discussion is the statement made in 12:1 which places the events of 11:40-45 (and probably Dan. 11:36-45) into the time frame of the period of tribulation and the final resurrections and judgment (Dan. 12:2). As chapter 11 ends, it does so with the prediction that a certain king (found at least in Dan. 11:40-45) will be destroyed. The twelfth chapter opens with *"and at that time"*, which is a clear chronological connector. So, the author unmistakably places the eschatological events of chapter 12 at the time when the king of chapter 11 is destroyed.

Several other chronological statements are found in this final vision of Daniel (chapters 10-12), which would indicate that eschatological events are in view. First, in 10:14, Daniel is informed that certain things would befall his people in *"the latter days"*, which is said to be *"the days yet future"*. The term "latter days" was discussed earlier (see pages 51 and 230) where it was indicated that this phrase, while being a general term, has definite eschatological significance in Daniel. It is a term that is "taken out of the previous prophetical literature of Israel, and always in Scripture includes some eschatological reference."[235]

It extends from the time of the prophet himself to the appearance of the Messiah and His kingdom. It is not a term that stops with the Maccabees or anywhere else except the times of the Messiah. It was used by the prophets of the eighth century as a technical expression for the time of Israel's restoration, which may well have influenced Daniel's usage of the term.[236]

The statement *"the days yet future"* simply reinforces the previous phrase and points to future events. A second chronological statement is found in 11:40 where events there recorded are placed *"at the end time"*. In and of itself this statement could simply refer to the end of the series of events being given by the author. However, because this section (Dan. 11:40-45) is connected by a clear grammatical link ("at that time", Dan. 12:1) to events that bring to an end the divine program with the advent of the Messiah (tribulation, resurrection and judgment in 12:2ff), it becomes another testimony to this section looking at the Antichrist and not Antiochus IV. Yet another chronological statement is found in 11:36 where the "willful king" is said to prosper in his endeavors until *"the indignation"* is completed. This is one of many terms used by the writers of the Old Testament to communicate the unparalleled times of future anguish for Israel.[237] This term is frequently, though not exclusively, used of God's wrath on men in the end times. It is used in Isaiah 26:20 in reference to the time of tribulation.

Finally, in the progress of revelation, a great amount of information was given by the New Testament writers about this coming evil ruler. What they reveal about this significant end time character fits the description given in 11:36-39. 2 Thessalonians 2, Revelation 13 and 17 agree with Daniel

---

235 Robert Culver, *Daniel and the Latter Days* (Chicago: Moody, 1954), 164.
236 Robert Chisholm, *Hosea: Bible Knowledge Commentary*, ed. Walvoord and Zuck (Wheaton: Victor, 1992), I. 1388.
237 Randall Price, *Old Testament Tribulation Terms: Terminology as an Indication of Timing*. (Paper presented at the Pre-Trib. Study Group, Chattanooga, Tenn., December, 1994), 3.

11:36-45 (as well as Dan. 7) that he will attain a level of arrogance and blasphemy not seen before. As much as 11:36-45 does not fit Antiochus IV, they do fit the coming Antichrist. And, of course, it should not surprise us that Antiochus IV had some of these same characteristics since he was to prefigure Antichrist.

It seems best, therefore, to see 11:36-45 as referring to the coming Antichrist who will appear at the end of the ages and completely fulfill these predictions of Daniel. Dr. John Walvoord observed that "many students of Scripture have recognized from antiquity that another king must be in view" and many of these (such as Jerome and Luther) identified him with the Antichrist of the New Testament.[238] We are, therefore, in good company when we identify this king as the "man of sin", "the beast", "the Antichrist."

THE PROPHECIES OF THE ANTICHRIST (Dan. 11:36-45)

11:36 The self-magnification of the Antichrist is one of the most obvious features of this future ruler, which is evidenced by the use of "he will" about a dozen times in 11:36-39. First, it is declared that this ruler *"will do as he pleases."* This opening phrase reveals him as an absolute ruler who dominates all others. His apparent unchallenged authority fits well with the revelation in Scripture concerning the Antichrist (but does not reflect the reality concerning Antiochus IV found in history). This succinct description goes along with Daniel 7:23 where he ("the little horn") will "devour the whole earth and tread it down and crush it", as well as Revelation 13:7 where he successfully makes war against the people of God and "authority over every tribe and people and tongue and nation was given to him." He will be one with unrivaled authority.

It is also said that *"he will exalt and magnify himself above every god."* These verbs used of Antichrist are "applied in the OT only to God and to

---
238 Walvoord, 270.

one who impiously asserts himself as being God and has judgment declared upon him (Isa. 10:15; 33:15)."[239] And the next phrase adds to the revelation that he defies the true God when it states that he *"will speak monstrous things against the God of gods."* This aggressive blasphemy of the true God by the Antichrist is uniquely evil and is what characterizes this man. Daniel spoke of his "boastful words" and that "he will speak out against the Most High" (Dan. 7:11, 25); John reveals that he will open "his mouth in blasphemies against God to blaspheme His name" (Rev. 13:6); and Paul teaches that he "opposes and exalts himself above every god or object of worship, so that he takes his seat in the temple of God, displaying himself as being God" (2 Thes. 2:4). His satanically generated blasphemy will set him apart from all who have come before him.

The final phrase in this verse indicates that he will have a measure of success, but that his career will be short and will be terminated at the end of *"the indignation"*, which we have previously identified as the end time of tribulation. The Antichrist's career will last only seven years, with a special period of success lasting 3 ½ years. This short period of prosperity has been determined by the God that he speaks arrogantly against. Daniel spoke of this period as "time, times and half a time" (Dan. 7:25) and as half of the final Seventieth Week (Dan. 9:27). John speaks of it as a period lasting for 42 months (Rev. 13:5).

11:37 This verse continues the explanation of Antichrist's rejection of all deities and his passionate desire to set himself above all persons and objects of worship. This text states that, *"he will show no regard for the gods of his fathers."* The way in which this phrase is translated pretty well determines its interpretation. When this phrase is translated as "the God of his fathers" (as in the KJV), it becomes a key support for the idea that the Antichrist is of Jewish origin.

---

239 Goldingay, 304.

If he is to pose for a while as the Jewish Christ (Messiah) it would appear necessary for him to be a Jew. The "God of his fathers" is, then, the Jehovah God of Israel. Some modern translations render the passage "gods of his fathers." But the many scriptural references to the "God of your fathers," or the "God of their fathers," or "Lord God", and others, make it close to certainty that the common expression for the Jewish God, Jehovah, is meant here. Beside, no true Jew will ever accept a known pagan as his Christ. At first he will appear to be a pious Jew. Afterward his true character will come to light.[240]

The King, Antichrist, shall not regard the God of his fathers. Here his Jewish descent becomes evident. It is a Jewish phrase "the God of his fathers" and besides this, to establish his fraudulent claim to be the King Messiah, he must be a Jew. Else the Jews would not own him as such.[241]

There are, however, arguments against the Jewishness of the Antichrist. It is pointed out that the word for "God" is the Hebrew word *elohim*, which is a name used in the Old Testament of both the true God and of pagan deities. It is used in the plural in this verse, which indicates plurality of gods since the word is used in the singular form in the next uses.

In the whole context, Daniel 11:36-39, the term *god* is used a total of eight times. In the Hebrew text, six of these times it is in the singular and twice in the plural, one of which is the phrase in verse 37. The very fact that the plural form of the word "god" is used in a context where the singular is found in the majority of cases makes this a reference to heathen deities and not a reference to the God of Israel.[242]

Although Daniel uses "God (*Elohim*) of my fathers" in Daniel 2:23 in view of this common usage elsewhere in Scripture, for Daniel to omit the Jehovah or Lord, (KJV) in a passage where

---
240 Robert Culver, *The Histories and Prophecies of Daniel* (Winona Lake; BMH Books, 1980), 179.
241 Arno C. Gaebelein, *Daniel* (Grand Rapids: Kregel, 1968), 188.
242 Arnold C. Fruchtenbaum, *The Footsteps of the Messiah*, Rev. Ed. (Tustin: Ariel, 2002), 211.

> a specific name for the God of Israel would be necessary, becomes significant.[243]

It is very difficult to come to a firm conclusion on this matter and it may be impossible to do so this side of the Seventieth Week. Several points do need to be kept in mind. First, the scriptures are quite clear that the Antichrist arises out of a gentile nation and not the nation of Israel (cf. Rev. 13:1; Dan. 7:19-20). However, does his national origin mean that it would be impossible for him to be of Jewish descent? If he emerges out of a gentile would that prohibit him from having Jewish blood in his veins? These questions probably cannot be answered either way with certainty. Second, some have observed that Israel would not accept as a messiah figure anyone that was not Jewish. But is that necessarily the case? It must be remembered that when the nation of Israel enters into the seven-year covenant relationship with the Antichrist that she is still deep in her apostasy. Would she really care at that point? It would seem that unbelieving Israel's only real concern is her safety in a hostile world and that she will jump at the chance to have that safety guaranteed regardless of the racial identity of the one with whom they are entering into a covenant agreement. So, the point that Israel would only accept a deliverer if he was Jewish may not be that strong an argument.

There is one final point of interest in the matter of whether the Antichrist is Jewish and that comes out of the New Testament. The Apostle John is the only one who uses the term "antichrist" (1 John 2:18, 22; 4:3; 2 John 7) and he uses it of a future individual along with present individuals who deny the Father and the Son. Does the word itself suggest the Antichrist is Jewish? In his discussion of "antichrist" in 1 John 2:18, B.F. Westcott deals with the use of the prefix "anti."

> The absence of the article shews that it had become current as a technical (proper) name. The word means far more than simply

---

[243] Walvoord, 273-274.

'an adversary of Christ.' As far as the form is concerned it may describe 'one who takes the place of Christ'…or 'one who under the same character opposes Christ…It seems to be most consonant to the context to hold that Αντιχριτοσ here describes one who assuming the guise of Christ opposes Christ.[244]

Other commentators make the same distinction. John Stott notes that the "antichrist's teaching is here recognized as being fundamentally against Christ and a denial of Christ. Perhaps both ideas are present in the word, 'counterfeiting and opposing.'[245]

And Curtis Vaughan adds that the prefix "suggests one who, assuming the guise of Christ, opposes Christ. He is both a counterfeit Christ and a rival Christ, a usurper and an adversary."[246]

If these authors are correct in their observations about the term "antichrist" including the idea of a "rival Christ" then is it suggesting that the Antichrist will be Jewish? Again, it is not possible to be dogmatic. Perhaps it will turn out that he, like Herod the Great of old, will have some Jewish blood flowing in his veins and will be called "king of the Jews." But even if not, the point in Daniel 11:37 is that Antichrist is absolutely irreligious and stands opposed to the object of worship of his ancestors.

The next phrase in 11:37 is just as difficult. It states that Antichrist will also have no regard for *"the desire of women."* This phrase has spawned many and varied interpretations. But in coming to some sort of conclusion on the meaning of the "desire of women" an important point should be made. "The word 'desire' is in the same construct form in Hebrew (*hemdat*) as in Haggai 2:7 and 1 Samuel 9:20, indicating that the noun following 'desire' is subjective not objective; hence it means "desired by women," not a desire for women."[247]

---

244 B.F. Westcott, *The Epistles of St. John* (Grand Rapids: Eerdmans, 1971), 70.
245 John R.W. Stott, *The Letters of John* (Grand Rapids: Eerdmans, 2000), 110.
246 Curtis Vaughan, *1, 2, 3 John* (Grand Rapids: Zondervan, 1983), 62.
247 Walvoord, 274.

This would eliminate all interpretations that see this phrase as referring to the sexual preference (or lack thereof) of the Antichrist. Instead it is the women's desire that is disregarded and not a desire for women. What desire is being spoken of? While we cannot be dogmatic on this either, it may be that Gaebelein has the correct idea seeing this as an expression for the messianic hope residing in Israel.

> The Lord Jesus Christ is here in view. Pious Jewish women in pre-messianic times had one great desire, they wanted to be mothers, with a view to Him, who is the promised seed of the woman. His birth was desired by these godly mothers of Israel.[248]

It is certainly evident that Satan's man, the Antichrist, will possess Satan's consuming hatred for the "seed of the woman" (Gen. 3:15), which Satan knows will bring him to complete and total defeat. Gaebelein's interpretation would certainly align itself nicely with the struggle and antagonism that has existed since Eden and will be culminated in the Seventieth Week of Daniel.

On the matter of the "desire of women" a number of commentators try and find fulfillment in one pagan goddess or another from ancient times (usually those who see Antiochus IV in this passage). But since we are viewing this as the days of the Antichrist it is highly unlikely that these goddesses will be objects of worship in the end times. Rather it seems that Daniel is simply reinforcing the point that this man is categorically irreligious. He holds no god, even the Messiah, in high esteem. This point is clearly emphasized by the next statement in the verse that he will not have regard for *"any god"*, which is a rather all-inclusive statement.

11:38-39 On the surface this verse, which states that Antichrist *"will honor a god of fortresses"*, seems to contradict the previous two verses where he has no god. But it is likely that the text is emphasizing

---

248 Gaebelein, 188

that the confidence, loyalty and focus of the Antichrist is on military power. In other words, his god is the "god of war". Bultema says that this is the best understanding because "the word *mauzzim* means strongholds, fortifications, and hence refers to battles and destruction."[249] The Antichrist will worship "the god of fortresses"; that is, the god of war and destruction. This would refer to warfare but might also include the "god of this world" who is a destroyer and murderer (cf. Rev. 9:11; John 8:44). The Apostle John sees this man as uniquely involved in war and destruction stating that no one is able to successfully make war against the Antichrist (cf. Rev. 13:4). And to this "god of fortresses" the Antichrist directs immense wealth.

He will successfully defeat all who would go to war with him because he will have the power and the authority of Satan, which makes it impossible for any to defeat him (cf. Rev. 13:2, 4, 7). "The Antichrist will lavish all his vast resources upon military fortifications and programs and will encourage cooperation by distributing positions of authority and valuable property to his followers."[250]

He will reward those who follow him and even in that he mimics the Lord Jesus who will reward His faithful followers when He establishes His reign upon the earth. The Antichrist will give those who align with him dominion and glory in his evil, short-lived world empire. Jesus Christ will give ruling authority and great reward to His loyal servants, which will not last 3 ½ years but at least one thousand years.[251]

11:40-45 These final verses speak of warfare in the end of time. The interpreter of this section in Daniel is challenged on several key matters; namely, when in the end times do these events occur, and how does this section relate to other prophetic scriptures (such as Ezek. 38, Zech. 14 and Rev. 16) that reveal military

---

249 Bultema, 336.
250 Whitcomb, 155.
251 Paul Benware, *The Believers Payday* (Chattanooga: AMG, 2002), 131-181.

conflict in the last days. Interpreters of Daniel hold to widely divergent opinions on these verses, and even among premillennial interpreters there are a variety of views. This reality makes dogmatism unwise and is a reminder to us that Bible prophecy was not given so that we could become prophets. We can only go as far as the text will allow us to go and not to engage in "newspaper exegesis".

11:40 The verse begins with the phrase "at the end time", which was used earlier by Daniel (Dan. 11:35) and contextually (Dan. 12:1) places these events at the very end of time during the Seventieth Week. There are three kings spoken of in this verse: the king of the North, the king of the South and the Antichrist. The kings of North and South were at the center of the prophecies in 11:5-35, and the events recorded in those verses have already been fulfilled historically in the conflicts of the Grecian period. These verses established the identification of these kings as those of Syria (north) and Egypt (south). In Daniel 11, the terms were always used to refer to Syria and Egypt. And while the borders of these kingdoms were not static and did change depending on military successes or setbacks, the terms "north" and "south" should not be stretched beyond their basic boundaries as found in Daniel 11. It is, therefore, probably unwarranted to say that in 11:40 the north "probably includes all the political and military force of the lands to the north of the Holy Land; hence the term could include Russia as well as related countries."[252] The reason for expanding the "north" to include Russia or the Islamic countries of the former Soviet Union is to tie in the "Gog and Magog" prophecy of Ezekiel 38 and 39 with Daniel 11 because Ezekiel 38 and 39 also speaks of a great force from the north invading Israel. Dr. Renald Showers is likely correct when he observes that the meaning of the terms "north" and "south" should remain as they were earlier in the chapter.

> Inasmuch as Christ did not tell Daniel that the king of the South and the king of the North of verse forty are different from those of verses two through thirty-five, it would appear that

---
[252] Walvoord, 277.

Christ intended them to be understood as being the same. This would mean, then, that in verse forty the king of the South is still Egypt, and the king of the North is still Syria.[253]

Normally it is only the king of the North that is controversial in this verse, since the king of the South is seen as Egypt, which is referred to in 11:43-44, and the "him" obviously refers back to the subject of 11:36-39, which is the Antichrist.

The text states that "**he** will enter countries…" The question at this point is the identification of "he". Does this refer to the king of the North or does it refer to the antecedent "him", that is, the Antichrist. The main subject of this portion of Daniel's prophecy (Dan. 11:36-39) has been on the "willful king" who has been identified as the Antichrist. And this along with the following context appears to make it preferable to take the "he" as referencing the Antichrist. We believe that the "he" refers to the Antichrist and, therefore, the activities in the remaining verses focus on him.

The events being described commence with an attack by the ruler of Egypt against the Antichrist, which is then followed by an attack from the North (Syria). The Antichrist must be in the land of Israel since he is said to be attacked by the already identified kings of the North and South. What is he doing in Israel and when in the Seventieth Week is this occurring? Obviously, we can only speculate since many details are missing from the text. However, we would suggest that this attack comes sometime in the first half of the Seventieth Week prior to the Antichrist becoming world ruler and the object of worship by the world. It should be remembered that by this time the Antichrist has cemented a relationship with the nation of Israel when he signed the covenant with Israel (cf. Dan. 9:27), which started the final seven-year period. By this covenantal agreement the Antichrist has committed himself to the safety and protection of Israel, which

---

253 Renald Showers, *The Most High God* (Bellmawr, N.J.: Friends of Israel, 2002), 166.

would mean that an attack on Israel was also an attack on the Antichrist.[254] But it would probably also require some kind of military presence of Antichrist's western forces in Israel, and from the text, it appears that he himself is actually in the land.

We can assume that the nations that surround Israel will not appreciate the Antichrist's covenant with Israel nor the presence of a Jewish temple (under construction or in use) on the temple mount. Their intent is most likely to remove the protector of Israel and take back the holy site. And they will come against him with all of their military resources ("with chariots, with horsemen, and with many ships"), which shows something of the respect that these nations will have for the military power of the Antichrist. The response of the Antichrist will be quick and powerful as he appears to faithfully respond to his covenant commitment with the nation of Israel. He will repel the attack and then proceed to invade and take over those who attacked.

As we think about wars in the seven-year period, it should be remembered that in the first half of Daniel's Seventieth Week there is much warfare in the world. The Scriptures say that during this time there will be "wars and rumors of wars" (Matt. 24:6) and that it will be "granted to take peace from the earth, and that men should slay one another; and a great sword was given to him" (Rev. 6:4). The Antichrist himself will conquer three kings in the early days of the Seventieth Week as he is establishing his western confederacy of nations (cf. Dan. 7:8, 24). It will certainly be the case that hatred, rivalry and revenge will be everywhere in the world and that the Antichrist will likely be at the center of it all. Though he will eventually become world ruler, the hatred of him and desire for retaliation, which is embedded in the heart of man, will manifest itself many times and in many ways. It may be that for a period of time no one can successfully wage war against him (cf. Rev. 13:4), but that hardly means they will not try. It appears that the land of Israel will be exempt from any devastation from these wars in the early days

---

254 Ibid., 167.

of the Seventieth Week, according to the Lord's words in Matthew 24:6-9. He seems to be saying that Israel will not become directly involved in these worldwide events until they become the focus of tribulation at the mid-point of the seven-year period (Matt. 24:9).

11:41-43 Assuming that the "he" of 11:40 refers to the Antichrist, the text now speaks generally of his conquests following the initial attack by the leaders of Egypt and Syria. It is stated that many countries will fall before him and that will include Egypt, which will be stripped of its wealth. Libya and Ethiopia will also submit to him. However, the text notes that Edom, Moab and Ammon will somehow escape his wrath. This area is now modern-day Jordan and includes some areas that are extremely hard to conquer because of the uniquely rugged terrain of the region. It is unclear as to the full significance of this area remaining outside the control of the Antichrist though in the Seventieth Week it will probably be as clear as crystal as to its significance. One author believes that the absence of the Antichrist's rule over these areas will provide a place of escape for God's people.

> All three of these ancient nations currently comprise the single modern kingdom of Jordan. The city of Bozrah in Mount Seir is located in ancient Edom or southern Jordan. Since this area will escape the domination of the Antichrist, it is logical for the Jews to flee to this place. Thus, God will provide a city of refuge outside the Antichrist's domain for the fleeing Remnant. It will be a very defensible city located in Mount Seir…Furthermore, as they flee and while they are living there, food and water will be miraculously provided.[255]

What is of special interest in these verses is the mention of the "Beautiful Land", which is the land of Israel, and the fact that the Antichrist enters it. As stated earlier, it appears that the Antichrist is likely in the land of Israel already. If so, then the point being made in 11:41 is that Antichrist will bring

---
255 Fruchtenbaum, 297.

in his western forces (as ruler of the Eleven Nation Western Confederacy) in numbers that will overwhelm the enemies.

That these events found in Daniel 11:40-45 take place in the middle of the Seventieth Week seem to be confirmed by the statement in Daniel 12:1 that "at that time" (the time of Dan. 11:40-45) Michael will rise up to support and defend Israel. It is at the mid-point that Israel is in deep trouble and persecution of the nation begins at the hands of Satan and the Antichrist and, therefore, there is the special need for the support of the Archangel Michael. The Lord Jesus was clear that it was at the mid-point that terrible persecution would come to Israel (Matt. 24:9, 15). The Antichrist will break his covenant commitment to Israel and set up the "abomination of desolation", terminate temple worship and commence a new holocaust against the people of Israel (cf. Dan. 9:27; Rev. 12:7-14; 2 Thes. 2:4; Matt. 24:15).

11:44 Although the Antichrist will have these notable military victories, he has little time to relax and enjoy the spoils of his success. He hears troubling reports from the "East" and from the "North", which most likely are rumors of yet more military activity targeting him. The content of the "rumors" are not given to us, but in light of the focus of the context on wars against the Antichrist, it would seem logical that military activity with the Antichrist is the subject. The text does not directly tell us what the end result of this new military battle will be but seems to imply that the Antichrist confidently responds to this new aggression. Some have suggested that this new military encounter is referring to the battle of Gog-Magog of Ezekiel 38 and 39. But this assumes that the Ezekiel battle occurs at the mid-point. And in the Ezekiel passage it is the Lord God that does the destroying, but no such fact is indicated in Daniel 11:44. There is simply not enough information given in this brief statement to equate it with Ezekiel or any other battle. Others identify this battle as referring to the Antichrist's warring against the ten western rulers (which may in fact occur much earlier in the Seventieth Week) and still others have seen it as reference to the "battle of

Armageddon" in the final days of the Seventieth Week when there is an invasion of the land by a huge army from the east (cf. Rev. 9:13-21; 16:12). But if we are right that the context is placing this at the mid-point of the Seventieth Week, then it may that none of the above-mentioned battles is in view, but rather separate ordained events which will catapult the Antichrist into his role as the ruler of the world. This may be one of those events that will only become clear when the Seventieth Week is actually in progress (cf. Dan. 12:4, 9). We do know, however, that the Antichrist will get his power, throne and great authority from Satan and will rule the world for a period of 42 months; that is, the final half of the Seventieth Week (cf. Rev. 13:2-7).

11:45 In connection with these many battles, the Antichrist will establish his presence in the land of Israel in a new and frightening way.

> The word for *tent* refers to a military tent of a general, and word for *palace* to a royal tent. It is a royal tent of a military general (the Antichrist) that is set up. It is set up *between the seas,* meaning between the Mediterranean Sea and the Dead Sean. Furthermore, it is *at the glorious holy mountain,* meaning the Temple Mount, or Mount Moriah or Mount Zion.[256]

Although the Antichrist apparently has been in the land since the covenant was made with the nation of Israel, it would appear that 11:45 reveals that he now establishes his presence in a new, aggressive way. It is then declared in the verse that "he will come to his end, and no one will help him." A common, and possible, understanding of this statement interprets it as a reference to the termination of his career at the very end of the Seventieth Week. So then the statement is understood to be a brief summary statement something like the Apostle Paul's pronouncement about his end in 2 Thessalonians 2:8.

> In the holy land, the place where the Antichrist has carried out his greatest destructions, he will also find his downfall He shall

---
256 Ibid., 245.

come to his end. In the battle at Armageddon, in the battle of the great God, he together with his army will be completely defeated by Christ and His saints (see Rev. 16:16; 19:19-20) ... seized by Christ Himself and cast into the lake of fire burning with brimstone (see Rev. 19:20).[257]

However, if the text remains focused at the mid-point of the Seventieth Week, then "his end" would be referring to his death. Randall Price is one interpreter who holds to this viewpoint.

> The "royal pavilion" in Daniel 11:45 refers to the military command center of the Antichrist in Jerusalem. Why in Jerusalem? Because apparently he will already be there. It is for this reason that the attack by the other kings will be aimed at Jerusalem (Daniel 11:44) and why the Antichrist will be killed there..."[258]

It is at the mid-point of the Seventieth Week that the Antichrist dies and shortly thereafter returns back to life. Three times in Revelation 13, the death of the Antichrist is mentioned along with his return to life (cf. Rev. 13:3, 12, 14). These verses forcefully declare that this individual will be "slain" and that he will have a "fatal wound" which will be healed. Furthermore, Revelation 13 states that he "had the wound of the sword and has come to life", which indicates that he will not die from natural causes (like the flu, cancer or old age) but will die a violent death of some sort. And it is equally clear that he has returns back to life. He really does die and really does come back to life.

It is important to overserve that the scriptural words used about the death and the return to life of the Antichrist, are also used of the Lord Jesus Christ in the Book of Revelation. In the heavenly scene, in Revelation 5:6, the Lamb is declared to be One that had been slain, and the words *hos esphagmenen* are used. These are the identical words used of the Antichrist

---

257 Bultema, 339.
258 Randall Price, *Jerusalem in Prophecy* (Eugene: Harvest House, 1998), 139.

being slain (*hos esphagmenen* is used in Rev. 13:3). So, since Jesus really did die and wasn't just badly hurt, then we must conclude that the Antichrist really does die as well. The Greek word "come to life" (*ezesen*) is used of Jesus in Revelation 2:8 and of the Antichrist in Revelation 13:14. Again, since Jesus did in fact come back to life again, then we have compelling support that the Antichrist comes back to life again after having been killed.

The question then arises whether or not Satan has the power to do this. There are several important points to keep in mind when dealing with this issue. First, the Tribulation period is an absolutely unique period of time. Jesus said (Matt. 24:21) that there has not been a time like this in the past, nor shall there be a time like this in the future. It is a totally unique period of time. Second, the Tribulation will be a time of amazing supernatural activity, coming from both God and Satan. The words used in the Scriptures of Satan's workings (through the Antichrist and the False Prophet) are the same ones used of the miracles of Christ and the Apostles. Signs (*semeion*), wonders or marvels (*teras*) and miracles (*dunamis*) are used of God's supernatural work (e.g. John 2:11; 2 Cor. 12:12; 1 Cor. 1:22; Rev. 13:13-14; 2 Thes. 2:9; Matt. 24:24). So, the miracles worked by Satan and his forces are of the same kind as God's people work. Third, ultimately God is the source of all in the realm of the supernatural. God has allowed, and will allow in the future, Satan and his followers to do supernatural things. He has even done so in biblical history. For example, the magicians of Egypt actually produced life when they threw down their inanimate staffs which then turned into snakes, and they also replicated the plague of frogs by producing frogs just like Moses and Aaron did. Now, no created being can do these things unless it was allowed by God. According to the Apostle Paul, it is part of God's plan to "send upon them a deluding influence so that they might believe what is false" (2 Thes. 2:11).

Some have suggested that this return to life is a reference to a revival of the Roman Empire in the last days. But according to Revelation 13, the response of people in the world, after this coming back to life, is to worship the Antichrist and also Satan. It does not seem at all plausible to have people worship revived Rome, but it does make a great deal of sense to have them worship a man. However, we would suggest that technically he is not "resurrected" but that he comes back to life. In other words, he does not have a resurrection body that is fitted for eternal living given to him at this point. It is problematic that God would grant the ability to resurrect people to Satan, something which is the prerogative of the Lord Jesus Christ (cf. John 5:28-29). And so, while we are amazed that even such a thing even as a return to life could take place, we must not forget that really awesome supernatural events are going to characterize these days. These supernatural acts are not only powerful acts, but they are also amazingly deceptive so that even believers would be fooled if it were not for the protecting work of the Father (Matt. 24:24). These days are unlike any other days.

We must not overlook the fact that if all this is at the mid-point of the Seventieth Week that an incredibly important event has taken place. At this moment, Satan is forcibly removed from heaven and is confined to the earth. And as the heavenly voice declares in Revelation 12:12, there are terrible days ahead for the people on the earth because Satan with great wrath will enter the earth's realm knowing that his days are numbered. Using the Antichrist and the False Prophet, Satan will do his very worst to harm and destroy God's people.

At the mid-point of the Seventieth Week a number of highly significant events will take place. As just noted, Satan will be removed from heaven and the Antichrist will be violently killed but return to life. At that time, he will break his covenantal agreement with Israel, end the Levitical worship in the Jerusalem temple, set up the "abomination of desolation" in the Jerusalem temple and set himself up as God in the temple and will begin his aggressive persecution of Israel. It is no wonder that Jesus' counsel to the Jews was to flee the land of Israel (Matt. 24:15-21) and why it is that the great prince Michael will rise up to support and defend Israel *"at that time"* (Dan. 12:1).

QUESTIONS TO CONSIDER

1. In what ways might this chapter contribute to a biblical worldview and remind us that we are strangers and aliens in this world?

2. What perspectives on the peace process currently going on in the middle-east might this chapter give to us? Knowing about these coming events in Daniel 11, should we even support peace efforts in that part of the world?

3. How does this chapter contribute to our confidence in the inspiration of the Scriptures? What specific encouragement does it give to you?

4. Give two spiritual lessons that you have received from a study of this chapter in Daniel that can be translated into your personal life?

5. What portions of scripture outside of Daniel became clearer to you as you correlated Daniel 11 with them?

6. What do sections of scripture like this one teach you concerning the character of God; such as omniscience, sovereignty, holiness and love?

CHAPTER TWELVE

FINISHING THE PROPHECIES

Preview: This chapter completes the final vision that aged Daniel was given concerning his nation. The chapter speaks of the terrible tribulation facing Israel, but also the absolute certainty of their deliverance, which includes resurrection and reward. Daniel himself was given instructions concerning this revelation as well as words of encouragement about his own future.

There is unanimous agreement that the chapter division here was poorly placed since it interrupts the flow of thought. The opening verses of this chapter (Dan. 12:1-4) clearly are part of the final revelation of the previous chapter (Dan. 11:36-45). The previous chapter was discussing the military conquests and activities of the Antichrist. And, we are now informed, that these activities would be resisted by the angel Michael when they pertained to the nation of Israel.

THE PROPHECY OF COMING TRIBULATION (Dan. 12:1)

12:1 It was observed previously that the time notation given in this verse is critical to the interpretation of these final revelations given to Daniel. Three times the words "that time" occur in this verse. It is "at that time" when Michael will rise to support Israel's cause; which we know from the previous paragraph is the time when the Antichrist is involved in his noteworthy military conquests (Dan. 11:40-45). And, if the previous discussion is accurate, then we are looking at the middle of Daniel's Seventieth Week as the specific time when this particular angelic activity will take place. Michael will rise up to support and defend Israel in a special way at the mid-point of the Seventieth Week. The mighty work of this preeminent angel will be so needed by the nation during these worst of days.

Michael is called the "great prince" (chief prince or supreme leader), which informs us that he ranks as the great leader of the holy angels. Michael was mentioned previously in this prophecy (cf. Dan. 10:13, 21) where he was seen keeping the demonic world forces from destroying the people of Daniel (Israel). It becomes apparent that Michael has received the special assignment to protect the covenant people of Israel. It would appear that these dark days of tribulation would bring about the annihilation of many peoples (cf. Dan. 11:44), and that would include Israel if it were not for the mighty efforts of Michael. It is safe to say that if Michael did not "arise" on Israel's behalf at the mid-point of the Seventieth Week that Israel would indeed be wiped from the fact of the earth. But the Lord God of Israel is committed to fulfilling the Abrahamic covenant with Israel and Michael is God's agent here in insuring that fulfillment. Adolph Hitler and those like him have failed to understand that Israel's covenant keeping God will never ever allow His people to be destroyed from off the face of the earth.

The middle of the Seventieth Week will prove to be a very busy time for this angel of God. Revelation 12:7 reveals that at this middle point there will be an unprecedented war in heaven where a pitched battle will be waged between the holy angels led by Michael and the demonic forces led by Satan. The outcome of this battle will be the final removal of Satan from the realm of heaven and his confinement to the earth. This will be a first for Satan. He will no longer be able to roam at will but will be restricted by God to this planet where he is the "god". There is great rejoicing in heaven over the defeat and removal of this longtime adversary (Dan. 12:10-12). However, the earth is issued a stern warning from heaven that terrible days are coming and will last for "one thousand two hundred and sixty days" (Dan. 12:6, 12). In essence the battle shifts from heaven to the earth. Satan who no longer can battle God's angels will now do battle as never before with God's people Israel and will dedicate himself to the destruction of Israel. This time of intense persecution will take place in the second half of the Seventieth Week. Daniel is informed that this persecution is aimed directly at his people ("your people").

Daniel records this unprecedented time of tribulation for Israel as "a time of distress such as never occurred since there was a nation until that time." The Lord Jesus undoubtedly had these words of Daniel in mind when He declared that at this moment in history "great tribulation" (Matt. 24:21) was to come on Israel to a degree that they had never experienced before in their entire history. And Jesus would have had the clear words of others in mind as well. Moses spoke of the "latter days" when there would be a time of "distress" (Deut. 4:30); Joel spoke of judgment in the day of the Lord and noted that "there has never been anything like it, nor will there be again after it" (Joel 2:2). Zechariah spoke of the worthless shepherd (the Antichrist) who would appear and do great harm to the nation of Israel (Dan. 11:15-16) before salvation and rest came from the returning Messiah (Zech. 12-14) and also of the coming time when two-thirds of Israel would be destroyed (Dan. 13:8-9). Jeremiah spoke of these days as the "time of Jacob's trouble" and Daniel himself had spoken of the fact that the Antichrist would have success in persecution God's people Israel (Dan. 7:25).

> In the Holocaust under Hitler, one-third of the world's Jewish population died. Under the fierce persecution of the Antichrist, controlled and energized by Satan, two-thirds of the Jewish population will die. This will be the largest and most intense persecution of the Jew ever known in Jewish history.[259]

---

259 Arnold Fruchtenbaum, *The Footsteps of the Messiah* (Tustin: Ariel Ministries, 2002), 289.

The combined scriptural voices reveal how important it will be for Israel to be defended during those three and a half years by the Great Prince Michael.

In all of the scriptures just mentioned it is equally clear that this time of tribulation will not destroy the nation, but rather deliverance and salvation will come to Israel. Even though many will experience physical death during those dark days, so many of these and others will come to faith. Some will live through the period until Messiah comes. The powerful proclamation of the gospel of the kingdom by the 144,000 will bring about everlasting life to untold numbers of gentile and Jews. Of these many will not survive those terrible times of tribulation but will die as martyrs (cf. Rev. 7:9, 10, 14). Is it not possible that many from every "tribe" (Rev. 7:9) could refer to the tribes of Israel who will be saved in great numbers? (The same word was used for the tribes of Israel 13 times in Dan. 7:4-8). And Daniel 12:1 confirms the future deliverance of Israel with the statement that "everyone who is found written in the book will be rescued." God's purposes for the Seventy Weeks, and particularly the Seventieth, were spelled out in Daniel 9:24-27. God's purpose is to bring Israel into the New Covenant so that the rest of the Abrahamic Covenant can be fulfilled. Israel will have been brought to repentance when Messiah comes and, therefore, God who keeps covenant will fulfill His promises given to Israel (cf. Rom. 11:25-28).

Daniel says that those who are rescued are the ones found "in the book." Daniel does not call this the "book of life" though it is generally assumed that is what he means. The "book of life" of the Lamb in the New Testament is a roster of the redeemed who cannot have their names removed from it (e.g. Rev. 13:8; 20:15). It may be that this is not what Daniel is speaking of though the end result is the same. In his imprecatory prayer in Psalm 69:28, David prays for names to be "blotted out of the book of life" and in Exodus 32:32 Moses prays for his name to be "blotted out" from God's book if the Lord does not forgive Israel's sin. While it could be argued that this is hyperbole and not to be taken literally, there is the possibility that it can be understood that names can be removed from this particular book. It may be that "the book" spoken about in the Old Testament is a book related to the covenant people Israel and is not the same book as the New Testament's "book of the Lamb". (There are number of "books" mentioned in the scripture and it is evident that they are not all the same). All Israelites were in a covenant relationship with God by the fact of physical birth. If they were descendants of Abraham, they were covenant people. However, they had to come to faith in the true God. Not to would mean spiritual death for them, and thus the removal of their names from that book. John the Baptist and Jesus spent considerable time trying to convince the Jews of their day that being a covenant person (with the blood of Abraham flowing in their veins) was not sufficient to enter God's kingdom (cf. John 3:1-16). It may be that Daniel was referring to a book other than the Lamb's book of life. In either case, the point is that the ones who are rescued are those who are regenerated people.

It should also be noted that not every single living Jew, by the end of the Seventieth Week, will have come to faith in Jesus the Messiah. The prophet Ezekiel says that there will be some "rebels" in Israel that will be purged out of the nation by the Messiah (Ezek. 20:33-38).

THE PROPHECY OF COMING RESURRECTION (Dan. 12:2-3)

12:2 The previous verses have dealt with those who would be rescued by the Messiah at His coming (according to later revelation). These verses seem to address the problem of those who will not rescued because they will not be alive at the Messiah's coming. They have died before the Messiah rescued Israel from the clutches of Satan and the Antichrist. Will they have a place in the Messiah's kingdom? The answer is that they will have a place because of their resurrection. In fact, in Revelation 20:4, these who die as martyrs in the Seventieth Week are seen in places of preeminence in Messiah's kingdom.

It is important to observe that the text very clearly states that it is "many" (Heb. *rabbim*) who will be raised and not "all." The subject is not mankind in general being raised from the dead, but believers, especially those who die during the "time of distress" and are not "rescued." This verse speaks of "many" who were dead and buried ("in the dust of the ground"). The word "many" allows for and seemingly suggests that there is not a future general resurrection in which *all people* from *all of history* are raised from the dead. C.F. Keil notes that the text of Daniel 12:2 does not say "all", and thus support a general resurrection, correctly states that interpreters cannot "obtrude upon *rabbim* the meaning of "all", a meaning which it has not and cannot have."[260]

> The fact that Christ said "many" rather than *all* indicates that He was not teaching a general resurrection of all the dead at the same time. The Bible teaches that there are different orders of resurrected, separated from each other by time (1 Cor. 15:20-24). It would appear, then, that Christ was saying that many will be resurrected at one time, but others will be resurrected at another time.[261]

There are then two distinct groups being spoken of here. One group of "those who sleep in the dust of the ground" will come to life and experience everlasting life. These are believers. The other group is simply identified as "the others" and these are heading for everlasting unpleasantness. "The metaphor of sleep for death is used in Scripture exclusively of deceased saints. The wicked are not said to be sleeping but are merely referred to as 'those over there'".[262] The New Testament supports the idea of several different times for resurrection. 1 Corinthians 15:20-24 states that Jesus Christ was raised first (as the firstfruits of the "first resurrection") and then He is followed by believers (at both the rapture and the Second Coming) and then by the unbelievers.

---

260 C.F. Keil, *Daniel* (Grand Rapids: Eerdmans, nd), 482.
261 Renald Showers, *The Most High God* (Bellmawr, N.J.: Friends of Israel, 2002), 172
262 Harry Bultema, *Commentary on Daniel* (Grand Rapids, Kregel, 1988), 345.

Revelation 20:4-6 speaks of two distinct resurrections, one before the millennial reign of Christ and one following His thousand-year reign. The resurrection of believers is called the "first resurrection" and the resurrection of unbelievers is simply called "the rest of the dead." Daniel suggested two distinct resurrections and John specified the distinctiveness by showing that there would be a thousand years between them. We should note that amillennialists have attempted to get around this stated chronology in Revelation 20 by stating that the first mentioned resurrection is a spiritual one (i.e. the new birth). But this position has significant problems with it.

> The same Greek word is used of both resurrections, so there is no justification for making these two resurrections different in kind. If the second one is a physical resurrection (which nearly all amillennialists agree is the case), the first one must also be a physical resurrection. Nothing in the context of Revelation 20 suggests that these are two different kinds of resurrection. The verb translated "came to life" is used about a dozen times by John in Revelation to refer to physical life, which would suggest that he is speaking of physical life also in Revelation 20.[263]

> The word *anastasis* (resurrection) is never elsewhere in the New Testament used of anything except physical resurrection, except in Luke 2:34, in which the context furnishes another meaning. The word appears forty-two times in the New Testament. Of the thirty-nine appearances outside this chapter (Rev. 20), thirty-eight have clear reference to physical resurrection. It will surely require overwhelming evidence to establish spiritual resurrection as the meaning of the word *anastasis* in Revelation 20.[264]

Daniel does, therefore, point to the fact of two coming resurrections involving two different groups of people with two different outcomes. It should be noted that the Old Testament does refer to, or suggest, the

---

[263] Paul Benware, *Understanding End Times Prophecy* (Chicago: Moody, 1995), 115.
[264] Robert Culver, *Daniel and the Latter Days* (Chicago: Moody, 1954), 208-209.

physical resurrection from the dead in other places besides this one in Daniel (cf. Gen. 22:5 with Heb. 11:19; Job 19:25-26; Ps. 16:9-10).

12:3 The text teaches that following the resurrection of the righteous there will be a time of their rewarding. (Note that Daniel does not speak of the "rewarding" of the unsaved at this point, which would support the idea that the two resurrections are at different times). The righteous ones, who have faithfully done the will of God, will be honored by the Lord for their faithful efforts. These are said to have "insight" which would surely speak of them being knowledgeable of the truth of God and living according to its precepts. In other words, they are those characterized by spiritual wisdom (cf. Dan. 11:33, 35). This concept of rewarding of believers mentioned in passing by Daniel is greatly developed and expanded by Christ and the writers of the New Testament.[265] The rewarding of believers is associated with the return of Christ and not with the death of the believer (e.g. Rev. 22:12). The rewarding of church age saints will take place when the Lord Jesus returns at the rapture and the rewarding of the Old Testament and tribulation saints will take place in connection with the Second Coming (cf. Matt. 16:27). It is said of faithful saints that they will shine brightly like the stars (bringing glory to the Creator). As the stars in the heavens give continual witness to the greatness and power of God, so also righteous believers will give the same testimony. They will do so "forever and ever", which may suggest that these rewards have eternal results. The Apostle Paul would later speak of the "eternal weight of glory" that would be his for faithfully serving Christ (cf. 2 Cor. 4:18). So Daniel is assured that righteousness does indeed pay and that the Lord has a wonderful forever for His children. And with this promise, the main content of the vision ends. Daniel is now given a command and also some information in response to his questions.

---

[265] Paul Benware, *The Believer's Payday* (Chattanooga: AMG Publishers, 2002).

THE COMMAND GIVEN TO DANIEL (Dan. 12:4)

12:4 With the giving of the prophetic information being concluded, Daniel is commanded to "conceal" and "seal up" the words of his prophecy. This does not mean that Daniel was to keep the message hidden from God's people. Rather, the command was to protect and preserve the prophecies "until the proper parties might open and read them." In fact, the Lord Jesus exhorted believers to come to an understanding of the prophecy of Daniel (cf. Matt. 24:15).[266] We should also observe that a few verses later in Daniel (Dan. 12:10), it is clear that if God had intended to keep the meaning of the vision hidden then the wise could not understand it any better than the wicked. But the godly were to understand it and as the centuries went by, God raised up many other men to be the channels of His revelatory truth, which resulted in greater clarity relating to the revelations given to Daniel. This would especially be true of the messages of Zechariah, the Apostle Paul and the Apostle John in the Book of Revelation.

Therefore, Daniel's orders were to protect and preserve these prophecies, not to hide them. It is interesting that Jeremiah, when buying a field, made two copies; one was "sealed" and the other was "open" (Jer. 32:9-15). The sealed document was not to be altered in any way, but rather was designed to preserve the conditions of the sale, while the "open" document could be viewed by others. Perhaps this is what Daniel did in obeying this command. The reality is, of course, that we today (3500 years later) do have the preserved document of Daniel. And as time has progressed along, the additional prophecies plus the accumulated understanding of godly people have increasingly opened the understanding of God's people to God's prophetic truth.

So, the first concern of Daniel must be to safeguard it well and confirm it as a divine revelation by ratifying it with his seal rather than making it known immediately to Israel.[267]

---

266 Robert Culver, *The Histories and Prophecies of Daniel* (Winona Lake: BMH Books, 1980), 188.
267 Bultema, 348.

The preserving of the prophecies of Daniel was to be "until the end of times." Showers notes that the word "until" can be translated to mean "during", thus indicating that the prophecies of Daniel would be preserved throughout the end times. If the end times is here understood as the time between the two comings of Messiah, then we can conclude that additional understanding will be given to God's people during this time. As suggested above, this would be through the New Testament writers and godly teachers given to the church. And we can certainly imagine that during the Seventieth Week itself believing Jews and believing gentiles will understand these prophecies as no one else has every understood them.

The final phrase of the verse has spawned numerous interpretations. Many are said to "go back and forth" and that "knowledge will increase." The idea that these are predictions of the increased ability of man to travel here and there is without any solid exegetical basis. And the view that the increase in knowledge is prophesying the great advancements in science and technology is also without solid basis. The going back and forth should be taken as the pursuit of God's knowledge by godly men. Some believe this is a reference to the eyes of a person going back and forth on page of a book. Others see it as a metaphor for the effort needed in the pursuing of God's truth (cf. Prov. 2:2-7). In either case, the emphasis on knowledge in this last vision has been on the knowledge that comes from God, which benefits the righteous (cf. Dan. 11:33, 35; 12:10). It is helpful to note that the definite article is used with knowledge indicating that something specific is being referred to. This "insight" and "knowledge" has essentially been used as a synonym for the spiritual understanding of the righteous and it probably should be that way here also. It is, therefore, the truly righteous person that will gain insight and understanding from God's prophetic word as time goes by and not simply that mankind will get smarter or more advanced in his knowledge of things. And John Walvoord is probably correct when he states that "those living in the time of the end will have far greater understanding of these things than is possible today."[268]

THE PROPHECIES OF THE TIME OF THE END (Dan. 12:5-12)

12:5-7 At this point we are returned back in the text to the Tigris River where the prophecy was originally set (cf. Dan. 10:4-10). Two individuals (most likely angels) were observed standing on opposite banks of the river. These angelic beings clearly do not understand the significance of the events just revealed to Daniel and so pose a question to a third individual. This third individual was dressed in linen and was seen to be above the river. This is the individual identified previously (Dan. 10:5-9) as the pre-incarnate Christ. He alone has the insight to answer to the question posed by the angel and the fact that He is said to be above the river speaks of His power and authority. The question that was asked by the angel was "how long will it be until the end of these wonders?" The answer from Christ indicates that the "wonders" being spoken of have to do with the truly awesome events which will take place in the second half of the Seventieth Week.

When giving the answer, Christ raised His hands and in doing so was taking an oath. He is probably doing so because of the tendency of man to disbelieve what God has said. This is a solemn oath that Christ is making. In the Scriptures, the raising of the hand indicated that a very solemn oath was being made (cf. Gen. 14:22; Deut. 32:40; Rev. 10:5). Here two hands are raised which apparently is making the oath even more serious (if that is possible).

In answering the question of the angel, two basic truths are affirmed by Christ. First, the duration of the time of these awesome, but awful, wonders is "time, times and half a time", and second, the obstinate rebellion of Israel will be ended. The duration of the time will be "time, times and half a time". God has limited the time of Israel's intense persecution by the Antichrist to

---
268 John F. Walvoord, *Daniel* (Chicago: Moody, 1971), 292.

3 ½ years. This phrase was used earlier in the prophecy of the Four Beasts (Dan. 7:25) and it was there concluded that it stands for the last 3 ½ years of the Seventieth Week (cf. Rev. 11:2; 3; 126, 14; 13:5). When these 3 ½ years have run their course, the Messiah will return and take control of the earth and establish His wonderful kingdom.

The second point in the answer has to do with the critical matter of the salvation of Israel. The Lord Jesus was quite clear that Israel, which had rejected Him at His first coming, would never see Him again until they became a regenerate nation (Matt. 23:39). In order for Messiah to rule over the land area of Israel, seated on the throne of David, Israel *must* enter into the New Covenant and experience the cleansing of their sins. The primary purpose of the Seventieth Week is to tear off the spiritual blindfold of Israel and cause them to see that Jesus of Nazareth was, in fact, their Messiah, and to bow before Him and become party to the New Covenant (cf. Dan. 9:24). In Daniel 9:24 one of the clearly stated purposes of the Seventy weeks of years was to "finish the transgression", which refers to the apostasy of Israel. The oath taken here is that this apostasy of Israel will indeed be shattered, and a humble, contrite nation will turn in faith to their Messiah.

12:8-10 In spite of hearing Christ's answer, Daniel still did not really comprehend what had been said by the Lord. His question is not the same as the one asked by the angel. Daniel apparently did understand the length of time involved but did not know how the deliverance of his people Israel was to be accomplished. That is the point of his questioning. In response to Daniel's inquiry, he is told that his concerns will be answered, but much later on. For now, the prophecy would be secured and preserved until further enlightenment would be given. As suggested earlier, this would refer to later writers of the Scriptures, particularly Zechariah, Paul and John

One of the wonderful realities of these future days is that many will come to know the Lord and walk with Him in purity and righteousness. Many sinful people will be cleansed by the precious blood of the Lamb of

God, resulting in the penalty of sin being totally removed, and the power and the presence of sin disappearing out of their lives. Only the powerful and gracious Lamb can do this with His blood, the greatest cleansing agent in all the universe.

On the other hand, the wicked among men who refuse to listen to the prophetic word from God will descend into greater and greater wickedness to the point that they cannot be salvaged. For example, these will know that the judgments in the Seventieth Week are from God, and yet they will blaspheme Him and absolutely refuse to repent of their many sins (cf. Rev. 16:9, 11, 21). Hearing the truth proclaimed, they refuse to listen and obey.

> The understanding of prophecy peculiarly requires spiritual insight and the teaching of the Holy Spirit. Even though the Scriptures describe in great detail the time of the end, it is obvious that the wicked will not avail themselves of this divine revelation; but it will be a source of comfort and direction to those who are true believers in God. Divine revelation is often given in such a way that is it hid to the wicked even thought it is understandable by those spiritually minded.[269]

And this reality is probably never truer than it will in these years that will end human history as we know it. And the Apostle Paul's discussion of the wisdom of God and the wisdom of man will never be truer either (cf. 1 Cor. 1:18-31).

12:11-12 Daniel is then given some additional facts about the length of the end time events, which would aid in his understanding of those very last days. The two crucial events of the termination of the Jewish sacrificial system and the setting up of the "abomination of desolation" have already been discussed (cf. Dan. 9:27). It is abundantly clear from Daniel and the Lord Jesus that these startling events take place at the midway point of the Seventieth Week (cf. Dan. 9:27; Matt. 24:15). The desecration of the Jewish

---
269 Ibid., 294.

temple will begin the "great tribulation", which will especially focus on the nation of Israel. The period of time from these events to the Second Coming of Christ are clearly established as 1260 days. However, the text of Daniel speaks of two other periods of time, both of which extend beyond the Second Coming. There is a period of 1290 days (30 days beyond the Second Coming) and 1335 days (75 days beyond the Second Coming).

Why will there be these additional days? While absolute certainty eludes us, we can make some legitimate suggestions based on a number of other passages of scripture. It is normally assumed that the Messianic kingdom (the Millennium) begins at the Second Coming, but this may not be the case. Actually, there will probably be a total of 75 days between the Second Coming and the commencement of Messiah's rule in order to deal with some necessary matters.

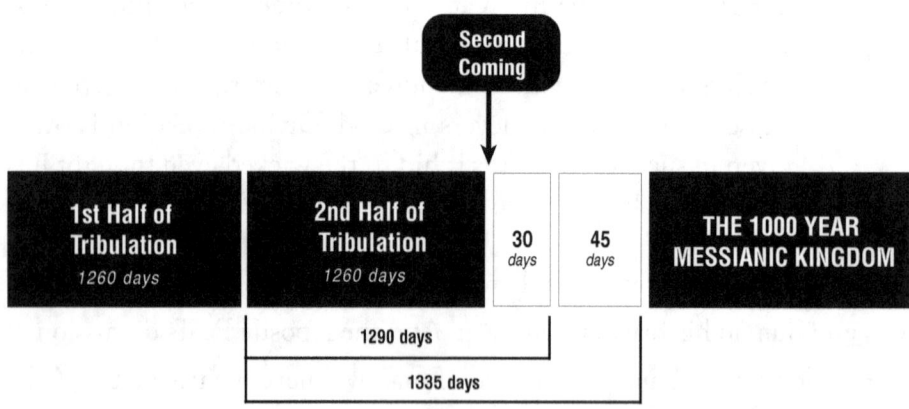

The 1290 days is closely associated with the "abomination of desolation" (in Dan. 12:11). The temple was desecrated by the Antichrist when he took his seat in the temple (cf. 2 Thes. 2:4) and by the False Prophet when he set up the idol with supernatural powers in the holy place (cf. Matt. 24:15; Rev. 13: 14-15). Apparently, there will be a thirty-day period for the cleansing and dedication of the temple.

He will presumably initiate a 30-day cleaning and purification of the Temple of God (cf. 2 Thes. 2:4). Similarly, King Hezekiah postponed by one month the celebration of the Passover "because the priests had not consecrated themselves in sufficient numbers, nor had the people been gathered to Jerusalem. Thus, the thing was right in the sight of the king and all the assembly" (2 Chron. 30:2-4). Likewise, Judas Maccabaeus and his army went to great lengths to cleanse the Jerusalem Temple of the abominations of Antiochus Epiphanes in 164 B.C. (1 Macc. 4:36-51).[270]

It is also possible that during this additional 30-day period that several necessary judgments will take place. These judgments are needed before the kingdom can begin. First, there is the judgment of the Antichrist (and the False Prophet as well). The Antichrist will be slain by Christ at His return (cf. 2 Thes. 2:8). It is most probable that this will be the fate of the False Prophet as well. These will then be raised immediately for their unique and personal judgment, being cast into the Lake of Fire (Rev. 19:20). Second, Satan will be bound and cast into the abyss (Rev. 20:1-3). This occurs prior to the start of the Messianic kingdom and is required to achieve righteousness in Christ's kingdom. It is important to observe that this judgment of Satan removes him totally and completely from any involvement on the earth during the one thousand years of Messiah's rule. Those in the Amillennial and Postmillennial camps view the binding of Satan as simply a restriction of his activities, often noting that you cannot bind up a spirit being with a chain, lock and key. But they fail to acknowledge that spirit beings can indeed be bound and confined. Jude 1:6 speaks of sinful angels who are kept in eternal bonds awaiting their judgment and Satan himself is confined to the earth after his removal from heaven by Michael (Rev. 12:7-12). Furthermore, Satan is not simply bound in this judgment but is placed into the abyss.

The abyss as the place of imprisonment for the demons is referenced in Luke 8:31, where the Lord Jesus met a man who was inhabited by demons. When confronted by Jesus, the demons entreated Him not to order them to the Abyss. They knew full well that their days of living in

---

270 John C. Whitcomb, *Daniel* (Chicago: Moody, 1985), 168.

that man were over and did not bother to debate the matter with Christ. What they feared was confinement in the Abyss, and they begged Jesus not to send them there.[271]

There are several other judgments, which are preparatory for the start of the millennial reign of Christ and which may fit into the 30-days. There is the judgment of living gentiles, commonly known as the "sheep and goat" judgment (Matt. 25:31-46). This is a judgment of gentiles who have made it through the horrors of the time of tribulation physically alive. This judgment will determine which of them are believers. These believers will be welcomed into the Messianic kingdom. According to Joel 3 this judgment of the living gentiles will take place in the Valley of Jehoshaphat. The proof of the genuineness of their faith is seen in how they treated the Jews during the time of "great tribulation" (Matt. 25:31-40; Rev. 12:15-16). There will also be the judgment of living Israelites. It is true that by the end of the Seventieth Week almost all living Israelites will have come to faith in Jesus the Messiah. But it is also true that some will remain rebellious and will be removed from entrance into the kingdom. This is the testimony of the prophet Ezekiel who said that God would "enter into judgment" with Israel and will "purge from you the rebels" (Ezek. 20:33-38). Jesus said much the same thing as He spoke of the days of fellowship in His kingdom with many believing gentiles but declared that "the sons of the kingdom shall be cast out into the outer darkness" (Matt. 8:11-12).

If these judgments of men, fallen angels and the Jerusalem temple take place in the 30-day period, what will be the events in the additional 45 days which adds up to the 1335 days. Again, it is impossible to be absolutely certain of the chronology and location of these events, but we do know that there are other events beyond the judgments. Daniel 12:12 indicates blessing for the person who makes it through the 75-day period after the Second Coming. This clear, unwavering statement of blessing ahead obviously indicates that

---

[271] Benware, *Understanding End Times Prophecy*, 112.

something really wonderful is going to take place at the end of 1335 days. What will be more blessed than being part of Messiah's kingdom, which will be characterized by joy, peace, righteousness, prosperity and the presence of the glorified Lord Jesus. This is most likely the meaning of blessing coming to the person who makes it through those days of judgment.

But what will take place during the 45 days? It is possible that this is where the rewarding of the Old Testament and tribulation saints will take place. Referring to His Second Coming, the Lord Jesus said: "For the Son of Man is going to come in the glory of His Father with His angels; and will then recompense every man according to his deeds (Matt. 16:27; Luke 14:14). The Scriptures indicate in many places that faithful believers will rule and reign with Christ when He comes and establishes His kingdom on this earth (e.g. Matt. 19:28; Luke 19:17, 19; Rev. 20:4-6). Time will be needed to set up the governing administration of His kingdom after the rewarding has taken place.

Once the judgments determining who can enter that kingdom have been concluded, it may take another forty-five days to form the government structure necessary to operate in the kingdom… After the saints and unbelievers have been separated, it will take time to appoint saints to different government posts and to inform them of their various responsibilities.[272]

The scriptures do give us some glimpses of life in the future, forever kingdom of God, but they are only glimpses. We are convinced that what people do here and now in this life will absolutely determine what will happen to them in the eternal state. Evil men do not get away with their evil. And saints who are either faithful or unfaithful in this life will see the consequences of their lives. As the song says, "it will be worth it all when we see Jesus."

12:13 The book ends with the Lord telling Daniel several important truths. Daniel was to continue living as he had until he died ("enter into rest"). Faithful Daniel is told that he will be resurrected and then he will, as

---

[272] Showers, 180.

a rewarded man, participate in Messiah's kingdom ("your allotted portion"). Daniel had been informed through the prophecies of chapters 2 and 7 that this kingdom of God would appear at the end of the age when man's kingdoms are destroyed. And Daniel is guaranteed his place in that coming kingdom.

QUESTIONS TO CONSIDER

1. When thinking back over the prophecies found in Daniel, what particular characteristics (attributes) of God have been impressed on your thinking?

2. What from Daniel's prophecies would be supportive of the view of premillennialism (Christ's return before an earthly 1,000-year rule) and the view of pre-tribulationalism (the Church is removed out of the world before the Seventieth Week begins)?

3. What can we learn from this chapter about angelic activities as they pertain to events in heaven and on earth?

4. What does this chapter (and related chapters in the Bible) teach us about God's judgments of men and nations?

5. As you reflect back over the Book of Daniel, which chapter had the greatest impact on your thinking? Why?

6. As you reflect back over the Book of Daniel, which godly characteristic of Daniel impacted you the most and your own walk with Christ? Are there any adjustments that you might make to become more like Daniel?